FnDeR

33.

The Metaphysics of Beauty

The
METAPHYSICS
of BEAUTY

NICK ZANGWILL

CORNELL UNIVERSITY PRESS

ITHACA AND LONDON

First published 2001 by Cornell University Press

Printed in the United States of America

Library of Congress Cataloging-in-Publication Data
Zangwill, Nick.
The metaphysics of beauty / Nick Zangwill.
p. cm.
Includes bibliographical references and index.
ISBN 0-8014-3820-9 (hardcover : alk. paper)
1. Aesthetics. I. Title.
BH39 .Z39 2001
111'.85—dc21   00-013259

Cornell University Press strives to use environmentally responsible
suppliers and materials to the fullest extent possible in the publishing
of its books. Such materials include vegetable-based, low-VOC inks
and acid-free papers that are also either recycled, totally chlorine-free, or partly
composed of nonwood fibers. Books that bear the logo of the FSC
(Forest Stewardship Council) use paper taken from forests that have
been inspected and certified as meeting the highest standards for
environmental and social responsibility. For further information, visit
our website at www.cornellpress.cornell.edu.

Cloth printing   10 9 8 7 6 5 4 3 2 1

For my mother, Hilda Zangwill,
and in memory of my father, Louis Zangwill

Contents

Acknowledgments

I have been thinking and writing about beauty and other aesthetic properties for about a decade. In this book, I have gathered that work together into what I hope is a unitary statement. All but one of the chapters have appeared as articles in journals. They have all been more or less retouched. In most places the alterations I have made are minor, but in some places I have made more substantial changes. This is particularly the case in chapter 3, which originated in a couple of essays where I replied to Robert Wicks. I wanted what appears here to be independently intelligible. Chapters 9 and 10, on Hume and on metaphor and aesthetic realism, have been modified and extended. The introduction is completely new, as is half of the last chapter, where I compare my views with those of others. Appendixes B and C of chapter 4 and the appendix to chapter 7 are also completely new.

The original places of publication of these essays are as follows:

"The Beautiful, The Dainty and the Dumpy," *British Journal of Aesthetics*, vol. 35 (1995)

"The Concept of the Aesthetic," *European Journal of Philosophy*, vol. 6 (1998)

"Long Live Supervenience," *Journal of Aesthetics and Art Criticism*, vol. 50 (1992)

"Supervenience Unthwarted," *Journal of Aesthetics and Art Criticism*, vol. 52 (1994)

"Feasible Aesthetic Formalism," *Noûs*, vol. 33 (1999)

"In Defence of Moderate Aesthetic Formalism," *Philosophical Quarterly*, vol. 50 (2000)

"Defusing Anti-formalist Arguments," *British Journal of Aesthetics*, vol. 40 (2000)

"Formal Natural Beauty," *Proceedings of the Aristotelian Society*, vol. 101 (2001)

"Aesthetic/Sensory Dependence," *British Journal of Aesthetics*, vol. 38 (1998)

"Hume, Taste and Teleology," *Philosophical Papers,* vol. 23 (1994)

"Metaphor and Realism in Aesthetics," *Journal of Aesthetics and Art Criticism*, vol. 49 (1991)

"Skin-Deep or in the Eye of the Beholder? The Metaphysics of Aesthetic and Sensory Properties," *Philosophy and Phenomenological Research*, vol. 61 (2000)

"Against the Sociology of Taste," *Cultural Values,* vol. 5 (2001)

I am grateful to the editors and publishers of these journals for permission to use this material.

Over the years, many people have helped me by offering criticism and advice. For their comments on the original articles, I would like to thank Kendall Walton, Roger Scruton, Crispin Sartwell, David Novitz, Carolyn Korsmeyer, Gary Kemp, Jim Edwards, Allen Carlson, and Malcolm Budd. I am especially grateful to Jerry Levinson and Berys Gaut for comments on several articles. I am also grateful for the help with specific points or short extracts that I received from Eddy Zemach, Ed Winters, Tim Williamson, Zena Ryder, Philip Percival, Alex Neill, Mike Martin, Peter Lamarque, Vassiliki Kolocotroni, Richard Hooker, Bob Hale, Bob Grant, Karen Fearing, and Ursula Coope. Gary Hagberg gave much-appreciated help and encouragement. I owe many thanks to Roger Haydon of Cornell University Press for his patience, fortitude, and much else. I am grateful to the anonymous referees for Cornell University Press, who made useful suggestions. And since much of the work included here was originally submitted to philosophy journals, I would also like to thank the anonymous referees for those journals, who offered valuable criticism.

Most of the work was done while I was employed by Glasgow University, though some of it originated when I had my first appointments in America after I got my doctorate from London University. Much of the work was completed during a year free of teaching in 1997–98. One semester was made possible by a sabbatical from Glasgow University, while the other semester was funded by an award of a *Mind* Bursary. I was lucky enough to be a visiting scholar at the philosophy departments of Princeton University, the Australian National University, and New York University. I am grateful for the hospitality and intellectual stimulation I received at these places.

This book is dedicated to my mother, Hilda, and sadly only to the memory of my father, Louis, who died in November 1998. My mother has always taken great pleasure in the beauty of nature and art, and she thought it important, not just for herself and her family, but also for the hundreds of children whose lives she enriched as a teacher and headmistress. My father would have been pleased to see this book. He enjoyed gardening, painting, playing his violin, conducting an amateur orchestra, driving his family to the countryside, smoking his pipe, drinking beer, and making terrible puns.

The Metaphysics of Beauty

Introduction

What does beauty entail?

Beauty does not stand alone. It cannot exist by itself. Things are beautiful because of the way they are in other respects. Beauty is a property that depends on other properties. Moreover, when we appreciate the beauty of a thing, we appreciate its beauty as it is realized in its other properties. For example, suppose we find a rose beautiful. What we find beautiful is a specific arrangement of colored petals, leaves, and stems. Beauty cannot float free of the way things are in other respects, and we cannot appreciate beauty except insofar as it is embodied in other respects. Beauty cannot be solitary and we cannot appreciate it as such.[1]

What then is this beauty, which is so closely tied to other features? To say that beauty is a property that depends on other properties is not enough. It is not all we want to know. It tells us something that is indeed *essential* for a property to be the property of beauty, but it does not tell us all that beauty *consists* in.

Someone might say that we cannot ask what beauty consists in like this because beauty is not independent of the human mind. Well, this may or may not be so, and I shall have quite a lot to say about it. But there is much that we can say about beauty without prejudging that issue. It is uncontroversial that beauty is an object of human thought and experience. We think about beauty and we experience it. The experience of beauty is something we value and desire; and we take our judgments of beauty seriously, in that we think that some judgments are better than others. There are important questions about the deep psychological nature of our experiences and judgments of

How do we know what beauty is?

---

1. Plato seems to deny this. I shall comment on Plato's views in the last chapter of this book.

I

Handwritten annotations:

OUR CONCEPT OF BEAUTY

TWO main interests in the book
1. FOLK METAPHYSICS: concept of beauty; what we represent beauty to be in our experience : Judgement
2. PURE METAPHYSICS: What beauty is itself

beauty.[2] In this book, however, I shall not broach these important issues in any great depth. Insofar as I shall be concerned with our experiences and judgments of beauty, I shall confine myself to considering our *concept* of beauty.

I take our concept of beauty to be what we represent beauty to be in our judgments and experiences. We can say a great deal about this while leaving open questions about the deep psychological nature of the judgments and experiences in which we deploy the concept. Since issues about our concepts are issues about how we represent the world, they are issues about what I like to call "folk metaphysics." These are indeed issues about the human mind. But investigating folk metaphysics stops short of inquiring into the deep psychological nature of the states that deploy the concept.

In this book I shall consider both the concept of beauty—what we represent beauty to be in our experience and judgment—and also what beauty really is, in itself, whether or not we represent that nature in our experience and judgment. That is, I am interested both in our *folk metaphysics* and in the *pure metaphysics* of beauty.

(1) This book has three parts. I begin the three chapters of part 1 with the idea that beauty is one among many aesthetic properties, such as ugliness, elegance, daintiness, and dumpiness. But the property of beauty has a preeminent place. I argue that beauty depends on other aesthetic properties. This enables us to get a clear view of the place of the concept of beauty among other aesthetic concepts. It also enables us to give a unitary account of what makes properties and judgments *aesthetic* properties and judgments. I articulate and defend the more general idea that it is essential to all aesthetic properties to stand in a dependence relation to nonaesthetic properties. Not only is this relation essential to aesthetic properties, it is definitive of aesthetic concepts that we represent aesthetic properties as standing in this essential relation. I examine the relation of aesthetic/nonaesthetic dependence, and I defend the claim that it holds against some objections.

(2) That much is probably part of what once would have been called the "analysis" of the concept of beauty—what I prefer to call folk metaphysics. But there are also issues about the relation between aesthetic and nonaesthetic properties that are more substantive. I address these issues in the five chapters of part 2. Discussions of formalism about various arts—especially painting, architecture, music, and literature—are, I think, best interpreted as being about the *scope* of dependence. The issues are about exactly *which* nonaesthetic properties sustain aesthetic properties. These issues are controversial, and they have been disputed among those who think and write about

2. I believe that Kant had many illuminating things to say about this.

Handwritten annotation: (# 1, 2, 3 = 3 parts to the book)

the various arts, among those who practice those arts, and among those who think and write about the aesthetics of nature. I consider what can be said for aesthetic formalism and I assess the role of sensory properties in determining aesthetic properties. I argue that a moderate version of aesthetic formalism can be defended and that sensory properties do have a special role in determining aesthetic properties. These issues go beyond reflection on what we take to be essential to the property of beauty that we represent in our experience and judgment. The issues do not turn merely on an adequate "analysis" of our concept of beauty. Either our concept leaves open these more controversial matters or, if it does not, the disputes are about how we *ought* to represent beauty in our experience and judgment. The issues are substantive first-order ones. But that is not to say that they are not also metaphysical issues. Insofar as the issues are about the scope of dependence, they are both substantive and metaphysical.

The theses advanced in parts 1 and 2, concerning the dependence of aesthetic properties on nonaesthetic properties and the scope of the relevant nonaesthetic properties, leave open the deepest, purely metaphysical questions about the property of beauty. These questions are addressed in the four ③ chapters of part 3. Is beauty a projection of the human mind? In particular, is beauty a projection of our sentimental nature? Or is beauty a real property? If so, is it a mind-dependent or a mind-independent property? I first argue against Hume's sentimentalism. I then defend aesthetic realism against an argument of Roger Scruton's. Next I argue against extreme aesthetic realism, in favor of a certain kind of mind-dependent view of aesthetic properties. Lastly, I compare my view with several rival metaphysical views, and end by rejecting sociological skepticism about the aesthetic. Once again, it might be that we represent beauty in our experience and thought as having a certain metaphysical status, even though beauty itself does not in fact have that status, or else there is no such thing as beauty as it is represented. The metaphysical truth about the property of beauty may or may not be built into our experience and thought. In part 3, I am concerned only with the pure metaphysics of beauty.[3]

Here in somewhat more detail is what I do in each chapter.

In the three chapters of part 1, I analyze the notions of beauty and of the aesthetic so that they can receive more substantive treatment later. I begin chapter 1 ("The Beautiful, the Dainty, and the Dumpy") by arguing that J. L.

---

3. It should not need to be said, but to be on the safe side I will mention that nothing in this book is intended to be a general theory of the nature of *art*. Moreover, I am not providing a theory of *artistic value*, although I do of course think that aesthetic values are important artistic values.

Austin was wrong to recommend that aestheticians should cease concentrating on "verdictive" judgments of beauty and ugliness, and of aesthetic merit and demerit, and he was wrong to recommend that they ought instead to focus their attentions on "substantive" aesthetic judgments, such as judgments about the dainty and the dumpy. I defend the more traditional idea that the judgment of beauty is an apt paradigm of aesthetic judgment. I argue that verdictive properties are determined by substantive properties and that they are both determined by nonaesthetic properties.

Ch. 2

In chapter 2 ("The Concept of the Aesthetic") I defend the modern concept of the aesthetic, which embraces both verdictive and substantive judgments while excluding judgments about representational properties. I consider a neo-Kantian program of showing how verdictive and substantive judgments are subjectively universal in something not too far from Kant's sense, but representational judgments are not. I eventually abandon that approach. Instead of the neo-Kantian program, I recommend appealing to the determination of verdictive properties by substantive properties. I argue that this determination is built into the meaning of substantive judgments, and here there is a contrast with representational judgments. This close link between verdictive and substantive judgments justifies grouping them together in one category. But I argue that this does not commit us to the view that there can be reasoning about aesthetic judgments.

Ch. 3

In chapter 3 ("Aesthetic Supervenience Defended") I defend aesthetic supervenience against three objections. First, I consider the *extent* of the supervenience base of aesthetic properties. I argue that the view that aesthetic properties supervene on nonaesthetic properties is consistent with the contextualist view that the aesthetic properties of a work of art supervene on relational properties, such as the history of production of the work. Second, I argue that the vagueness affecting aesthetic/nonaesthetic supervenience should not lead us to reject it. And third, I argue that it is a mistake to expect supervenience to have any interesting epistemological consequences.

Ch. 4

In the five chapters of part 2, I give a limited defense of the much-despised doctrine of formalism. My claim in chapter 4 ("Feasible Aesthetic Formalism") is that there is considerable truth in formalism. I give an account of how nonformal aesthetic values are related to formal values and other aspects of works of art. The account of formal properties deploys Kant's notion of dependent beauty and it allows us to formulate a "moderate formalist" view. I explore the way that account deals with the arts of representational painting, architecture, literature, and music. In each case I show that the phenomena of the art form can best be understood in terms of moderate formalism.

Ch. 5

In chapter 5 ("In Defense of Moderate Aesthetic Formalism") I argue against Kendall Walton's anti-formalist argument that we must always take the history of production into account in ascribing aesthetic properties to works of art. I concede that he is right about representational properties and about what I call "contextual" properties of works of art. But that conclusion cannot be generalized to abstract and noncontextual art, and it cannot be generalized to the nonrepresentational and noncontextual features of representational and contextual works of art. I then dispute Walton's intriguing *guernicas* argument. I also consider Walton's other counterexamples. I argue that art historical categories can be put to one side when we consider the aesthetic nature of abstract and noncontextual abstract works of art. There is no doubt, however, that many other works of art possess significant nonformal aesthetic values.

In chapter 6 ("Defusing Anti-Formalist Arguments") I propose a systematic method for resisting anti-formalist arguments. The method is to apply one of three strategies for dealing with potential counterexamples to moderate formalism: tactical retreat, irrelevance, and benign dilemma. I show these neutralizing strategies at work with seven objections to formalism.

Next I defend moderate formalism about the aesthetics of nature. My claim in chapter 7 ("Formal Natural Beauty") is that anti-formalists cannot account for the incongruousness of much natural beauty. This failure shows that some natural beauty is not kind-dependent. I then tackle several anti-formalist arguments that can be found in the writings of Ronald Hepburn, Allen Carlson, and Malcolm Budd.

The thesis of chapter 8 ("Aesthetic/Sensory Dependence") is that aesthetic properties always depend on sensory properties. I tackle cases which at first sight seem to be counterexamples. In the case of architecture and representational painting, I contend that sensory properties are necessary even if they are not sufficient to determine the work's aesthetic properties. But I deal differently with literature and with the symbolic and narrative properties of painting. Here I argue that any properties that do not depend on the sound of words or the colors on the surface are not in fact aesthetic properties. We sometimes make value judgments that deploy typically aesthetic terms about literature and about the symbolic and narrative properties of painting, but I argue that in fact we are using these terms metaphorically and that the properties we describe are not aesthetic properties. Lastly, I consider various other cases—proofs, theories, chess moves, machines, goals, and deaths—where we are inclined to talk about "beauty" and "elegance." But here too the use is metaphorical, and that the properties that we are describing are not aesthetic properties.

I consider the reality of beauty and the other aesthetic properties in part

3. In chapter 9 ("Hume, Taste, and Teleology") I examine Hume's various strategies for reconciling his sentimentalist account of aesthetic judgment with the normativity implicit in our aesthetic judgments. As possible sources of excellence or fault in our sentiments, Hume appeals to fine-grainedness, practice in judgment, a broad experience, being in the right mood, and the absence of prejudice. I argue, in turn, that none of these features delivers the normativity we require. In addition I observe that what underlies all of Hume's strategies is what I call his optimism—the idea being that our faculty of taste will function well if we merely develop the potential that lies within it and isolate it from extraneous interference. But I argue that this assumption helps itself to the normativity that needs to be earned. So I conclude that Hume does not succeed in capturing normativity for a sentimentalist account, and thus, in the absence of any other suggestions, we are entitled to think that sentimentalism is unsatisfactory.

The subject matter of chapter 10 ("Metaphor and Realism in Aesthetics") is Roger Scruton's argument that aesthetic realism cannot give a satisfactory account of the prevalence of metaphor in aesthetic descriptions. Scruton argues that an aesthetic realist cannot account for the sameness of meaning of the descriptive terms which are deployed both in and out of aesthetic contexts. I reply by distinguishing aesthetic thought from aesthetic talk. I argue that the realist can allow for the sameness of meaning at the linguistic level, but I insist on a difference at the level of thought. Thus there can be distinctively aesthetic thoughts which can be expressed only by means of metaphor. I give an explanation and defense of the idea that some aesthetic thoughts are literally inexpressible.

Chapter 11 ("Skin-Deep or in the Eye of the Beholder?") begins by presenting a physicalist aesthetic realist view of aesthetic properties. I then argue against this view on the basis of two premises: the thesis of aesthetic/sensory dependence defended in chapter 8, and the denial of a mind-independence thesis about sensory properties. I give an argument for the latter claim. I then put these two premises together and conclude that physicalist aesthetic realism is false. I articulate and give a limited defense of the view that if aesthetic properties exist at all, they are a certain kind of mind-dependent property.

In the final chapter ("Differences") I briefly discuss some authors who hold different views from the ones I favor, and I finish with a rejection of sociological approaches.[4]

---

4. I have written two lengthy surveys, on beauty and on aesthetic properties, which cover some of the terrain of this book. They can be found in the *Oxford Handbook of Aesthetics*, ed. Jerrold Levinson (Oxford: Oxford University Press, 2002).

PART ONE

DEPENDENCE

CHAPTER I

The Beautiful, the Dainty, and the Dumpy

How important is beauty? Should judgments of beauty be accorded their traditional pivotal status in aesthetics? Or should they be dethroned?

For centuries if not millennia it has been assumed that beauty is a central object of philosophical inquiry. But in the middle of the twentieth century, writers such as Austin, Goodman, and Wittgenstein changed that. In the last years of the century, beauty has made something of a comeback.

I want to stick up for beauty. I shall argue that judgments of beauty should indeed be the central concern of aestheticians who are interested in the nature of aesthetic judgment.

We are going to need some terminology. Let us call *verdictive* aesthetic judgments those judgments to the effect that things are beautiful or ugly, or that they have or lack aesthetic merit or value. (I group these together for the time being.) We also judge that things are dainty, dumpy, graceful, garish, delicate, balanced, warm, passionate, brooding, awkward, or sad. Let us call these judgments *substantive* aesthetic judgments. The question we have to consider is: What is the relation between verdictive and substantive judgments?

The most common sort of reason that philosophers have had for downplaying judgments of beauty is the thought that substantive judgments are equally important or more important. But there are also philosophers who have had other worries about judgments of beauty. I shall begin by breezing through these other worries in section 1, so that I can then deal at greater length with the relation between verdictive and substantive judgments. After tackling some of the standard issues in section 2, I propose my own view in section 3.

1 BEAUTY AND AESTHETIC MERIT DEFENDED

1.1   The first argument for downplaying verdictive judgments that I want to consider appeals to the fact that we rarely *say* that things are beautiful or have aesthetic merit. According to Wittgenstein, when we are at the tailor, we only tend to say things like "Too long" or "Too short," and we do not make explicit evaluative statements.[1]

I do not know which tailor Wittgenstein frequented, but I doubt that he is right about what most people say at the tailor. I am sure I have heard "Too long!" "No, too short!" and "There—just right; that looks great! Just beautiful!" (Perhaps in certain stuffy Viennese or Cambridge circles, it was the done thing to be rather stiff and restrained.) But even if what Wittgenstein says were true and we do not make explicit evaluative *statements*, that would not show that verdictive *judgments* are irrelevant. For when we *say* "Too long!" that would only be because we *think* that the garment would look better if it were shorter. We must postulate a judgment of aesthetic value in order to explain why someone performs the actions of saying "Too long" or of buying one suit rather than another. Consider that it is common, in the contexts of films, plays, or exhibitions, to say that people "vote with their feet." When they vote with their feet, they act in a way that we can only explain if we attribute to them a judgment of aesthetic value. An aesthetic evaluation moves us even if it is not voiced. Aesthetic *language* is not of great importance in itself. We do not always voice aesthetic value judgments out loud; we often just *think* them. And the judgment may be a standing disposition or state, rather than an occurrent event.

1.2   A second argument is that works of art often have other purposes and values besides aesthetic purposes and values. They can be sources of knowledge, of moral uplift, of political comment, and much more. Moreover, these other purposes and values are sometimes more important than their aesthetic value.

But this observation could not show that the aesthetic purposes and values of works of art are not significant and interesting. It may be that aesthetic merit is not the preeminent aim of many works of art. But this does not imply that aesthetic merit is completely irrelevant. Judgments of aesthetic merit may be important in their own right, even if there are many other things to be said about works of art.

1. See Wittgenstein's *Lectures and Conversations on Aesthetics, Psychology and Religious Belief* (Oxford: Blackwell, 1966), p. 5.

Notice that this means that the notions of *artistic* value and *aesthetic* value come apart. The overall artistic value of a work is a composite of all the types of value—including aesthetic value—which it attains. There is no such thing as artistic value per se, and there is no such thing as *the* value of a work of art considered as a work of art.[2] But for all that, there may be such a thing as aesthetic value among the other values of the work. Different sorts of works of art (music, literature, painting) have different sorts of artistic values, and the same goes for different genres or particular works of art. Aesthetic value may be more or less important relative to other values.

1.3   The third argument is concerned specifically with the concept of beauty and its relation to aesthetic merit. People sometimes say things like "Many of *Constable's* paintings are beautiful, but not Picasso's *Guernica!* *Guernica* is a *great* but not a *beautiful* painting." It is then inferred that beauty is not particularly important in aesthetics.[3]

This argument would be ineffective if it rested merely on the thought that many valuable works of art are not particularly beautiful. It could not show that we should separate beauty from aesthetic merit because, as we have just seen, we should distinguish aesthetic from artistic values. Once we make that distinction, it could be that *Guernica* excels in nonaesthetic dimensions. And so we have no reason for separating beauty from aesthetic merit.

But perhaps the point is that 'beauty' *is* often used as a substantive aesthetic term, not as a pure evaluation. If so, the aesthetic value of beauty might be upheld or disputed. People sometimes want to reject the value of beauty. It is true that the *word* "beauty" has picked up unbecoming overtones recently, rather like the word "moral." The word "beauty" is sometimes used to indicate a certain *style*. 'Beauty' in this sense means a kind of sentimental prettiness. Consider the similar scenario in morality: the use of the word "moral" is sometimes taken to imply a perverse denial of pleasure.[4] One might call these senses of 'moral' and 'beauty' the *inverted commas* senses. Now if such senses are what is in question, then we can doubt whether being "moral" is morally good, and we can doubt how much aesthetic merit "beautiful" things possess. However, someone who thinks that beauty is a substantive aesthetic concept may not want to denigrate beauty; it might be that beauty

2. Contrast Malcolm Budd, *Values of the Arts* (London: Penguin, 1995).

3. See, for example, J. A. Passmore's somewhat dreary "The Dreariness of Aesthetics," *Mind* 57 (1948): 50.

4. Recall the wonderful passage of Hume, where he lampoons the "monkish virtues." See *An Enquiry concerning the Principles of Morals*, ed. L. A. Selby-Bigge (Oxford: Clarendon, 1958), p. 270.

is just one way of achieving aesthetic merit, rather like being graceful or dainty.

I think that we need not worry too much about this concern with ordinary aesthetic language. Whatever we say about the *word* "beauty," what is important is that there is a *mental act* of making a pure judgment of aesthetic value or merit. We could just insist that this is all that the word "beauty" should express, even if there is no one word in natural language unambiguously marking out that concept. Or else we could allow that the word "beauty" sometimes denotes a substantive aesthetic quality, just as the word "moral" might mean obeying a certain narrow class of moral rules. If 'beauty' is substantive, then aesthetic merit and beauty are distinct. If 'beauty' is not substantive, then they are the same. I cannot see that we need to decide this matter because those who think that the word "beauty" denotes a substantive quality should admit that we also have a notion of pure aesthetic merit—and we can then focus on that—while those who think that beauty and aesthetic merit are the same have no problem. (In general, we are not interested in aesthetic *language* except as a means to enlightening us about aesthetic *thought*.)

There is plenty more to be said about what exactly a judgment of aesthetic merit is. But the above three reasons for thinking that judgments of beauty are not important are unconvincing. We should not eliminate beauty from aesthetics.

2 Verdictive and Substantive Judgments

2.1   The preceding arguments were concerned to denigrate judgments of beauty and aesthetic merit, but they did not seek to do so by means of an unflattering comparison with other kinds of aesthetic judgment. However, many aestheticians have shied away from verdictive judgments because they think that substantive aesthetic judgments are equally important or more important.

J. L. Austin recommended that aestheticians should focus on substantive aesthetic judgments rather than the judgments of beauty and ugliness. He lamented famously, or perhaps infamously:

> If only we could forget for a while about the beautiful and get down instead to the dainty and the dumpy.[5]

5. See J. L. Austin, "A Plea for Excuses," in *Philosophical Papers* (Oxford: Clarendon, 1961), p. 131.

Nelson Goodman's complaint was similar but not exactly the same. He wanted us to see judgments of merit as subordinate to substantive aesthetic judgments.

> Rather than judgments of particular characteristics being mere means toward an ultimate appraisal, judgments of aesthetic value are often means toward discovering such characteristics. If a connoisseur tells me that one of two Cycladic idols that seem to me to be almost indistinguishable is much finer than the other, this inspires me to look for and may help me to find the significant differences between the two. Estimates of excellence are among the minor aids to insight.[6]

Goodman recommends concentrating on substantive judgments rather than verdictive judgments, and Austin recommends something similar, at least in the short term. It is conceivable that Austin's intent was merely to redress the balance in the long run. He may have thought that substantive and verdictive judgments are of equal importance overall. But in the short term, both Austin and Goodman urge us to focus our attention on substantive judgments and turn away from judgments of beauty.

2.2   In her book *Beauty Restored*, Mary Mothersill retorted heroically:

> If we "forget about the beautiful," we shall not get very far with the "dainty and the dumpy."[7]

In support of this, she pointed out that Frank Sibley failed to give a philosophical *explanation* of the distinction between aesthetic and nonaesthetic concepts, even if he *described* that distinction very well.[8] So far so good, except that it is difficult to see how that negative point—Sibley's failure to ground the distinction between aesthetic and nonaesthetic concepts—supports Mothersill's view that *within* aesthetic concepts beauty has some kind of priority. So far as I can see, her argument and conclusion are disparate. Mothersill's heart is in the right place, but she ends up—disappointingly—having little to offer in support of her heroic retort.

2.3   Those who take the pro-substantive line hardly ever *argue* for their view. They usually put it forward as if, once stated, it is undeniable. The only

---

6. Goodman, *Languages of Art* (London: Oxford University Press, 1969), p. 262.

7. Mothersill, *Beauty Restored*, (Oxford: Oxford University Press, 1984),p. 253.

8. Ibid., pp. 253–56. Frank Sibley, "Aesthetic Concepts," *Philosophical Review*, vol. 68 (1959); Sibley, "Aesthetic/Nonaesthetic," *Philosophical Review*, vol. 74 (1965).

argument I have come across is the following very weak argument of Good-man's, which I might as well dismiss before I argue in the other direction. Goodman complained as follows:

> To say that a work of art is good or even to say how good it is does not after all provide much information, does not tell us whether the work is evocative, robust, vibrant, or exquisitely designed, and still less what are its salient specific qualities of colour, shape, or sound.[9]

Goodman thinks that to call something by a substantive term is to give quite a lot of information about what it is like, whereas to give a pure evaluation of a thing is to give very little idea what it is like. But it is surely silly to complain on this score. For to call something good *is* to give some idea what it is like. Obviously, it is to say that it is good! Why is that any less informative than calling it robust or vibrant? What is certainly true is that to say that something is good is to say something *different* from saying that it is robust and vibrant. But that is irrelevant to the question of priority. Maybe Goodman's idea was that if one knows that a thing has a substantive aesthetic property then one has some idea what it is like *in nonaesthetic respects*, by contrast with knowing that it is good. But this is not true. Something which is delicate might be made of sounds, paint, or words, and even within these media vast divergences are possible. We are just as much in the dark about a thing's nonaesthetic properties as we are with judgments of merit. This more-information complaint is in fact utterly baseless, and little more than an expression of preference.

2.4   Let us try to introduce some order into the list of substantive judgments. To recall, the list of substantive aesthetic judgments that I produced earlier was this: we judge that things are dainty, dumpy, graceful, garish, delicate, balanced, warm, passionate, brooding, awkward, and sad. These substantive judgments are all commonly classified as aesthetic, in addition to the purely verdictive judgments. (Let us here put aside the question of the rationale for including substantive judgments together with judgments of beauty in the class of aesthetic judgments. I take up that question in the next chapter.)

2.5   Let us note in passing that there is an important division in the list between metaphorical and nonmetaphorical judgments. To call something delicate, balanced, warm, or passionate, in an aesthetic context, is to describe it metaphorically. A painting with warm coloring is likely to be at no higher

---

9. Goodman, *Languages of Art*, p. 261.

a temperature than one with cool coloring. But to describe something as beautiful, dainty, dumpy, graceful, elegant, or garish is not typically metaphorical. Indeed, these descriptions are only metaphorical in *non*aesthetic contexts! For example, if we describe someone as being in an *ugly* mood, or as having a *beautiful* hand at cards, or as having made an *elegant* take-over bid, our description is metaphorical. But in aesthetic contexts, such description is nonmetaphorical. Any general account of aesthetic judgments needs to span metaphorical and nonmetaphorical aesthetic descriptions. I shall not say much about this here. Notice, however, that describing things as graceful, dainty, and garish involves distinctively aesthetic *terms*, unlike the metaphorical aesthetic descriptions. Thus many aesthetic *descriptions* do not employ distinctively aesthetic *terms*.[10]

2.6   However, we are more concerned with how substantive aesthetic judgments—metaphorical or not—relate to evaluation. There seems to be *some* kind of distinction between evaluative and nonevaluative substantive aesthetic descriptions. Some substantive aesthetic descriptions, such as 'dainty' and 'sad', *seem* to be nonevaluative; they do not obviously imply an evaluation. But what about 'delicate', 'balanced', 'graceful', 'garish', 'dumpy', and 'awkward'? These seem to involve an evaluation. 'Graceful', 'delicate', and 'balanced' seem to imply a positive evaluation, and 'garish', 'dumpy', and 'awkward' seem to imply a negative evaluation. They seem to evaluate a thing in addition to giving a substantive description of it. If so, there is then an issue about whether we can factor out or disentangle the evaluative and nonevaluative components of these judgments.

The issue is a difficult one, and it parallels the issue in moral philosophy about so-called thick moral descriptions, such as 'courageous' or 'honest'. The usual line in both moral philosophy and aesthetics is that these terms are intrinsically evaluative, so that when we describe something as graceful or courageous, it is part of the meaning of our judgment that we also praise it. Given such an intrinsically evaluative view, there is an issue about whether or not we can in principle separate the evaluative component from a purely descriptive component. Some say we can and some say we cannot.

2.7   However, there is another option. On this view, we do not have to choose between whether we can or cannot factor out the evaluative content.

---

10. See the often ignored note 1 of Sibley's "Aesthetic Concepts," where he says that his distinction is really one among *uses* of terms. A more controversial question is whether the metaphorical aesthetic judgments employ aesthetic *concepts*. I suggest that they do in chapter 10.

The debate over thick concepts is always set up as if we have to make a choice, but perhaps we should refuse to choose. What we might say instead is that these substantive descriptions have *no evaluative content whatsoever*; but when we use substantive descriptions—such as 'graceful', 'delicate', 'garish', or 'awkward'—we *conversationally imply* an evaluation. So evaluation is not part of the *content* or *sense* of the judgment. Instead, we infer that the person making the judgment also makes the evaluative judgment from the use of the language in a context. Here for once language *is* important, not just thought. There is no evaluative component of meaning to factor out, although from someone's linguistic utterance of the substantive description we can often infer that an evaluative judgment was made.

A similar approach might be recommended in moral philosophy. The idea would be that concepts such as 'courageous' or 'honest' have no evaluative content at all; it is just that when we use these words we often conversationally imply an evaluation. Crooks discussing the honesty of their colleagues might have different conversational presuppositions from the rest of us. (One crook to another: "What's Big Joe like as a crook?" Answer: "Too honest.") Those with different moral outlooks might see courage and honesty as morally neutral or negative.[11]

A disanalogy between aesthetics and moral philosophy would be that on the conversational implicature model in aesthetics, concepts like 'graceful', 'dainty', and 'garish' are all aesthetic concepts, it is just that they are not verdictive aesthetic concepts. Whereas on a conversational implicature model in morality, the allegedly thick moral concepts like 'courageous' and 'honest' are not moral concepts at all; they turn out to be purely psychological concepts.

2.8   How might one *argue* for the conversational implicature view? According to Paul Grice, conversational implicatures are "cancellable."[12] So in order to argue that judgments of daintiness and dumpiness only conversationally imply a judgment of merit, we need to show that we can cancel the conversationally implied judgment of merit without retracting the substantive aesthetic description. Thus we need to consider whether we can say or think that a certain substantive aesthetic description applies to a thing even though it lacks the aesthetic value which is normally associated with it. And

11. The so-called shapelessness of these properties with respect to their non-thick base would just be due to the shapelessness of a psychological property with respect to physical properties and more basic psychological properties. Such variable realization is a common phenomenon with little to teach us about 'thick' concepts.

12. Paul Grice, *Studies in the Way of Words* (Cambridge: Harvard University Press, 1989), pp. 39, 44.

to think about this is to think about an application of the *open question argument* in aesthetics. We could show that the conversational implicature model is preferable to the intrinsically evaluative approach if we can establish that there is always an open question as to whether something with a substantive aesthetic property is aesthetically good or bad.[13]

One must be careful how one sets up the open question. An object which has some substantive feature S might not be a meritorious work of art because of its *other* features. Those other features might *outweigh* the merit of feature S. Nevertheless, it could still be that S was necessarily a merit. It might be a *pro tanto* merit in a work which could be *outweighed* by other *pro tanto* defects, so that overall the work lacks merit. S might still be a merit as far as it went. The feature S might still have a positive evaluative *direction*, and that might be built into the concept of S.

2.9   Now, what about 'daintiness', 'dumpiness', and 'garishness'? Is daintiness always a *pro tanto* merit? And are dumpiness and garishness always *pro tanto* defects? Well, some things are horribly dainty—porcelain figurines, for example. So daintiness can be an aesthetic vice or a virtue. What goes for the dainty also goes for the dumpy. Some things are wonderfully dumpy—some prehistoric sculptures of women, for instance. And some garish things are wonderful for their very garishness—for example, some neckties. There seems to be an open question in all these cases. And the conversational implicature model is the only option for explaining how there is *some* connection with evaluation, even though the descriptions have no evaluative content. 'Daintiness', 'dumpiness', and 'garishness' *appear* to have evaluative content only because of the usual conversational implications which surround the use of these terms. But we can cancel the evaluation without retracting the substantive description. So daintiness, dumpiness, and garishness are not necessarily good or bad in themselves.

However, other cases are less clear-cut. Can the elegance of something ever be a demerit? It is difficult to see how it could. If something is elegant, it seems that that necessarily counts toward its being beautiful or aesthetically meritorious, even if other features can outweigh that merit in an overall judgment of value. And some metaphorical aesthetic descriptions are equally problematic. Take delicacy. One can agree that something is delicate but deny that it is beautiful without contradiction. This is because there may be more to the thing than its delicacy. Other features might let it down. But it is

---

13. See Stephen Ball's sympathetic reconstruction of Moore's open question argument in "Reductionism in Ethics and Science," *American Philosophical Quarterly*, vol. 25 (1988).

not obvious that one can always raise the question: I agree that it is delicate, but is its delicacy a virtue of it? The same goes for other metaphorical descriptions, such as 'balanced', 'brooding', and 'passionate'. It is not obvious that there are open questions in these cases. They all seem to be *pro tanto* merits.

It might be said that in certain special contexts, delicacy is not a virtue at all. For example, perhaps delicacy is out of place in a triumphal arch.[14] One line of reply would be to concede that these are very special contexts but insist that in normal contexts delicacy is necessarily a merit. But need we make this concession? What is going on in the triumphal arch case is that the delicacy does not merely *outweigh* some important positive feature of the rest of the design, instead it *destroys* it. But then the positive value of the delicate part or aspect still remains. What makes the triumphal arch case special is that we are dealing with what Kant calls "dependent" beauty.[15] The triumphal arch has a nonaesthetic function. Even though delicacy destroys the dependent powerfulness of the arch, the delicacy itself remains a valuable quality.

2.10   At any rate, it looks as if some substantive features always count in one evaluative direction, and some others don't.

One problem with the present discussion is that people have different intuitions concerning substantive descriptions. Intuitions differ over the application of the open question argument to substantive descriptions. In my view, many substantive descriptions—many more than is usually supposed—succumb to a conversational implicature model. But there may well be a residual class of substantive aesthetic descriptions which are intrinsically evaluative.

There seems to be no uncontroversial, clear, and uniform answer to the quite general question of whether substantive judgments involve evaluation as part of their content. This is rather disappointingly inconclusive. It would have been nice to come down firmly on one side or the other. But as we shall see, this matters less than we might think.

3 THE DETERMINATION VIEW

3.1   And now, after some delay, for my own view. I shall first outline this view, and then elaborate it by contrast with Monroe Beardsley's suggestion.

14. This is Stephan Burton's example, from "Thick Concepts Revised," *Analysis* 52 (1992): 32.
15. Kant, *Critique of Judgement* (Oxford: Oxford University Press, 1928), section 16; and chapter 4 below.

My view is that the issue is best thought of as one about *determination, dependence,* or *supervenience.*[16] We have a three-layered cake. Aesthetic properties depend on nonaesthetic properties.[17] But also, *within* the aesthetic, verdictive properties depend on substantive aesthetic properties.[18] (Verdictive properties are those described by verdictive judgments, and substantive properties are those described by substantive judgments.) Something which is beautiful cannot be *barely* beautiful. It must be beautiful *because* it has various substantive properties. This dependence has three aspects or perhaps three consequences: If two things differ in evaluative respects, then they differ substantively. If something changes evaluatively, then it changes substantively. And something could be different in evaluative respects only if it were different in substantive respects. There are equivalent contraposed versions of these three aspects of dependence.

(Talk of aesthetic properties and their determination does not necessarily involve a commitment to a realist metaphysics of aesthetic properties. There could be some kind of Humean analysis of aesthetic properties in terms of projections of sentiment.[19] Such an account would have to try to explain the determination of such projected properties as a requirement of consistent projection in nonaesthetically similar cases.)

3.2   We can now see why the issue about the evaluative content of substantive descriptions drops out. The role of substantive aesthetic descriptions, *whether or not they have an evaluative content,* is to pick out properties that *determine* aesthetic merit or beauty.[20] If they have evaluative content, then it is analytic that they determine them. If they do not have evaluative content, then it is not. Either way, these properties stand midway between earth and heaven—the earth of nonaesthetic properties and the heaven which is beauty.

Suppose that some substantive aesthetic description *is* analytically connected with merit (much as 'murder' is with 'wrongdoing'). Mothersill says exactly the right thing about this when she notes that the application of such

16. For our purposes, it will not matter if we use "determination" and "dependence" and "supervenience" interchangeably. So G properties determine F properties if and only if F properties depend on G properties if and only if F properties supervene on G properties.

17. I defend this thesis in chapter 3.

18. Here I follow a hint of Alan Goldman's. See his "Aesthetic Qualities and Aesthetic Value," *Journal of Philosophy* 87 (1990): 24. See also his *Aesthetic Value* (Boulder, Colo.: Westview, 1995).

19. See chapter 9.

20. This *may* be what Mary Mothersill has in mind when she writes: "when a point about a poem or a musical performance is made, the concept of beauty is in the background" (*Beauty Restored,* p. 257).

a substantive aesthetic description will be as controversial as whether the thing has the evaluative aesthetic feature.[21] Just as murder is a particular way of acting wrongly, so grace, say, is a certain way of achieving aesthetic excellence. You might offer a thing's grace as a reason for thinking that it is beautiful. But someone who does not think it beautiful may well deny that it is graceful. Perhaps it is effete rather than graceful. One person thinks that its beauty is determined by its grace, and the other thinks that its ugliness is determined by its effeteness. The difference then devolves on a disagreement about whether the agreed nonaesthetic features determine grace (and thus beauty) as opposed to effeteness (and thus ugliness). On the other hand, if the substantive aesthetic description is not one which is analytically connected with beauty, then agreement over substantive properties may well coexist with disagreement over verdictive properties. (There is a parallel scenario concerning thick descriptions in moral philosophy.)

As I mentioned, I have not broached the question of what judgments of merit or beauty and substantive aesthetic judgments have in common. We need a rationale for subsuming substantive judgments and judgments of aesthetic value under one category. Luckily, the determination account of the relation between verdictive and substantive judgments does not depend on such an account. Whether or not verdictive and substantive properties can be usefully subsumed under one category, the latter determines the former.[22]

3.3   Let us now compare this view with that of Monroe Beardsley in his essay "What Is an Aesthetic Quality?"[23] I am not confident that I have properly understood Beardsley's view, but at the very least he definitely holds that what is essential to substantive descriptions is that they can be offered as *reasons* or *grounds* for aesthetic evaluations. What is less clear is whether he thinks that substantive descriptions are intrinsically evaluative. On the one hand, it looks very much as if he does want to say this when he says of substantive properties (he calls them "A qualities") that "An A quality is an aesthetically valuable quality of that object" and "Unity and gracefulness . . . contribute to the value of the objects which have them." But on the other hand, he also says that "Goodness is not entailed by 'unity' or 'gracefulness', and hence it is not part of their meaning," and "The proposal is not to regard A properties . . . as themselves normative." He seems to think that judgments

21. Ibid., pp. 119–21.

22. This account fits nicely with the account of thick aesthetic descriptions given by Stephan Burton in his insightful "Thick Concepts Revised."

23. Beardsley, "What Is an Aesthetic Quality?" in *The Aesthetic Point of View* (Ithaca, N.Y.: Cornell University Press, 1982).

of unity or grace are not *themselves* value judgments, although they *support* such judgments.[24] But either grace and unity are intrinsically good or they are not. I could not get clear about whether or not Beardsley thinks that substantive judgments have evaluative content.[25] Is it that such features just have a mysterious *tendency* to be positive features? I suspect that Beardsley backs off from saying that they have evaluative content because he is thinking of a value judgment as an *overall* or *all-things-considered* judgment of value about a thing. What I think Beardsley was reaching for was a theory of the *pro tanto* goodness of grace, unity, and the like. On such a view, grace and unity always count in a positive evaluative direction. Such features definitely have a *pro tanto* value which, though outweighable, counts toward its overall value.[26]

But then, if Beardsley's view *is* this *pro tanto* view, there is a problem. How can substantive judgments function as *reasons* for *pro tanto* judgments of value if evaluation enters into the content of the substantive description. For if these descriptions *have* an evaluative content, then they cannot be offered as reasons for a *pro tanto* evaluation without begging the question. If Beardsley is right to think that substantive descriptions are offered as reasons in support of *pro tanto* aesthetic evaluations, it seems that we should conclude that they do not themselves have evaluative content.

3.4   On the determination view, there are three determination relations: they run from nonaesthetic properties to aesthetic properties, from nonaesthetic properties to substantive properties, and from substantive properties to verdictive properties. But there is no reason to think that these determination relations mean that we can give reasons for our verdictive judgments, as Beardsley thinks. (I assume that reasons are non-question-begging.) The combination of a determination relation together with epistemic autonomy is a common one in many areas of philosophy.

It is true that so far I have not said enough to definitely rule out a determination relation running in tandem with a reason-giving relation. On the other hand, nothing in the determination view should encourage it. Moreover it is not plausible that there are reason-giving relations corresponding to the determination relations.

There is a dilemma: either there are analytic entailments between substantive judgments and verdictive judgments or there are not. If there *are*, then not

---

24. Ibid., pp. 103–5.

25. Beardsley's cake example (ibid., p. 105) involves a causal process, so it is surely a distraction.

26. At one point Beardsley worries that some substantive descriptions—such as 'grotesque'—appear to be evaluatively neutral. His response is not at all convincing (ibid., p. 106).

only are there are no *interesting* reason-giving relations (that is, non-question-begging ones) between them, there are also no reason-giving relations between nonaesthetic judgments and these substantive judgments. On the other hand, if there are *no* analytic entailments between substantive and verdictive judgments, then it is also plausible that there are no reason-giving relations between them. That is, where there are analytic entailments linking substantive and verdictive judgments, there are no reason-giving relations between substantive judgments and nonaesthetic judgments, and where there are no analytic entailments linking substantive and verdictive judgments, there are also no reason-giving relations between them. So for any substantive judgment, either there are no nonaesthetic-to-substantive reason-giving relations or else there are no substantive-to-verdictive reason-giving relations. In either case, there is a dearth of reasons.[27]

Thus I think that Beardsley was wrong to think that substantive judgments are those which are offered as reasons for evaluations. *Retrospectively*, we might say that a thing has a certain merit property *because* it has a certain substantive property. But this is the *because of* determination. The lower-level substantive ascription is a not a warrant for the upper-level merit ascription. Rather they are offered as descriptions of the *way* that a thing *achieves* aesthetic merit.[28] Substantive judgments describe that which *determines* merit. We are then invited to try to perceive the determining substantive aesthetic properties.

Beardsley was almost right, but not quite. The right view is a neighbor of his. The issue is one about *determination*, not about *reasons*.

3.5   On the determination view, the substantive properties of a thing determine its verdictive properties; and verdictive properties are those which are determined by substantive properties. And our verdictive and substantive judgments describe the properties that are so related. Someone blind to the beautiful would also be blind to the dainty and the dumpy; and someone blind to the dainty and the dumpy would also be blind to the beautiful. So far, it seems that the relationship is mutual. We have parity between the

27. Where we know that the property F is determined by the property G, we might say that the "reason" that something is F is that it is G. That is a reason of a sort, but only in the sense of pointing to a determination relation. No *interesting* generalizations can be derived from it apart from 'all G things are F'. There may be no properties roughly similar to G which will be caught in such generalizations. A very slightly different property may not determine F. For discussion of the "uninterestingness" of certain laws linking subvenient to supervenient properties, see my "Supervenience and Anomalous Monism," *Philosophical Studies*, vol. 71 (1993).

28. Compare again Burton, "Thick Concepts Revised."

dainty and the dumpy, on the one hand, and the beautiful, on the other. But I would like to try to push this a little further.

Consider once again Goodman's connoisseur, who distinguished two similar Cycladic sculptures.[29] Ironically, Goodman's example nicely illustrates the determination view. On the determination view, verdictive properties are determined by substantive aesthetic properties. So Goodman is right: an aesthetic value difference between two similar idols entails a substantive difference between them. Goodman put forward the case as if it were one where the sole point of the judgment of aesthetic value is to get us to investigate the substantive properties of the thing. But that tells only half of the story. Goodman's example carries weight only because the point of the judgment of aesthetic value is to get us to investigate the substantive properties of the thing *which are the basis of that aesthetic value.* Goodman's case is in fact one in which substantive judgments are crucially related to evaluative judgments. Contrary to Goodman, substantive aesthetic differences between two Cycladic idols are significant *just because* of the different aesthetic values that they determine. Understanding a work of art is a matter of understanding not just which substantive aesthetic features it has, but *which substantive aesthetic properties determine its aesthetic value.* The suggestion is that the point of substantive judgments is to describe that which determines aesthetic value. And this is why it is misguided to loose interest in beauty and focus instead on the dainty and the dumpy, or forget about aesthetic goodness and concentrate instead on robustness or vibrancy. Substantive judgments have no point except to describe that which determines merit or demerit. And this is asymmetrical. Beauty is the icing on the aesthetic cake.

Coda

I have not dealt with the question of whether we should lose interest in *all* aesthetic concepts. Perhaps we should take an eliminative line with respect to substantive *and* verdictive aesthetic judgments. But so long as we are investigating aesthetic thought as it is, beauty must take pride of place. Austin, Goodman, and Wittgenstein were dead wrong. Among aesthetic concepts, beauty is top dog.

29. In my view, one of the finest is number GR 1971.5–21.1 in the British Museum. An added bonus is that it still has traces of paint.

CHAPTER 2

The Concept of the Aesthetic

Can the contemporary concept of the aesthetic be defended? Is it in good shape or is it sick? Should we retain it or dispense with it?

The concept of the aesthetic is used to characterize a range of judgments and experiences. Let us begin with some examples of judgments which aestheticians classify as aesthetic, so that we have some idea of what we are talking about. These paradigm cases will anchor the ensuing discussion. Once we have some idea of which judgments are classified as aesthetic judgments, we can go on to ponder what, if anything, they have in common.

We judge that things are beautiful or ugly, or that they have or lack aesthetic value or aesthetic merit. Let us call these judgments *verdictive* aesthetic judgments. (I group judgments of beauty and aesthetic value together.)[1] We also judge that things are dainty, dumpy, graceful, garish, delicate, balanced, warm, passionate, brooding, awkward and sad. Let us call these judgments *substantive* aesthetic judgments. The objects and events about which we make verdictive and substantive judgments include both natural objects and works of art.

Aestheticians have traditionally been concerned to understand the nature of verdictive judgments. Interest in substantive judgments, by contrast, is a novelty—something that has surfaced only since the Second World War. Interest in judgments of beauty and ugliness has a millennia-long history, whereas interest in substantive judgments has been around for only a few decades.

---

1. I justify grouping these judgments together in chapter 1.

The contemporary category of aesthetic judgments, as it is usually conceived, includes both verdictive judgments and substantive judgments. But "aesthetic" is a term of art, and there is no right answer concerning how the word should be used. For example, the modern usage is quite unlike Kant's. What is in question is the *point* of a classification which groups the beautiful together with the dainty and the dumpy. Is there anything to be said for such an classification? Or is it arbitrary? Are there relevant similarities which would make such an inclusive classification illuminating and worthwhile? The other problem is representational judgments. Examples of representational judgments are judgments to the effect that a work of art is of Napoleon or of a tree. Representational judgments are usually, but not always, excluded from the category of aesthetic judgments. Are there relevant *dis*similarities which would make such exclusion illuminating and worthwhile?

The issue is not one about aesthetic *terms*, since, as Roger Scruton has emphasized, there are many aesthetic descriptions which do not deploy aesthetic terms.[2] These are the *metaphorical* aesthetic descriptions. For example, we say that works of art are "delicate" or "balanced." A subclass of metaphorical aesthetic descriptions are the *expressive* metaphorical descriptions; for example, we say that works of art are "sad" or "brooding" or "serene." Moreover terms which are paradigmatically aesthetic are used metaphorically in judgments which are not aesthetic judgments (a "beautiful" hand at cards). We are interested in a kind of mental act, not in language.

What we need to do in order to vindicate the modern concept of the aesthetic is to give an account which makes sense of the categorization of the examples. The threat is that the list of examples of aesthetic judgments is not as unified as it has been thought to be; and perhaps items off the list have a lot in common with items on it. The task is not the dull neo-Wittgensteinian one of analyzing our concept of the aesthetic, but the more interesting and possibly the more truly Wittgensteinian task of uncovering the *point* of the classification.[3]

2. Roger Scruton, *Art and Imagination* (London: Methuen, 1974). See also Frank Sibley, "Aesthetic Concepts," *Philosophical Review* 68 (1959): 422–23, 446–48.

3. The topic of this chapter is not art. So I shall not be concerned with whether or not there are some works of art which have no aesthetic purpose.

1 THE NEO-KANTIAN PROGRAM

1.1 The Judgment of Taste

Let us begin with what we can say, relatively uncontroversially, about judgments of beauty and ugliness. In his *Critique of Judgement*, Kant characterized what he called the "judgment of taste," by which he means what I have called verdictive judgments. In Kant's view, the most basic feature of judgments of taste is that they have *subjective universality*.[4]

A subjective judgment is one that is based on a felt response to a representation, such as pleasure or displeasure. We can take a representation to mean a cognitive state such as a belief or perceptual experience, which might be true or veridical in virtue of how things stand in the world. A felt response such as pleasure or displeasure is not a cognitive state.[5]

A judgment which claims universal validity at the very least aspires to a kind of *correctness*. In this respect, Kant thinks that judgments of taste contrast with judgments of niceness and nastiness, which he calls "judgments of the agreeable." Judgments of taste aspire to be correct and they run the risk of failure. There are some judgments that we ought to make. There is more to be said about Kant's specific version of the universality requirement, since for Kant, it is restricted to human beings or those like us; but we need not worry about this here.

On the Kantian story, judgments of taste occupy a midpoint between judgments of niceness or nastiness and empirical judgments about the external world. Judgments of taste are like empirical judgments in that they claim universal validity, but they are unlike empirical judgments in that they are made on the basis of a subjective response. Conversely, judgments of taste are like judgments of niceness or nastiness in that they are made on the basis of a subjective response; but they are unlike judgments of niceness and nastiness which make no claim to universal validity. To cut the distinctions the other way: with respect to the claim to universal validity, judgments of taste are like empirical judgments and unlike judgments of niceness or nastiness; but with respect to subjectivity, judgments of taste are unlike empirical judgments and like judgments of niceness or nastiness. So we have threefold division: empirical judgments, judgments of taste, and judgments of niceness or nastiness.

4. Immanuel Kant, *Critique of Judgement*, trans. James Meredith (Oxford: Oxford University Press, 1928). Kant's account develops from, but goes beyond, the views of the British sentimentalists.

5. On the distinction between cognitive and noncognitive states, see my "Direction of Fit and Normative Functionalism," *Philosophical Studies*, vol. 91 (1998).

And judgments of taste have the points of similarity and dissimilarity on each side which I have just noted.[6]

For Kant, then, judgments of taste—that is, judgments of beauty and ugliness, of aesthetic merit and demerit—are subjectively universal. And in my view, Kant is right about that. What I now want to do is to explore the prospects for *extending* Kant's account of verdictive judgments of taste to the other judgments which in the twentieth century have been categorized as aesthetic judgments. How does Kant's characterization fit with the dainty and the dumpy? Given that verdictive judgments are subjectively universal, can the same be said of substantive judgments?

Let us call the project of showing how all aesthetic judgments are subjectively universal "neo-Kantian." If there were a common thread of subjective universality running through all aesthetic judgments, that feature would make the list of aesthetic judgments nonarbitrary. This is surely the natural approach to the issue, given the history of the concept—an expansion from its initial core. If such a project were successful, the category of the aesthetic would be vindicated. The concept would have a point.[7]

---

6. On this minimal account of aesthetic judgments, there is kind of pleasure we take in the representation of a thing, and we take that pleasure to ground a judgment that aspires to be correct. Will our judgments and experience of *literature* be aesthetic on such a minimal account? It might seem so. Our experience of literature affords us pleasure, and the pleasure is one that we take to be appropriate. This combination of pleasure and normativity makes the case similar to our experience of the beauty of abstract paintings and absolute music. This might tempt us to classify our pleasure in literature as aesthetic. However, we might want to move beyond the minimal account and say that subjectivity and normativity are *necessary but not sufficient* for the aesthetic. This is independently plausible if we consider that emotions such as pride, grief, and hate are feelings that can be *morally* evaluated, even though they do not ground aesthetic judgments. Kant, in particular, has much to add to subjectivity and normativity. He insisted that the pleasure in the beautiful is also "disinterested" in his special sense. (See my "UnKantian Notions of Disinterest," *British Journal of Aesthetics*, vol. 32 [1992], and "Kant on Pleasure in the Agreeable," *Journal of Aesthetics and Art Criticism*, vol. 35 [1995].) If we think that Kant was right to add that proviso, the question is whether our judgments of works of literature have this extra feature of genuine judgments of taste. Some judgments might, and some might not. See chapter 8, where I argue that many valuable properties of literature are not aesthetic properties.

7. Frank Sibley famously claimed that the correct application of aesthetic terms "requires an exercise of taste, perceptiveness, or sensitivity, of aesthetic discrimination or appreciation" ("Aesthetic Concepts," p. 421). He seemed to many to be explaining "aesthetic" qualities in terms of the faculty of taste, and then also explaining the faculty of taste (or appreciation, sensitivity, etc.) in terms of aesthetic qualities. Ted Cohen and Peter Kivy complained that this is too tight a circle to provide illumination (Cohen, "A Critique of Sibley's Position," *Theoria*, vol. 39 [1973]; Kivy, "What Makes 'Aesthetic' Terms *Aesthetic*?" *Philosophy and Phenomenological Research*, vol. 36 [1975]). But Sibley's approach has a Kantian pedigree insofar as he explains a range of properties (or qualities) in terms of a faculty of mind. There is nothing wrong with trying to give sense and unity to the aesthetic by describing a certain faculty of mind, so long as we don't try to take the explanation

1.2 Substantive Judgments

If the neo-Kantian project is to succeed, the reconstructed concept of the aesthetic must include the dainty and the dumpy and exclude representational properties.

Substantive judgments do well with the second feature of judgment of taste. They claim universal validity or correctness. Imagine someone who thought it appropriate to call Hawaiian music or Alpine yodeling "passionate" and flamenco or rebetika "cheerful." Such a person would not have judged as well as someone who found Hawaiian music or alpine yodeling cheerful, and flamenco and rebetika passionate. One description is more apt than the other. So the aspiration to correctness is true of substantive judgments as well as judgments of beauty.

The more problematic question is whether substantive judgments are subjective in Kant's sense.

As Kant rightly affirmed, following the British sentimentalists, judgments of beauty or ugliness, or of aesthetic merit or demerit, are made on the basis of a response of *pleasure* or *displeasure*. Both Kant and the British sentimentalists agree that we do not *perceive* beauty, although we do perceive things which are beautiful. The question is whether we can generalize Kant's claim and say that applying *any* aesthetic concept requires some kind of response or feeling— although not necessarily pleasure or displeasure. Just as pleasure and displeasure correspond to judgments of beauty and ugliness, so, perhaps other sorts of response or feeling correspond to judgments of elegance and delicacy. And perhaps there is no subjective response or feeling in the case of representational judgments. However, if substantive judgments are *not* based on a subjective response or if representational judgments *are*, then substantive judgments will not be distinguished by their subjective universality in the way the neo-Kantian program requires.

In one sense, it is necessary that the judgment that something is graceful or delicate is based on the experience of it. The difficult question is whether this is *perceptual* experience. That is, do the concepts of elegance or delicacy enter into the content of perceptual experience?[8] If so, the neo-Kantian account will *not* include judgments of elegance and delicacy as aesthetic judgments. But if such judgments are based on some response or feeling that

---

back in the other direction. Kant is prepared to go a lot further than Sibley in what he says about the faculty of mind.

8. I don't take possession and deployment of concepts to involve sophisticated linguistic abilities. I assume that perceptions are intentional states in which we deploy concepts of objects and properties.

we have as a *consequence* of perceptual experience with no such content, then the neo-Kantian account *will* include them as aesthetic.

The trouble is that it does seem plausible that we perceive elegance and delicacy. When we judge that something is graceful or delicate, it is plausible that we experience the thing *as* graceful or *as* delicate. And descriptions of music in emotional terms, or in terms of movement, are also based on, or rationally caused, by experiencing it in a certain way. For example, the judgment that a melody is sad or that it twists and turns is founded on the experience of hearing the melody *as* sad or *as* twisting and turning.[9] The problem is that this seems to be part of our perceptual experience. It is not that we have some neutral *perception* of the music, and we then *react* by finding it sad or twisting and turning. Rather, these concepts enter into the content of our perceptual experience. One *hears* the sadness, or whatever, *in* the music. And this seems not to fit the neo-Kantian model.[10] If judgments of elegance or delicacy are not essentially subjective, then they fall outside the bounds of the aesthetic and we have a fragmentation of our initially tidy list of aesthetic judgments.

There is an important reply at this point, which is to say that although the dainty and the dumpy and the elegant and the delicate do indeed enter into the content of our experiences, that does not necessarily mean that we are *applying* these concepts to objects in the world, so that we form beliefs. We might merely be *imagining* that a thing is delicate or sad, not *believing* that it is.[11] The judgment is an *as if* one. Perhaps judgments made on the basis of such experiences are usefully classified as subjective. Such an imagination-based account is plausible for metaphorical judgments of delicacy and sadness. But it is also plausible for nonmetaphorical substantive judgments, such as judgments of daintiness and dumpiness. We see a thing *as* dainty or *as* dumpy.

Suppose I judge that a certain table is austere. This feature is, in a sense, a perceptible feature of the table. It is not *narrowly* perceptible in the way that its primary and secondary qualities are perceptible. But it does seem to be a feature that we see *in* the primary and secondary qualities of the table. We see the austerity *by* seeing its primary and secondary qualities. So the judg-

---

9. See Roger Scruton, "Understanding Music," in *The Aesthetic Understanding* (London: Carcanet, 1983).

10. For this reason, it is a good idea to avoid talking vaguely of *aesthetic experience*, since "experience" does not distinguish between a perceptual experience of things in the world and a felt response such as pleasure. Kant warns us against the very same confusion with the word "sensation" (*Critique of Judgement*, section 3). Commentators have been very unfair in their discussion of this important passage. (See my "Kant on Pleasure in the Agreeable.")

11. See Scruton, *Art and Imagination*.

ment is not a subjective one in a strict sense. On the other hand, if a judgment of austerity does not involve applying concepts to the world in an empirical judgment but merely imagining that they apply, then such judgments could be said to be subjective in a more relaxed sense. For such judgments are based on an imaginative response to ordinary perception.

There is a problem about exactly what sort of experience this imaginative experience could be. One might think that it is a form of aspect perception—like seeing a duck-rabbit picture as a duck, or a face in a cloud. However, it seems that aesthetic imaginative perception cannot be exactly like ordinary aspect perception, where we can switch aspects at will. For there are normative constraints on aesthetic judgments of austerity which are connected with normative constraints on perceptions of austerity. One ought not to see the table as austere if in fact it is more appropriately seen as fussy and extravagant. It is not that we can see the table as austere if we feel like it, and we need not if we don't feel like it. We *ought* to see it that way. Seeing it a quite different way would be incorrect or inappropriate. But our ordinary aspect perception is not subject to such normative constraints: it is not the case that we ought to see one aspect rather than another. Even if we cannot help but see a man in the moon or a face in a cloud, there is no *requirement* that we see them there. Someone who sees an animal or a flower instead is not wrong. So if we embrace the theory that substantive aesthetic qualities just *are* aspects, as Roger Scruton does in his *Art and Imagination*, then they must be a very special kind of aspect. An account needs to be given of how there *can* be normative constraints on seeing aspects. How can it be that there are some aspects that we ought to see and others that we ought not to see? The imagination theorist needs to answer this question.[12]

At any rate, it seems that any theory of substantive aesthetic judgments has to say that they involve *some* kind of perception. If neo-Kantianism is to remain afloat, the kind of perception must be one in which concepts are not *applied* to the world, so that we form beliefs on the basis of those perceptions. This seems to open up the possibility that we could move the boundary between subjective and nonsubjective judgments so that the category of the subjective comes to include *either* judgments based on felt responses to perceptual experiences *or* judgments based on imaginative perceptual responses to ordinary perceptual experiences. If we are allowed to stretch the concept of the subjective just a little, substantive judgments can be said to be subjective. It is still the case that such imaginative experiences

---

12. For other problems with thinking of aesthetic properties as aspects see Peter Kivy, "Aesthetic Qualities and Aesthetic Aspects," *Journal of Philosophy*, vol. 65 (1968).

are not cognitive in the sense that such experiences ground beliefs. It seems that we can save the neo-Kantian program by being somewhat flexible about subjectivity.

1.3 Representational Judgments

The trouble is that if we stretch at one place, we may bulge at another. Maybe changes in conceptual shape cannot be isolated. Modifications may lead to ramifications.

The question is: Does the notion we have now stretched continue to exclude representational judgments?

Judgments of representational properties have normative aspirations. Of course, there is the relativist tradition pursued by Barthes, Derrida, and many others, who, despite their differences, think that the aspiration to correctness of judgments of meaning is in some sense an illusion. Where not incoherent, relativists make the error of elevating a fair epistemological point into a metaphysical point.[13] The fair point is that the ascription of meaning is not passive; rather it is creative, and it involves drawing on one's own beliefs and values. (In fact, Donald Davidson said as much, without the chic obscurity.)[14] The non sequitur is to conclude that any ascription of meaning is as valid as any other. ("The author is dead, all interpretation is permitted.") There are surely better and worse ascriptions of representational properties. If someone interprets *Guernica* as being about the invasion of earth by Martians, that interpretation would be inferior to many others. So let us ignore the relativists and accept that representational judgments claim universal validity.

What about subjectivity? This is where the real problem lies.

The ascription of representational properties to visual art does not require that we experience *pleasure*. But Richard Wollheim seems to be right to say that to ascribe to a picture the representational property of being of a tree, we must see it *as* a tree, or that we must see a tree *in* the picture.[15] But then

---

13. An excellent clear exposition and critical discussion of Derrida and his ilk can be found in Stuart Sim, "Structuralism and Post-structuralism," in *Philosophical Aesthetics*, ed. Oswald Hanfling (Oxford: Blackwell, 1992). This is a good survey for students. See also Robert Grant, "Anti-meaning as Ideology: The Case of Deconstruction," in *Verstehen and Humane Understanding*, Royal Institute of Philosophy Supplementary Volume 41, ed. A. O'Hear (Cambridge: Cambridge University Press, 1996).

14. Donald Davidson, "Belief and the Basis of Meaning" and other essays in *Inquiries into Truth and Interpretation* (Oxford: Clarendon, 1982).

15. Richard Wollheim, "Seeing-as, Seeing-in, and Pictorial Representation," in *Art and Its Objects*, 2d ed. (Cambridge: Cambridge University Press, 1980). Notice that this means that the cat-

the concept "tree" enters into the content of our perceptual experiences. It is not that we think that there is a representation of a tree because we have some subjective response *to* the perceptual experience.

The problem is that if we have conceded that the ascription of some *substantive* properties involves aspect perception, or something very like that, and that makes *them* subjective, then we seem to be committed to saying the same of *representational* properties. Once we widen the category of the subjective to include substantive judgments, it seems that representational properties will also slip in. But the category of the aesthetic is usually supposed to include the former but not the latter.

It might be argued that there is a difference. Representational properties are a matter of *meaning*—substantive properties are not. Someone must *make* something a representation, but substantive properties can be possessed by natural things. Suppose that something is a representation of a tree. Then, as Wollheim insists, the correctness or incorrectness of seeing a tree-aspect is determined in part by something outside the work of art—the artist's intention; and it might be argued that this is *not* true of the aspect perception that is involved in verdictive or substantive judgments. In the case of representational judgments, what makes an aspect perception the right one is determined in part by the artist's intention. A relativist might affect to say that the *Mona Lisa* can with perfect justice be said to be a representation of a spaceship; but if its maker did not intend it to represent a spaceship, then it doesn't. Something represents a tree only if it can be seen as a tree, or a tree can be seen in it, and the artist intended that it can be seen as a tree, or that a tree can be seen in it. Representation is "derived intentionality" not "intrinsic intentionality," in John Searle's terms.[16] And that means that representational properties are partly determined by the artist's intention. Intentions in part determine representational properties, even if it is true that the best way to *get at* the artist's intentions is usually not to dig up bibliographical information about him but to go in for creative interpretation of the work of art.

So it might be argued that although there are normative constraints on representational judgments—some are correct and others incorrect—this normativity is unlike the normative aspirations of verdictive judgments and substantive judgments. The point is not merely that what determines the correctness or incorrectness of certain aspect perceptions is something

---

egory of representational properties excludes the purely symbolic properties of visual art, the understanding of which does not involve perceiving-as or perceiving-in. Meaning, in this sense, can outrun what can be seen *in* the picture. See Norman Bryson, *Word and Image* (Cambridge: Cambridge University Press, 1981).

16. John Searle, *Intentionality* (Cambridge: Cambridge University Press, 1983).

beyond the object. For that is arguably also the case with the beautiful, the dainty, and the dumpy, where we need to see the work in the context of a stylistic tradition of other works.[17] The point is that representational properties are *constituted* in part by the artist's intentions. By contrast, it is not part of what constitutes the beauty or daintiness of a thing that an artist intends that it will be beautiful or dainty. (That's what he might *strive* for, but he might fail.)[18] Maybe both representational and substantive judgments involve aspect perception. But the correctness of seeing a tree-representation as a tree is constituted in part by the artist's intention that it should be seen as a tree, whereas the correctness of seeing something as dainty is not constituted in part by the artist's intention that it should be seen as dainty. The artist's intention is a cause but not a constitutive part of its being dainty, whereas the artist's intention is both a cause and a constitutive part of its representing a tree.

It seems, then, that the normative constraints on aspect perception which are involved in representational judgments are different from the normative constraints on aspect perception which are involved in substantive judgments. Representational judgments do not make the same kind of intention-independent normative demand on our aspect perceptions that substantive judgments make.

Now, once we have got this far enmeshed in the dialectic, this last move might seem like progress—it might seem to help the neo-Kantian. But if we step back and think about it, we can see that something has gone wrong. What was supposed to be a significant difference between aesthetic and nonaesthetic judgments has turned out to rest on some vanishingly subtle difference in normative demand. But if we were so generously easygoing with the concept of subjectivity in order to accommodate substantive judgments, why not be equally easygoing with normative constraints on representational judgments? And anyway, is it really so uncontroversial what kind of normative demand aesthetic judgments make? It may prove rather hard to hold on to the neo-Kantian distinction between aesthetic judgments and representational judgments. Establishing the neo-Kantian program has become a fiddly exercise which fails to preserve any real interest or point in the category of the aesthetic. It is not that we could not operate with such a category, but that given the neo-Kantian epicycles we have been through, it would be difficult to see

17. See Kendall Walton, "Categories of Art," *Philosophical Review*, vol. 79 (1970).

18. It is also true that an artist might intend to make a tree-representation, and fail, because the thing cannot be seen as a tree or a tree cannot be seen in it. But that does not affect the fact that when something has a representational property, the correctness of an aspect perception is determined in part by intention, whereas in the case of substantive properties it is not.

why we would bother. What initially seemed to be a fundamental category—
the Aesthetic—has turned out to involve a lot of finicky distinctions. We have
lost a clean and illuminating way of characterizing a significant category.

2 THE DETERMINATION ACCOUNT

2.1 Aesthetic/Nonaesthetic, Meaning, and Necessity

We need a different approach. The neo-Kantian route is not stupid, and in
many ways it is the natural program to explore. But instead of working *out-
ward* from judgments of beauty and ugliness, I believe that we should work
downward.

On what I call the *determination* account, verdictive judgments are subjectively universal, just as Kant said. But there is a certain necessary link
between substantive and verdictive judgments, and there is no such necessary
link between representational and verdictive judgments. So we can retain a
tight grip on subjectivity and normativity. On this account, we need not
compromise or start bending concepts.

What exactly is this necessary link? The necessary connection between
verdictive and substantive judgments that I have in mind is that it is part of
our concept of substantive properties that they determine aesthetic value
and disvalue. Suppose that I make the verdictive judgment that a certain
table is aesthetically excellent. The point of a substantive judgment about
the table is to describe exactly *why* and *how* it is aesthetically excellent. What
this claim presupposes is not just the determination of the aesthetic by the
nonaesthetic, which was well described by Frank Sibley,[19] but a determination relation *within* the aesthetic.[20] Substantive judgments do not describe
neutral features of things but ways of being beautiful or ugly. We can put
the point in terms of the *function* of the judgments. The function of verdictive judgments is simply to pick out aesthetic value and disvalue; and the
function of substantive judgments is to pick out the substantive properties
that determine aesthetic value and disvalue. Substantive judgments are there
to *serve* verdictive judgments. Substantive and verdictive judgments are inex-
tricably locked together in this way.

There are two related theses here. First, there is a connection of meaning
between particular substantive and verdictive judgments. And second, it is

---

19. See Frank Sibley, "Aesthetic/Nonaesthetic," *Philosophical Review*, vol. 74 (1965).
20. I say more about this determination in chapter 1.

constitutive of thinking in substantive terms to realize that substantive judgments are deployed in order to describe and explain why and how things are beautiful or ugly. This is a 'framework principle' for aesthetic judgments.

Two of points of clarification.

(a) The necessary link I describe is between *judgments*. It is plausible that there are also necessary links between aesthetic and nonaesthetic properties. Suppose a painting has a large unbroken expanse of blue. That nonaesthetic property of the picture might determine boldness. But there is no connection of *meaning* between the token judgment that the painting has a large unbroken expanse of blue and the judgment of boldness in the way that there *is* a connection of meaning between the judgment of boldness and the judgment of aesthetic merit. Judgments of primary and secondary qualities may describe that which determines aesthetic merit, but this is not their raison d'être. We can make such judgments with no thought of aesthetic merit. The same is true of representational judgments. Representational judgments describe representational properties, which in part determine aesthetic properties. This relation between the *properties* is necessary, but there is no connection of meaning between *judgments* about these properties.[21]

(b) The claim is that there is no such thing as a neutral substantive aesthetic *judgment*. This is a thesis about thought, not about language. (Judgments are mental acts which may or may not be expressed out loud.) It is true that some substantive *terms* have no evaluative direction. An example might be 'dainty'. Such terms contrast with 'dumpy' and 'elegant', which do have evaluative direction. There are also metaphorical substantive descriptions which seem to be evaluatively neutral. For example, calling something "heavy" seems neutral by itself. But *particular uses* of such terms *on particular occasions* are never evalu-

21. Perhaps we can distinguish between what we say about substantive *judgements* and *concepts* from what we say about substantive *properties*. Is there a claim about substantive properties to accompany the claim that there is a connection of meaning between substantive and verdictive judgments? Someone might propose that a suitable metaphysical cousin would be the modal principle that substantive properties *necessitate* verdictive properties. However, that would be a mistake. For if aesthetic/nonaesthetic supervenience holds, the same is true of physical and sensory properties, and perhaps also of representational and art-historical properties. Now although all these properties might be *necessarily* linked to aesthetic properties, perhaps only substantive properties are *essentially* linked to verdictive properties. (See Kit Fine, "Essence and Modality," *Philosophical Perspectives*, vol. 8 [1994] on the distinction between essence and necessity.) It is not part of *what it is* to have such and such shapes and colors to be beautiful, even though it might be *necessary* that those shapes and colors are beautiful. But it *is* part of what it is to be elegant to be beautiful. Unlike the modal principle, this principle is the true metaphysical cousin of the analytical entailment principle.

atively neutral. They always serve to describe *ways* of achieving aesthetic value or disvalue.[22]

2.2 Hierarchy

In order to find any kind of uncontrived unity on the judgments that we classify as aesthetic, we must recognize *hierarchy* among them. Judgments of aesthetic value—of beauty and ugliness—are the fundamental sort of aesthetic judgment that we make. Such judgments move artists and audiences to make and experience works of art.[23] And such judgments move us to seek out, respect, and protect nature. Aesthetic value is important to us. But we also want to explain *how* and *why* things are beautiful or ugly. This is where the substantive judgments come in. Their role is entirely subsidiary to judgments of aesthetic value, and we completely misunderstand such judgments if we miss this.

So even if we *concede* that substantive judgments are *not* themselves subjective, it is still true that they are necessarily connected with judgments of aesthetic merit which *are* subjective. The raison d'être of substantive judgments is to describe that which determines aesthetic value, which we *do* apprehend by means of a subjectively universal judgment. And we could not make substantive judgments unless we made subjectively universal judgments of aesthetic value.[24] There is thus a close conceptual tie between substantive and verdictive judgments which warrants our putting them both in the same class. There is a rationale for saying that substantive judgments are aesthetic judgments.

This means that we do not need to stretch the concept of subjectivity in order to try to accommodate substantive judgments. We can group the beautiful together with the dainty and the dumpy without the messy terminological legislation that the neo-Kantian program involves. On the determination account, we do not have to worry about whether substantive and representational judgments both involve seeing aspects, and we do not have to worry

---

22. This move evades Peter Kivy's argument against the "value-tending" account of aesthetic concepts in his "What Makes 'Aesthetic' Terms *Aesthetic?*" He argues that many aesthetic terms have no evaluative direction or polarity. But like many others, Kivy casts the issue in terms of aesthetic *terms*, which I think muddies the issue, since we are interested in aesthetic *judgments* and *concepts*.

23. See my "Groundrules in the Philosophy of Art," *Philosophy*, vol. 70 (1995), and "Art and Audience," *Journal of Aesthetics and Art Criticism*, vol. 57 (1999).

24. I am less sure about whether someone could make verdictive judgments without substantive judgments. Maybe young children have no consciousness of what *makes* things beautiful besides their primary and secondary qualities. But I think that it is impossible for someone to make substantive judgments but not verdictive judgments.

about showing that substantive and representational judgments make a different kind of normative demand. The determination account is far simpler than the neo-Kantian epicycles. On the determination account, substantive judgments have *derivative* aesthetic status. Aesthetic judgments are those which are either themselves subjectively universal or necessarily tied to judgments which are subjectively universal.

Those who thought of themselves as exploring the variety of our aesthetic conceptual repertoire tended to share the assumption that their investigation necessarily involved a *leveling* process. They were led to a kind of conceptual egalitarianism according to which all aesthetic concepts are on a par. But conceptual investigation does not have to be like this. The alternative, which I believe that real conceptual probing reveals, is that there is *structure* among our aesthetic concepts and judgments. Aesthetic properties are hierarchically structured, and this is reflected in aesthetic concepts and to some extent in aesthetic terms.

2.3 Determination and Laws

Given the determination view that I advocate, I need to say whether I think verdictive judgments can be *supported* by substantive judgments. For it might look as if I am endorsing a certain position in the debate about reasoning in aesthetics. It looks as if I am siding with those who say that there can be general reasons for aesthetic judgments.[25] The generalist thinks that there can, whereas the particularist thinks not. Generalists need not go as far as Monroe Beardsley, who held that there are a select group of exceptionless principles; a generalist need only hold with Frank Sibley, that there are what we can call *pro tanto* reasons—reasons which can be overridden.[26] These principles derive from the fact that properties such as elegance and delicacy have inherent polarity or evaluative direction.

However, in this debate I am on the particularist side, even though I agree with the thesis about the inherent evaluative polarity of elegance and delicacy.

In thinking about this, we need to note that substantive judgments might be *pro tanto* reasons for a verdictive judgment even though the substantive property might be an *overall* defect in a complex work. The merit of an ele-

25. See John Bender, "General but Defeasible Reasons in Aesthetic Evaluation: The Particularist/Generalist Dispute," *Journal of Aesthetics and Art Criticism,* vol. 53 (1995).

26. Monroe Beardsley "On the Generality of Critical Reasons," in *The Aesthetic Point of View* (Ithaca, N.Y.: Cornell University Press, 1982); Frank Sibley, "General Criteria and Reasons in Aesthetics," in *Essays on Aesthetics,* ed. John Fisher (Philadelphia: Temple University Press, 1983).

gant part survives even in a complex work in which the elegance of that part detracts from the overall value of the whole. Perhaps the other substantive properties of the whole are power and dynamism, and the one elegant part prevents the many other powerful and dynamic parts from combining to realize an overall powerful and dynamic work. Nevertheless, the lonely elegance persists.[27] It does not commit suicide out of guilt. The defender of the view that substantive judgments are reasons for verdictive judgments should say that substantive aesthetic properties have evaluative direction or polarity on their own and not merely in the context of a whole work. Elegance is always an aesthetic merit even though in the context of a whole work, the elegant part might lower the work's overall aesthetic excellence.

Nevertheless, I do not think that substantive judgments supply even *pro tanto* reasons, in any interesting sense, for a verdictive judgment. Interesting reasons for a verdictive judgment must put *pressure* on someone to accept it. I think that a dilemma opens up at this point. Either substantive judgments have evaluative content or not. If substantive judgments have no evaluative content, then they provide no support for the verdictive judgment. For someone could easily accept the substantive judgment but reject the verdictive judgment. On the other hand, suppose they have evaluative content. Might such a substantive judgment be put forward in support of a verdictive judgment? Surely not. For the substantive and verdictive judgments are too closely linked. Someone who rejects the verdictive judgment will also reject the substantive judgment.[28]

Someone might reply that if a substantive judgment has evaluative direction, why complain that it is too good a reason? Surely it is as good as it could be! But this is beside the point. The reason-giving relation between verdictive and substantive judgments might indeed be uncontroversial in some or all cases. In such cases, there is a trivial and uninteresting reason-giving relation because of the connection of meaning. But in all cases, the relation between the *nonaesthetic* and the substantive remains controversial. To give reasons for an aesthetic judgment, in any interesting sense, we need an epistemic route from the *nonaesthetic* to the aesthetic, not just from the substantive to the verdictive. But this is just what Sibley rightly denied when he said that aesthetic judgments were not positively condition-governed.[29]

If we take something's being G to be a reason for its being F, then this commits us to the generalization that all G things are F, other things being equal.

---

27. Contrast Bender, "General but Defeasible Reasons," section 2.
28. See chapter 1, section 3.2.
29. Sibley, "Aesthetic Concepts."

(R. M. Hare was right about that.) Aesthetic laws cannot flow from aesthetic to nonaesthetic properties because of the variable realization of aesthetic properties in nonaesthetic properties. The things that share an aesthetic property may have no ordinary nonaesthetic property in common (apart from some wildly disjunctive nonaesthetic property). If there were aesthetic laws, they would have to flow the other way, from nonaesthetic to aesthetic. The trouble is that these laws will be highly specific. They will bind only complex conjunctive nonaesthetic properties to aesthetic properties. But even if we grant such laws, they will be too complex for us to grasp and use as a basis for prediction.[30] Therefore they cannot underwrite reasons. Of course, less complex laws might be proposed, such as that one should not have blue in the foreground of a painting or that music in a major key sounds happy. But such purported laws tend to be doomed—Gainsborough's *Blue Boy* or Hank Williams come along to refute them.

Nonaesthetic properties are *responsible* for aesthetic properties; they determine them. But when some particular nonaesthetic property determines an aesthetic property, there is no connection of meaning between the concepts that pick out the two properties. So if we know that a thing has a certain nonaesthetic property, we are not thereby in a position to know that it has the aesthetic property. Nevertheless, this is not to say that there is no connection of meaning at all between aesthetic and nonaesthetic concepts. What we know as part of understanding aesthetic concepts is that if a thing has an aesthetic property, then it has *some* nonaesthetic property which is responsible for it. This is a *framework* principle.[31] It is an a priori presupposition of aesthetic thought. But knowing this general framework principle does not put us in a position to know any particular determination relation. For that, as Sibley rightly said, we need something more like 'taste', 'sensitivity', or 'perceptiveness', where these words denote a faculty of mind, of some sort or other, which is radically different from the faculties of mind involved in knowing about nonaesthetic properties.

2.4 Reasoning and Rhetoric

If we seek a diagnosis of the epistemic autonomy of the aesthetic, it is not hard to find. It lies in the subjectivity of judgments of aesthetic value. Just as

---

30. See my "Supervenience and Anomalous Monism," *Philosophical Studies*, vol. 71 (1993), and "Supervenience, Reduction and Infinite Disjunction," *Philosophia*, vol. 26 (1998).

31. See my "Moral Supervenience," *Midwest Studies*, vol. 20 (1995), for a parallel claim in moral philosophy.

Donald Davidson argued that mental and physical concepts are governed by radically disparate constraints which render them anomalous with respect to each other,[32] so subjective and nonsubjective (or empirical) forms of judgment are so radically different that we cannot bring the two into lawlike relation. And we need to do that if we are to reason from one to the other.

There is a limit set to reasoning about aesthetic matters. We must ultimately look or listen, and feel. I take comfort in the fact that writers such as Ernst Gombrich and Clement Greenberg retain a keen sense that art has a value which we can only appreciate, at least in part, by looking and feeling. As Kant said, one cannot be reasoned into judgments of beauty: "I stop my ears: I do not want to hear any reasons or arguing about the matter."[33]

If substantive judgments do not give reasons for verdictive judgments, then what *is* their role? Substantive judgments are more like *rationalizations*, in the pejorative sense, than reasons. Having judged that something is good or bad, the substantive judgment says what is good or bad about it.[34] As Greenberg said in an interview: "In criticism, the value judgment comes first." It is true that listening to others expressing their substantive judgments may persuade us to revise our verdictive judgments. But that is because our attention has been drawn to ways in which things achieve excellence or its opposite. It is more like *rhetoric* than *reasoning*. Rhetoric is most usefully defined in the Socratic way, by contrast with reasoning. In general, I think that there is a lot to be said for Socrates' critique of rhetoric in the *Gorgias*. But rhetoric might be defended in some domain if it can be argued (!) that it is not possible to reason in that domain. For then, only nonrational persuasion remains. Given the limits set to critical argument and reasoning in aesthetics, it is legitimate that part of critical discourse is a certain kind of rhetoric. But its end is nothing disreputable—it is nothing less than proper experience and judgment.

Such rhetoric should operate in tandem with our rational faculties. While there may be no arguing from the nonaesthetic to the aesthetic, there is a norm of consistency constraining aesthetic judgments. This norm dictates that differences in aesthetic judgments between two things must be accompanied by differences in nonaesthetic judgments. (This norm derives from

32. Donald Davidson, "Mental Events" and "Psychology as Philosophy," in *Essays on Actions and Events* (Oxford: Clarendon, 1980).

33. Kant, *Critique of Judgement*, p. 140.

34. For such an account of the role of so-called thick concepts in moral philosophy, which also deals with substantive aesthetic concepts, see Stephan Burton, "Thick Concepts Revisited," *Analysis*, vol. 53 (1992). See also Simon Blackburn's "Through Thick and Thin," *Aristotelian Society Supplementary Volume* 66 (1992).

the framework principle.) Aesthetic rhetoric inevitably starts from other responses and judgments of the person being addressed. It typically works by trying to get us to see something as having an aesthetic likeness to something that we already have a view about. Having nonrationally been brought to see an aesthetic likeness, we can then reason according to cannons of consistency. There can be reasoning about aesthetic matters—but its role is derivative. Aesthetic reasoning is, and ought only to be, the slave of the aesthetic passions.

Coda

To some extent, I would have aesthetics return to a state of prewar innocence. Things were far simpler and more straightforward in the good old days when aestheticians only had to worry about judgments of beauty and ugliness. That concern demarcated a distinctive topic—a form of judgment unlike empirical judgment and unlike judgments of the agreeable.

In the good old days, aestheticians did not worry about daintiness, dumpiness, elegance, balance, and the rest. But since J. L. Austin's jibe and one aspect of Sibley's work, aestheticians have become sensitive to the complex and varied nature of aesthetic description. Insofar as such description occurs, I suppose this is a good thing, to an extent, since we do not want to overlook phenomena. But there has also been a serious downside, which is that we have been distracted from philosophical issues which have greater centrality than the conscientious surface exploration of the subtle variety of aesthetic description.

There is more in philosophical life than the investigation of our concepts. There are pressing questions about whether, and if so how, the commitments of a range of concepts can be legitimate. In aesthetics, we should be interested in the Kantian question of how a judgment of taste is possible. But if we are to get to the issue about what if anything legitimizes a form of judgment, we need a decent picture of what we are seeking to justify.

I have argued that the category of the aesthetic is in good shape. It is not hopelessly amorphous and we should not dispense with it. We need not panic and exclude substantive judgments from the category of the aesthetic due to their lack of subjective universality or include representational judgments due to their boasting subjective universality. The determination account shows how the concept of the aesthetic nonarbitrarily groups verdictive and substantive judgments together while excluding representational judgments along with judgments of primary and secondary qualities. So there is a rationale for the contemporary concept of the aesthetic. The concept reflects an important independently functioning kind of judgment. The aesthetic is, as it were, a *natural mental kind*.

In my view this conceptual repair is timely. We need to have the concept up and running, in order to deploy it in our understanding of many aspects of human life. And in particular, it is about time we brought it back to bear on our understanding of art.

3 Levels

determine BUT different kinds of properties

① Metaphysical : substantive & verdictive Properties

② Psychological :
Substantive & verdictive judgments

$\neq$

③ Conceptual :
Concept of substantive & verdictive judgments

---

① Metaphysical : $Sp \xleftrightarrow{X} Vp$ (substantive determines to find the judgments + CONCEPT)

Determine

② Psychological : $Sj \xleftrightarrow{X} Vj$ (substantive judgments function is to serve the verdictive and find its CONCEPT)

serves

③ Conceptual : $CSj \longleftrightarrow CVj$

CHAPTER 3

(Determination relation) [handwritten]

Aesthetic Supervenience Defended

① Broad + Narrow [handwritten]
② Vague [handwritten]
③ Metaphysical + Epistemological [handwritten]

Since I shall be depending on the claim that a supervenience relation holds between aesthetic and nonaesthetic properties, I shall defend that claim in this short chapter. I will rebut three arguments against aesthetic/nonaesthetic supervenience: a contextual argument, a slippery slope argument, and an epistemological argument.[1]

(what is beautiful in one culture, may be ugly in another .) . [handwritten]

1 BROAD AND NARROW SUPERVENIENCE

The first argument takes off from a point that Kendall Walton made in his essay "Categories of Art."[2] Walton argued that the aesthetic properties of a work of art do not depend only on its *narrow* nonaesthetic properties. (By a narrow nonaesthetic property I mean an intrinsic primary property or a secondary property; a broad nonaesthetic property is one that is not neither an intrinsic primary property nor a secondary property, such as a historical property of a work; see further chapter 4, appendix A.) Walton argued that the aesthetic properties of a work of art also depend on certain of its relational properties—in particular, its relation to its history of production. Walton has two main sorts of example where this is so. First, the representational properties of a work of art depend on the conventions current at the time of

---

1. Versions of these arguments can be found in Robert Wicks, "Supervenience and Aesthetic Judgment," *Journal of Aesthetics and Art Criticism*, vol. 46 (1990); and "Supervenience and the Science of the Beautiful," *Journal of Aesthetic and Art Criticism* 50 (1992): 322–24.

2. Kendall Walton, "Categories of Art," *Philosophical Review*, vol. 79 (1970). I discuss this essay in detail in chapter 5.

43

its creation, and on the representational intentions of the artist. So if we are to assign representational properties correctly to a work of art, we need to know about the work's history of production. Second, the art-historical categorization of a work of art depends on its relation to other works of art. So assigning stylistic categories to a work of art cannot be done solely on the basis of its narrow nonaesthetic properties. This second point applies equally to representational and nonrepresentational works of art. Consider, for example, two narrowly indistinguishable works of art with different titles, which intimate different representational intentions.[3] Or consider two narrowly indistinguishable mosaics from quite different periods. In each case, the two artworks seem to differ in their aesthetic properties. The Waltonian point—if it is right—shows that the narrow nonaesthetic properties of a work of art do not suffice to determine its aesthetic properties.

Let us assume here that Walton is right, and let us postpone the assessment of Walton's thesis until later in this book. The point I want to make now is that even if Walton is right, it does *not* show that *no* aesthetic/nonaesthetic supervenience relation holds. It just shows that we need to widen the supervenience base. Although aesthetic properties of an object do not depend only on its narrow nonaesthetic properties, they *do* depend on its *narrow* nonaesthetic properties *plus* some of its *broad* nonaesthetic properties. The situation is exactly parallel to developments in the philosophy of mind. Hilary Putnam and Tyler Burge argued that mental properties do not supervene only on what is "in the head"—that is, on intrinsic physical properties of a person.[4] The content of a person's propositional attitudes is determined, in part, by a person's causal interactions with his environment. A certain intrinsic neurological or computational setup in the brain may be necessary, but it is not sufficient to determine content. Putnam and Burge argue that mental properties have a wider supervenience base than we previously thought. And Walton argues similarly in aesthetics. In both cases *narrow* supervenience fails, but *broad* supervenience is intact.

For example, consider the aesthetic properties of two indistinguishable mosaics—Roman and Byzantine. The aesthetic properties of each of them are perhaps determined not just by their narrow nonaesthetic properties but also by the broad historical fact that it is a Roman or Byzantine mosaic. So the reason there is an aesthetic difference between the Roman and Byzan-

---

3. See Jerrold Levinson, "Titles," in *Music, Art, and Metaphysics* (Ithaca, N.Y.: Cornell University Press, 1990).

4. Hilary Putnam, "The Meaning of Meaning," in *Mind, Language, and Reality* (Cambridge: Cambridge University Press, 1978); Tyler Burge, "Individualism and the Mental," *Midwest Studies in Philosophy*, vol. 5 (1979).

tine mosaics is that the two indistinguishable mosaics do not have *all* their nonaesthetic properties in common. They have similar *narrow* nonaesthetic properties but different *broad* nonaesthetic properties. One was created in the context of Roman culture and other Roman mosaics while the second was created in the context of Byzantine culture and other Byzantine mosaics. So there is what Simon Blackburn has called a "releasing" property, which is a difference in the subvening base that explains a supervening difference.[5] The argument only defeats narrow supervenience, and broad supervenience is left in the field.[6]

2 VAGUE SUPERVENIENCE

(handwritten: some artworks in one category can be fragile and another artwork in a different category can be fragile)

The second argument is that if all we can say is that two absolutely non-aesthetically indiscernible things must be aesthetically indiscernible, that would make the supervenience relation trivial because supervenience "would have no scope of application."[7] And once we try to make the relation less trivial by relaxing our restriction on the underlying nonaesthetic properties, we are in for trouble because there is a danger that the aesthetic property will no longer be instantiated.

(handwritten margin: different natural properties can determine the SAME THING.)

There seems to be a straightforward reply to this, which is to appeal to the variable realization of aesthetic properties in nonaesthetic properties: the supervenience relation allows that necessities flow one way, up from the base to the supervening level, without requiring that there is something in common between all the base-level setups that determine a certain type of supervening property. So that which determines an aesthetic property can be a very specific particular nonaesthetic setup. Other instantiations of the same aesthetic property can be determined quite differently. Something can be elegant in virtue of its smooth and curving lines, but not any old smooth curving lines will determine elegance; they have to be smooth and curving in exactly that way. So maybe there is nothing wrong with disallowing flexibility in the subvening nonaesthetic base of a particular instantiation of an

(handwritten vertical margin: MULTIPLE REALIZED!)

5. Simon Blackburn, "Supervenience Revisited," in *Essays on Quasi-Realism* (Oxford: Oxford University Press, 1993), p. 50.

6. We must be careful: what the supervenience base includes are not properties like 'being *judged* as a mosaic' or 'being *judged* as a Roman mosaic' but properties like '*being* a mosaic' or '*being* a Roman mosaic'. To judge a mosaic which *is* a Roman mosaic as a Byzantine mosaic would be to make a mistake. (Cf. Wicks, "Supervenience and Aesthetic Judgment," p. 510.) If Walton is right, one should judge a Roman mosaic as a Roman mosaic.

7. Wicks, "Supervenience and Aesthetic Judgment," p. 511.

(handwritten: Example: a human brain state is pain; if a dog can have a brain state is also pain; then it is not just a human quality.)

It seems like there is room for ambiguity. (in supervience) → different PHYSICAL properties can have same AESTHETIC properties.

aesthetic property. Aesthetic supervenience seems to be perfectly consistent with allowing that aesthetic properties are acutely sensitive to small variations in their nonaesthetic base.[8]

But this reply is too quick. For when we have a particular aesthetic/nonaesthetic dependency, not *every* nonaesthetic property of the object is necessary for the aesthetic property. There are some *restrictions* on which nonaesthetic properties do the determining of the aesthetic property. There are interesting questions here about 'subvening relevance', which also crop up in moral philosophy and the philosophy of mind. Maybe the exact physical make up of our brains does not matter for the determination of mental properties, and all that matters is the functional system that our brains instantiate. And maybe whether a person stands in a certain relation to me is not of moral relevance.

The complaint against aesthetic/nonaesthetic supervenience might be that once we allow that very slight deviations in the supervenience base do not make any supervening difference, we then have no choice but to allow greater differences in the base; but then at some point there will be a nonaesthetic difference which makes an aesthetic difference. It is a slippery slope. Once we admit that some nonaesthetic properties are aesthetically irrelevant, where do we stop? We can also run the argument the other way. Imagine that someone thought that aesthetic/nonaesthetic supervenience involved dependencies like: the aesthetic property of delicacy depends on the nonaesthetic property of having smooth curving lines. But there are many very different ways that a line can be smooth and curving without being delicate. What this shows is that referring to something as having smooth curving lines is not sufficient to pick out the nonaesthetic properties that determine delicacy. We need to specify the nonaesthetic properties more exactly. But then the problem is whether we can stop before fixing absolutely every nonaesthetic property of a thing. In which case, there never could be two nonaesthetically identical things, and supervenience would be trivial. This is not so much an argument as a challenge.

We can approach this problem by a roundabout route. Consider a related problem which I believe throws light on the slippery slope problem. Suppose that an object is delicate in virtue of having the total property $N\star_1$. (An $N\star$ property of a thing conjoins *all* of the nonaesthetic properties of a thing that play a role in determining its aesthetic properties.) However, suppose that the object would also be delicate if instead it had the total property $N\star_2$. Now

8. Wicks puts the idea by talking of the "volatile" character of the aesthetic qualities of great works of art. ("Supervenience and the Science of the Beautiful," p. 323.)

suppose that someone asks the question: is the difference between $N^\star_1$ and $N^\star_2$ aesthetically relevant? We must be careful before answering this question. For $N^\star_1$ might be *very* different from $N^\star_2$ and yet the resulting object might still be delicate because of the variable realization of delicacy in nonaesthetic properties. It is plausible that delicacy is variably realized; very different things can be delicate (marks on paper, sounds, sentences). But then, the question is: what is the difference between this sort of radical variable realization case and the sort of case where we have a small nonaesthetic difference that makes little or no aesthetic difference? Perhaps $N^\star_2$ differs only very slightly from $N^\star_1$. The worry I am trying to induce is that there may be no real difference between the variable realization case and the tiny difference case. At very least, the challenge is to say what the difference is.

I suggest the following solution to this problem. Suppose that the aesthetic property is what I shall call a "total" aesthetic property, $A^\star$. An $A^\star$ property is the conjunction of *all* the aesthetic properties that the thing in fact possesses. We understand the idea of a thing's total aesthetic character, even if it might transcend our ability to state or know that character. (The idea of a conjunctive total property has been deployed for *subvening* properties, but not, as far as I know, for *supervening* properties.)[9] *Total* $A^\star$ properties contrast with *specific* aesthetic properties, like delicacy or elegance. We can then distinguish total and specific aesthetic determination. We can either consider the determination of *all* of a thing's aesthetic properties, that is, of its total $A^\star$ property, or we can consider the determination of a *specific* aesthetic property of a thing.

What we can say now is that in the variable realization case, the difference between objects which are $N^\star_1$ and $N^\star_2$, where the difference between them is huge, is aesthetically irrelevant for the determination of the instantiation of the *specific* aesthetic property of delicacy, but it is aesthetically relevant for the determination of the instantiation of the *total* $A^\star$ property. By contrast, in the tiny difference case, we can say that the difference between objects which are $N^\star_1$ and $N^\star_2$, where the difference between them is tiny, is aesthetically irrelevant *both* for the determination of the instantiation of the total $A^\star$ property *as well as* for the determination of $A^\star$'s specific aesthetic conjuncts. This is the difference between the two cases. The worry I tried to induce is removed once we see the contrast between the determination of a thing's $A^\star$ property by a certain narrow disjunctive range of $N^\star$ properties, and the wild and wide sort of variable realization of specific aesthetic properties by all sort of quite different $N^\star$ things. A vast nonaesthetic

9. See my "Supervenience, Reduction, and Infinite Disjunction," *Philosophia*, vol. 26 (1998), for a discussion of subvening conjunctions and disjunctions.

CONSIDER THE TOTAL AMOUNT/KINDS OF
PROPERTIES. Example: TA (Total aesthetic properties)
N_1 BIG DIFF. BETWEEN $N_2 \rightarrow$ TA is altered.
(of both natural matures)

departure will jeopardize the realization of the A★ property although some of A★'s specific aesthetic conjuncts may be intact. But the A★ property can only be realized by something pretty similar to what in fact did determine the A★ property.

To be less abstract: take a painting which is delicate in virtue of certain lines and colors (among other things, perhaps). It might still have been delicate even if it had very slightly different lines and colors. But things can be delicate which are not remotely like this delicate painting. For example, a delicate piece of music does not have much nonaesthetically in common with the delicate painting. But although the piece of music and the painting may both be delicate, they will not be delicate in the same way. There are *other* aesthetic differences. The two works of art share one specific aesthetic property—that of delicacy—but they differ with respect to many other aesthetic properties; therefore they possess different total A★ properties.

We were anxious about the difference between the case of the subvening difference which makes *no* supervening difference and the case of the subvening difference which *does* make a supervening difference. If we have not distinguished total and specific determination, this will be worrying. For we will want both to say that a rather large subvening difference may make a supervening difference and that it may not, which seems paradoxical. But there is no problem once we see that it will make a *total* supervening difference but that it may not make a *specific* supervening difference. A large subvening difference may leave *some* specific aesthetic properties intact, but it is bound to change others; so it will make an A★ difference. If we focus just on total determination, we can recast the issue as one about the difference between the case where a subvening difference makes an A★ difference and the case where it does not.

There is now no danger that supervenience will evaporate. For it is quite acceptable that this sort of determination is a matter of degree, just as determination elsewhere often is. There is only so much that you can do to a table before it ceases to be a table. But there is no sharp cutoff point. It is the same with aesthetic determination. Given some aesthetic/nonaesthetic dependency, something other than the actual nonaesthetic setup might have produced the same total A★ property. There is flexibility in the supervenience base. But while the disjunctive set of nonaesthetic properties which can realize any *specific* aesthetic property is very wide indeed (due to variable realization), for any *total* A★ property, there is a quite narrow disjunctive range of nonaesthetic setups which can do the job. Stick within that set and A★ will be preserved; stray too far outside that set and A★ will be jeopardized. The more the nonaesthetic base is altered, the more likely it is that A★ will be lost. It is a vague matter—a matter of degree. We can go some way before the supervening property is threatened. But eventually it is unclear whether it is realized. And there will come a point where it is clear that it is not realized. This is how we should expect it to be. The slope may be smooth but it is not slippery.[10]

If you can learn abat one, you can lean abut the other (KNOWLEDGE)

3 Metaphysical and Epistemological Supervenience

The third argument is that if a supervenience relation holds between two sorts of properties, then given our knowledge of one sort of property, we should be able to *infer* knowledge of the other; but we cannot, so supervenience fails.[11]

However, this objection assumes that supervenience should play an epistemological role. By contrast, I take supervenience to be a relation between two families of properties, and therefore a metaphysical relation. The supervenience claim is that if something has an aesthetic property, then it has some nonaesthetic property such that necessarily anything which has the nonaesthetic property has the aesthetic property, and that says nothing about anyone's knowledge of anything.[12] Supervenience is a relation of metaphysical determination between two families of properties, and we should concede that supervenience is pretty austere as a source of knowledge.

For example, if we do not *know* whether a mosaic is a Roman or Byzantine mosaic then, if Walton is right, we will not be in a position to ascribe aesthetic properties to it because we do not know its art-historical context. This is analogous to the way that we must know the motive for a piece of behavior if we are to be in a position to evaluate it morally. We cannot evaluate a thing unless we know something about its relevant nonevaluative properties. But this is irrelevant to the issue of whether a metaphysical determination relation holds. Such a relation may hold between aesthetic and nonaesthetic properties whether or not we know the nonaesthetic properties that do the determining. The only complication that arises in the mosaic example is that we know *part* of the relevant supervenience base—their narrow physical properties—without knowing the whole, which includes their art-historical context.

10. It is perhaps worth noting that we do not really have a proper slope here, never mind a slippery one. *Some* slight changes make no aesthetic difference whereas equally slight or perhaps less slight changes may make a substantial difference. It is not necessarily a linear matter.

11. Cf. Wicks, "Supervenience and the Science of the Beautiful," p. 322.

12. See Jaegwon Kim, "Concepts of Supervenience," in *Supervenience and Mind* (Cambridge: Cambridge University Press, 1993) on how best to understand and formulate the notion.

In spite of this, the claim of aesthetic/nonaesthetic supervenience is not totally devoid of epistemological consequence. For if we know that something has a nonaesthetic property and also that it has some aesthetic property, and that its having the aesthetic property supervenes upon its having the nonaesthetic property, then given our knowledge that something else also has the same nonaesthetic property, we can infer that it too has the same aesthetic property. So the notion does have *some* epistemological bite. But this does not give us the knowledge that a thing has an aesthetic property given only the knowledge that it has some nonaesthetic property. But there is no reason to think that the supervenience relation would illuminate our knowledge of supervening properties in that way.

We must distinguish between knowing that supervenience holds and knowing the particular dependencies which figure in the consequent of the overall supervenience conditional. Supervenience says that if something has an aesthetic property then it has some nonaesthetic property such that necessarily anything that has that nonaesthetic property has the aesthetic property. But one could know that without knowing that everything which has the nonaesthetic property necessarily has the aesthetic property. That is, one could know that a supervenience relation holds without knowing particular dependencies.

The epistemological austerity of supervenience is connected with the lawlessness of aesthetic properties that we encountered in the first two chapters. We should not confuse the supervenience relation with rules or laws of taste. Of course, given something which has certain aesthetic properties in virtue of certain nonaesthetic properties, then something almost exactly like the first thing in all relevant nonaesthetic respects will also possess the same aesthetic properties. That is a law of sorts; but it is an *uninteresting* law since the properties it binds are very complex.[13] The nonaesthetic properties that determine aesthetic properties are highly specific, very complex conjunctive nonaesthetic properties. So particular dependencies will not have the generality appropriate for laws or rules. Knowing that something has an aesthetic property in virtue of a specific complex conjunction of nonaesthetic properties, so that the conjunction of nonaesthetic properties suffices for the instantiation of the aesthetic property, would not be to know a rule for predicting aesthetic properties. Most obviously, we would not know anything to the effect that, say, graceful things will always be produced in certain nonaes-

13. See my "Supervenience and Anomalous Monism," *Philosophical Studies*, vol. 71 (1993), for the importance of the qualifier "interesting" when discussing laws.) There I argue that strong psychophysical supervenience is compatible with the absence of psychophysical laws which are "interesting" in the sense I define.

thetic ways. That confuses the sufficient conditions which supervenience involves with necessary conditions. Less obviously, the sufficient conditions of the dependencies will not generalize in an interesting way due to their conjunctive complexity. It is this which explains the sensitivity of aesthetic properties to variations in their bases. Specific aesthetic/nonaesthetic dependencies are too particular to generalize to form rules for predicting aesthetic instantiations, except for the uninteresting rule that given something which has an aesthetic property in virtue of certain nonaesthetic properties, anything just like it in nonaesthetic respects will have the same aesthetic properties.

Lastly, someone might argue that we should not believe in supervenience just because it is epistemologically sterile. This raises the question of how we might ever come to assert a supervenience relation if it is epistemologically useless in particular instances. We can imagine someone complaining that I have in effect agreed that we have no right to assert such a relation. We now run up against a deep and difficult issue—that of the status of the supervenience principle. In my view, no one has really come to grips with this issue in *any* area where supervenience is employed, although Nathan Salmon has an illuminating discussion of the status of essentialist principles in various areas.[14] My view is that aesthetic/nonaesthetic supervenience, like moral/natural supervenience, has an a priori status, by contrast with psychophysical supervenience and by contrast with essentialism about natural kinds and about species/genus subsumption. Part of knowing what moral or aesthetic properties are is knowing that they supervene on natural properties.[15] Supervenience is partly *constitutive* of thinking in moral or aesthetic terms. So we do not need to assert supervenience on the basis of its predictive usefulness on particular occasions.

We can persist in holding aesthetic/nonaesthetic supervenience as a metaphysical relation between aesthetic and nonaesthetic properties. The three arguments we have considered in this chapter need not give the devote of supervenience any sleepless nights. Long live supervenience!

14. See Nathan Salmon, *Reference and Essence* (Oxford: Blackwell, 1981), chapters 5, 6, and appendix 2.

15. See further my "Moral Supervenience," *Midwest Studies*, vol. 20 (1996).

PART TWO

FORMALISM

CHAPTER 4

Feasible Aesthetic Formalism

Aesthetic Formalism has fallen on hard times. At best it receives unsympathetic discussion and swift rejection. At worst it is the object of abuse and derision. But I think that there is something to be said for it. In this chapter, I shall try to find and secure the truth in formalism. I shall not try to defend formalism against all of the objections.[1] Instead I shall articulate a *moderate* formalist view which draws on aesthetic/nonaesthetic determination and Kant's distinction between free and dependent beauty. I shall examine four central art forms—painting, architecture, literature, and music—and I shall show that only moderate formalism provides a satisfactory understanding of them.[2]

in class, only discuss PAINTING & MUSIC.

1 FORMAL/NONFORMAL: A KANTIAN DEPENDENT BEAUTY ACCOUNT

1.1   I shall characterize formalism in terms of aesthetic/nonaesthetic *determination*. I assume as a fundamental principle that aesthetic properties are determined by nonaesthetic properties.[3] By the determination of aesthetic properties by nonaesthetic properties, I mean that if something has an aesthetic property, then it has *some* conjunction of nonaesthetic properties

---

1. I discharge the duty of critically examining the arguments against formalism in the next three chapters. But in this chapter, I put the defensive dialectic to one side and am concerned to spell out a tenable formalism.

2. I assume that the issue of formalism is one about the kind of aesthetic properties that works of art have and not an issue about the nature of art.

3. See Frank Sibley, "Aesthetic/Nonaesthetic," *Philosophical Review*, vol. 74 (1965).

which is *responsible for* the aesthetic property. It has the aesthetic property *in virtue of* the conjunction of nonaesthetic properties. Once we admit this thesis, there is then an issue about *which* nonaesthetic properties determine aesthetic properties. The determination thesis itself says nothing about the scope of the nonaesthetic properties that determine aesthetic properties. Which nonaesthetic properties are aesthetically relevant? This is where the issue of formalism should be located.

Let us fix the issue with some paradigm cases of formal properties—for those who believe in them. The formal aesthetic properties of abstract paintings are thought to be those aesthetic properties that are determined solely by arrangements of lines, shapes and colors on their surfaces.[4] (I include shininess and glossiness as color properties.) Similarly, the formal aesthetic properties of absolute music are thought to be those aesthetic properties that are determined solely by arrangements of sounds in time. In these two cases, sensory properties—colors and sounds—are crucial. But in abstract sculptures, some formal aesthetic properties are thought to be those that are determined by the three-dimensional spatial relations between the physical parts of the sculpture. So formal properties are not thought to be restricted to those aesthetic properties that are determined solely by sensory properties. By contrast, nonformal aesthetic properties are thought to be those aesthetic properties which are determined in part by the history or context of the work of art, such as the artist's intentions in making it, or the wider artistic culture or social circumstances in which it was created. We want a general account of formal and nonformal properties that makes sense of the classification of these paradigm cases.

The most straightforward account would be to say that formal properties are those aesthetic properties that are determined solely by sensory or physical properties—so long as the physical properties in question are not relations to other things or other times. This would capture the intuitive idea that formal properties are those aesthetic properties that are directly perceivable or that are determined by properties that are directly perceivable. The only trouble is that some philosophers think that all aesthetic properties are dispositions to provoke responses in human beings, and it is not clear whether any such dispositions would be formal properties on the straightforward account. In order to finesse this difficulty, and in order to keep things as simple as pos-

---

4. Kant asserts, bizarrely, that colors are irrelevant to a judgment of taste and that design is all (*Critique of Judgement*, trans. James Meredith [Oxford: Oxford University Press, 1928], pp. 67–68). But Roger Fry argues persuasively for the formal relevance of color in "Plastic Colour," in *Transformations* (London: Chatto & Windus, 1926).

sible, I shall stipulate that the word "narrow" includes both sensory properties, nonrelational physical properties, and also any dispositions to provoke
responses that might be thought to be partly constitutive of aesthetic properties. The word "broad" covers anything else. So we can blandly say:

> Formal properties are entirely determined by narrow nonaesthetic properties,
> whereas nonformal aesthetic properties are partly determined by broad non-
> aesthetic properties.

The history of production of a work is always a broad property of it, since it
is not a sensory property, nor is it a nonrelational physical property, nor is it a
dispositional relation to our responses. So the history of production of a
work of art does not partly determine its formal aesthetic properties. I give
the rationale of this characterization in an appendix to this chapter.

There is a difficulty with this notion of a formal property: although it captures most common uses of 'form', there are some rogue uses, in writings on
painting and literature which it does not fit so comfortably. (In fact it would
be surprising if the characterization fitted them all, given the proliferation of
uses.) In particular, we need to say something about the notions of three-
dimensional plastic form in painting and of structural form in literature. I
shall deal with these notions in sections 2 and 4.

1.2 I characterized formal properties as a certain kind of *aesthetic properties,* which requires comment.

(a) In the class of aesthetic properties, I include verdictive properties such as
beauty, ugliness, and also aesthetic value and disvalue if these are different from
beauty and ugliness. I also include substantive properties, such as elegance,
daintiness, dumpiness, power, balance and delicacy.[5] I assume that this is a significant grouping. I think that it can be argued that it is; but I shall not go into
this here.[6] I will return to this list later, as a touchstone of properties that
count as aesthetic.

(b) By an aesthetic property I do not mean any property of a work of art,
or a property which makes something art. This follows from the preceding
point. Natural things possess aesthetic properties; and works of art possess
many nonaesthetic properties. In particular, we should distinguish aesthetic
values from other values. Works of art have many values besides aesthetic val-

---

5. I have argued in chapters 1–3 that verdictive evaluative aesthetic properties are determined
by substantive aesthetic properties. Nothing here depends on that assumption.

6. See chapter 2.

ues—moral, political, religious or emotional values, for example. Works of art are multipurpose things, and there is no reason to suppose that aesthetic values are the only values they possess, even though these may be particularly important. Formal values (if there are any) are a subclass of aesthetic values, and in a work of art, aesthetic values are a subclass of artistic values.

(c) In speaking of aesthetic "properties," I do not mean to commit myself to aesthetic realism. I leave open controversial questions about the metaphysical nature of aesthetic properties. I want the discussion to be neutral between realist, projectivist and response-dependent views of aesthetic properties. All I assume is the falsity of an error theory according to which aesthetic thought and talk is a mistake.[7]

(1.3) So far we have been thinking about formal and nonformal *properties* but what about formal*ism*? *Extreme formalism* is the view that *all* the aesthetic properties of a work of art are formal. *Anti-formalism* is the view that *none* of them are formal. The extreme formalist believes that all aesthetic properties are *narrowly determined* (by sensory or intrinsic and contemporaneous spatial properties or dispositions to provoke responses) whereas the anti-formalist believes that they are all *broadly determined* (by the history of production of the work as well as its narrow nonaesthetic properties). The issue runs parallel to an issue in the philosophy of mind, where many have argued that mental properties are not determined solely by neurophysiological properties, but also by what is outside the head—in particular, by the causal origins of internal states. In the philosophy of mind, the issue is whether mental properties are determined solely by what is under the skin, whereas in the aesthetics of painting, for example, the issue is whether aesthetic properties are determined solely by what is within the frame or on the canvas. *Moderate formalism* is the view that while *some* aesthetic properties of a work of art are formal, others are not. As we will see, the moderate formalist *concedes* that representational works have nonformal aesthetic properties. And he *concedes* that what I shall call "contextual" works have nonformal aesthetic properties—where contextual works are works that are intended to be seen only in the light of other works.[8] But the moderate formalist insists that there are *some* works of art

---

7. See John Mackie, *Ethics* (Harmondsworth, England: Penguin, 1977), for an error theory in moral philosophy.

8. Duchamp's *Fountain* would be an obvious example, as would Arthur Danto's imaginary array of indiscernible red square paintings (see his "Works of Art and Mere Real Things," in *The Transfiguration of the Commonplace* [Cambridge: Harvard University Press, 1981]).

that *only* have formal aesthetic properties. The strategy of tactical retreat defines the moderate formalist view.[9]

1.4   Now, in order to defend and refine moderate formalism, we need to pursue a deeper understanding of what *non*formal aesthetic properties are. It is not enough merely to say that the nonformal aesthetic properties of a thing are aesthetic properties that are *not* determined by its narrow nonaesthetic properties, and which *are* determined in part by some facts or other about its history of production. Which historical facts are relevant? And why? Moreover, we need to understand how formal and nonformal aesthetic properties can figure *together* in the overall aesthetic nature of a work of art. How are formal and nonformal aesthetic properties related? How do they combine? Maybe it has been because we lack an understanding of these matters that people have made the mistake of assuming either that works of art only have formal aesthetic properties or else they have none.

I propose that we should reach for the invaluable but misunderstood and underappreciated distinction that Kant drew between "free" and "dependent" beauty.[10] We can best understand nonformal aesthetic properties in terms of dependent beauty, and formal properties in terms of free beauty. But we do not have to buy into Kant's exact way of making the distinction in order to use it with great profit. The distinction can be cut loose from Kant's terminology and his specific views about the judgment of taste. And as we shall see, the distinction can be put to work to help us to understand a wide range of art forms. Indeed I go so far as to say that without this distinction, or something like it, we cannot begin to understand the aesthetics of pictorial representation, poetry, architecture, nonabsolute music, and much more. Dependent beauty is the key to understanding the nonformal aesthetic properties of art.

Kant introduces the free/dependent distinction in terms of whether a judgment of beauty involves subsuming an object under a certain concept. Many have charged Kant with inconsistency, since he says earlier in the *Critique of Judgement* (in sections 1 and 6) that the judgment of beauty is not cognitive and does not derive its universality from concepts.[11] I believe that this charge can

---

9. There are also other cases where we should tactically retreat. As we shall see, there is a general principle at work determining when tactical retreat is in order, and representation and contextuality turn out to be instances of that principle.

10. Kant, *Critique of Judgement*, section 16.

11. See, for example, Ruth Lorand, "Kant on Free and Dependent Beauty," *British Journal of Aesthetics*, vol. 29 (1989).

be met in Kant's own terms. But I do not want to get tangled in exegetical concerns, except to note that it is absolutely crucial to see that Kant's view is not just that a judgment of dependent beauty involves a *concept* but that it involves a concept of an *end* or *purpose*. Judgments of free beauty do not.[12]

Kant is often thought to be the wellspring of formalism. But since he accepts the category of dependent beauty, this is a major error. In view of the abuse he has suffered for being a formalist, it is ironic that Kant is an *anti-formalist* about many art forms, because he thinks that they have a purpose that must be understood.[13]

Examples of both free and dependent beauty can be found in nature as well as art. Kant cites flowers, birds, and crustaceans as examples of natural free beauties; and he cites wallpaper designs and instrumental music as examples of artificial free beauties. Kant cites horses as natural dependent beauties, and buildings as artificial dependent beauties. To add some examples of my own: some natural things—such as feathers and butterfly wings—can be judged in terms of both free and dependent beauty. Rocks, however, are inanimate natural things that have no natural function; so only by committing an error can we see them as having dependent beauty. On the other hand, it would be difficult to find an arm freely beautiful; if an arm is beautiful it is beautiful *as* an arm—a thing with a certain function. As we shall see, it is the same with many representational works of art in that they are beautiful only as things with a certain representational function. Judging an abstract work to have representational beauty would involve an error. We find both natural and artistic things dependently beautiful in the light of what we believe to be their function.[14]

12. According to Kant, when we make a judgment of *dependent* beauty, a certain kind of concept figures *in* our representation of the object to which pleasure is a response. On the other hand, Kant's *general* claim about the judgment of taste in the first moment of the *Critique of Judgement* is that, *given* a representation of an object, a judgment of its beauty is based on a pleasure in that representation. So a judgment of beauty is not a cognitive judgment which would involve subsuming an object under a concept of beauty. A sympathetic reconstruction of Kant on free and dependent beauty can be found in Eva Schaper, *Studies in Kant's Aesthetics* (Edinburgh: Edinburgh University Press, 1979), chap. 4.

13. To make just one observation: when Kant made the free/dependent distinction he was not ranking free beauty above dependent beauty as is often erroneously alleged. Schaper is good on this point in her *Studies in Kant's Aesthetics*. Kant writes: "Taste, it is true, stands to gain by the combination of intellectual delight with the aesthetic" (*Critique of Judgement*, p. 73).

14. Human beauty is a special case. We cannot see human beauty as we see the beauty of flowers and rocks. We must see a beautiful person as such. We cannot appreciate a person as abstract sculpture, although a person may embody purely sculptural formal values. This point is illustrated by Kant's point (and I think he is right, although some will find this controversial) that tattooing defaces the human body even when the tattoo itself has intrinsic beauty. For Kant, tattooing is a dependently ugly thing to do to the human body. Moral philosophers and aestheticians might reflect on why this is so.

1.5   I would like to recast Kant's distinction as a point about the *property* of beauty rather than as a point about the *judgment* of beauty. I want to do this in order to abstract from Kant's terminology and his specific views about the judgment of taste. Let us say that something is dependently beautiful if it is *beautiful as a thing with a certain function*. A thing is not dependently beautiful merely in virtue of executing some function *and* being beautiful; instead dependent beauty is a matter of the *apt aesthetic embodiment or aesthetic realization* of some function. In a case of dependent beauty, a thing is not just beautiful *and* a functional thing of certain sort, but beautiful *as* a thing with that function. Ascriptions of dependent beauty are thus like 'large' or 'good' according to Peter Geach.[15] Ascriptions of free beauty are not like this. However, this appeal to the *as* locution does not take us very far.

We need to understand dependent beauty as beauty that has a certain broad determination base. (Kant chose an appropriate word when he talked of "dependent" beauty.) If a natural thing is dependently beautiful, its beauty is determined in part by the nonaesthetic property of having a certain evolutionary function. And if a work of art is dependent beautiful, its beauty is determined in part by the functional properties that were bestowed on it by a certain history of production. In particular, the artist's *intentions* are the source of the function. For example, a work may be intended to be a representation of a certain sort; and if that intention is successfully realized, the work ends up fulfilling the representational function that the artist gave it. Unless someone else intentionally modifies that function, the initial function persists. The work may then be beautiful as a representation of that sort.

On this approach, a work of art has nonformal aesthetic properties because of the way it embodies (realizes, expresses, articulates) some historically given nonaesthetic function. Formal aesthetic properties do not depend on the fact that the thing has some nonaesthetic function—or indeed any function at all. This distinguishes the two sorts of aesthetic properties.

1.6   There is an important additional level of complexity. So far, we have focused on the way different kinds of nonaesthetic properties determine aesthetic properties. However, it is also true that the aesthetic properties of a work are often (and are often intended to be) appropriate to *other* aesthetic properties of the work. For example, the dependent aesthetic properties determined by a representation in a painting might fit snugly with the aesthetic properties determined by the two-dimensional design in which the

15. Peter Geach, "Good and Evil," in *Theories of Ethics*, ed. Philippa Foot (Oxford: Oxford University Press, 1967).

representation is realized. Different aesthetic properties of aspects of a work can combine, where each is aesthetically appropriate to the other, to determine further aesthetic properties of the whole. This is the phenomenon of organic unity which interested G. E. Moore.[16] An aesthetic property of one aspect of a work of art can have a function with respect to its other aspects. And it can fulfill that function in an aesthetically interesting way. Formal aesthetic values, nonformal aesthetic values, and nonaesthetic artistic values can all combine so as to produce an aesthetic effect.

I have given a rather abstract account of the way we should understand nonformal aesthetic properties and the way they relate to formal aesthetic properties. Let us now consider how this applies to various art forms. This will allow us to appreciate the virtues of moderate formalism.

2 REPRESENTATIONAL PAINTING

2.1   Theories of formalism in the visual arts emerged at the beginning of the twentieth century when there was a tendency toward abstraction in painting, in the wake of Cézanne, Picasso, and others. The popularity of formalism at that time had much to do with that tendency. There is no doubt that much of what Clive Bell and Roger Fry say on this topic is propaganda for a particular artistic movement, dressed up as philosophical reflection.[17] However, the position that formalism defines is not one that is necessarily linked to any artistic movement or style. It has universal application.[18]

Bell and Fry did not deny the existence of representational properties, but for them aesthetic properties and representational properties stood side by side—independent of each other.[19] But—as thousands complained—this is very implausible. There is beauty in the *way* something is represented, which is a beauty over and above its beauty as abstract design. Something is not just

16. G. E. Moore, *Principia Ethica* (Cambridge: Cambridge University Press, 1903), chap. 6. The appellation "organic" is fitting in that the unity in question is like that of a living system where parts have a purpose with respect to each other and with respect to the whole.

17. Clive Bell, *Art* (London: Chatto & Windus, 1914); Roger Fry, *Vision and Design* (London: Chatto & Windus, 1920), and *Transformations*.

18. Noel Carroll makes this point in "Clive Bell's Aesthetic Hypothesis," in *Aesthetics: A Critical Anthology*, ed. George Dickie et al., 2d ed. (New York: St. Martin's, 1989).

19. Bell writes "a man will paint an execution and, fearing to miss with his first barrel of significant form, will try to hit with his second by raising an emotion of fear or pity" (*Art*, p. 39). At other places, nonformal values are not distinguished from aesthetic ones but rudely dismissed: "if a representative form has value, it is as form not as representation. The representative element in a work of art may or may not be harmful; always it is irrelevant" (p. 36). See also Fry, *Vision and Design*, pp. 23, 29, 197.

a beautiful pattern *and* a picture of a tree but beautiful *as* a picture of a tree. The two properties are not merely added but multiplied.

This is because representational beauty is a kind of dependent beauty, in the sense that I outlined in the last section. We have to understand a picture's *representational function* if we are to appreciate its beauty as a representation of a tree.[20] The purely formal properties of representational paintings should not be ignored even when the aesthetic properties determined by represen- tations are more important. That much should be conceded to Bell and Fry. But it is not enough to save their extreme formalist claim that all the aes- thetic properties of representational paintings are formal.[21]

2.2   Although I agree with the anti-formalist critics that Bell and Fry cannot do justice to the aesthetic properties of representational works, the usual argument at this point is not decisive. For all we have been offered is a range of counterexamples. But someone could simply insist, as Bell and Fry do, that the aesthetic and representational properties of a work of art are independent. Why should we think that there *are* any aesthetic properties that depend on representational properties? Why is it not aesthetically irrele- vant that a picture represents what it does?

At this point, we have to rely on our intuitive aesthetic judgments. The problem for Bell and Fry is that people make aesthetic judgments about both abstract patterns and representations, and they express these aesthetic judg- ments in similar words. In chapter 2 I offered a principled way of drawing the line between aesthetic and nonaesthetic judgments. But for our present purposes we do not need a full-blown theory of the distinction. We can draw on a list of paradigm cases of aesthetic properties that I offered in sec- tion 1.2(a). And given that an aesthetic judgment is one that ascribes an aes- thetic property, that list enables us to distinguish aesthetic and nonaesthetic judgments. The list included beauty, elegance, and delicacy; and people do make judgments of beauty, elegance and delicacy about both abstract pat- terns and representations. But if Bell and Fry are right, this is a huge mistake.

20. I assume something like Richard Wollheim's view of pictorial representation ("Seeing-in, Seeing-as, and Pictorial Representation," in *Art and its Objects*, 2d ed. [Cambridge: Cambridge University Press, 1980]). Being a representation with a certain content depends in part on the intentions with which the representation was produced. If the Aztecs did not intend their carvings to represent space aliens, then they don't.

21. Clement Greenberg explicitly addresses the issue of formalism in "Complaints of an Art Critic" and in his reply to Max Kozloff in *Clement Greenberg: The Collected Essays and Criticism,* ed. John O'Brian, vol. 4 (Chicago: University of Chicago Press, 1993). I believe that Greenberg was reaching for the idea of the dependent aesthetic value of representation when he talks about how difficult it is to "talk *relevantly* of the literary factor in painting and sculpture" (p. 274, his emphasis).

In the case of a beautiful representation of a tree (or of some particular tree), it is intuitive that its aesthetic properties are not merely *conjoined* with the representational properties but partly *determined* by them. There is beauty in the *way* it represents a tree. It is a case of dependent beauty. Bell's and Fry's view that representation has no aesthetic role at all is quite implausible. Of course, some of our judgments about representations are nonaesthetic; but it is not plausible that they all are. This implausibility is what almost everyone finds unappealing about Bell's and Fry's formalism. (By contrast, Clement Greenberg carefully distances himself from such a principled eradication of representational aesthetic values.)[22] The eradication of specifically representational aesthetic properties is out of synch with our ordinary aesthetic experience and thought. This means that a view like Bell's and Fry's implies that a large portion of our ordinary aesthetic experience and thought is in error. Of course, it is possible to reject common opinion. Philosophers sometimes do. Examples are eliminativists in the philosophy of mind, error theorists in moral philosophy, and consequentialists in first-order moral theory.[23] But such philosophers put forward arguments for disparaging common opinion. Bell and Fry provide none, or at least none that are remotely compelling.[24] Moreover Bell and Fry present themselves not as iconoclasts of this sort but as laying bare what has always been taken to be the central value of art. This unforeseen revisionism about our judgments about representational works is the basic problem with the hard-line, extreme formalism of Bell and Fry.

2.3   We must now address the complication that I noted earlier on. Bell and Fry also recognize a kind of formal property of pictures that inheres in the spatial relationships that hold between the items represented in them.[25] (Poussin's paintings are often said to be notable for such qualities.) These properties are sometimes referred to as "plastic form." But such properties are an aspect of what is represented; and representational properties are determined in part by representational conventions, which are determined in part

22. See Clement Greenberg, "The Case for Abstract Art," and "Modernist Painting" (esp. note 1), in *Clement Greenberg*, vol. 4.

23. Paul Churchland, *A Neurocomputational Perspective* (Cambridge, Mass.: MIT Press, 1992); Mackie, *Ethics*; and Shelly Kagan, *The Limits of Morality* (Oxford: Oxford University Press, 1989).

24. See Carroll, "Clive Bell's Aesthetic Hypothesis"; and Malcolm Budd, *Values of Art* (London: Allen Lane, 1995). Both Carroll and Budd do a good job of criticizing Bell and Fry's arguments *for* formalism, such as they are. But Carroll and Budd provide less in the way of non-question-begging arguments *against* formalism.

25. See, for example, Bell, *Art*, pp. 37–38. Fry unfairly criticizes Bell for ignoring such properties (*Vision and Design*, p. 206).

by the history of a work. So the three-dimensional plastic properties of paintings are not narrowly determined; they are not determined solely by what is on the canvas. How then do three-dimensional plastic "formal" properties of a work relate to the kind of formal properties that *are* determined by a work's two-dimensional abstract pattern? Is it a mere accident that the same word is used in both cases?

Although the three-dimensional plastic properties of paintings are not themselves formal properties in the sense defined earlier, it is understandable that they have been thought of as formal properties. For the idea of three-dimensional plastic form in painting derives from the idea of the genuinely formal properties that *would* be realized *if* the items represented actually existed. So the notion of three-dimensional plastic form in painting must be understood in terms of the notion of spatial form that is exemplified in abstract sculpture. Although plastic formal properties are not genuine formal properties, we can only conceive of them given a conception of genuine formal properties. There is a close conceptual tie. So we can understand why people might use the same word to describe plastic properties of paintings. But our basic notion of form, as those aesthetic properties determined solely by narrow nonaesthetic properties, is still conceptually fundamental.[26]

Moreover, even if we despair of discerning some intimate conceptual connection between genuine formal properties and plastic formal properties, moderate formalism is still safe. Suppose we generously allow a wide notion of a formal property, which includes both genuine formal properties as previously characterized as well as the aesthetic properties determined by three-dimensional representational properties. (This wide notion might be constructed on either a principled or an ad hoc basis.) It is still plausible that

---

26. Malcolm Budd notices that what is thought of as formally important in painting is sometimes not just "plastic form," in the sense of the representation of a spatial array of colored objects, but the representation of a spatial array of colored objects *as seen from a particular point of view* (*Values of Art*, pp. 51–54). In such cases, he suggests that we need a notion of form that involves an interplay or mutual dependence of plastic formal and two-dimensional formal properties. But Budd abruptly gives up on the project of forging such a notion of form because he says that the idea of the *relation* between represented three-dimensionality and two-dimensional pattern "lacks definition" (p. 54). It is unclear what Budd is asking for here, but the dependent beauty account can certainly illuminate that relation. Plastic form and two-dimensional form can play the mutual functional role that I described in section 1.6. We can also note, ad hominem, that if Budd has a criticism here, it applies equally to his own preferred account of form according to which form is a matter of the relation between the elements of a work (p. 60). Moreover, such an account is problematic because it allows that there are formal properties that are determined by the relation between different representational elements of a painting. But in many cases these "formal" properties would not in any sense be directly perceivable in the work. See further section 4 below on literary structure.

some paintings have aesthetically significant plastic properties but no *further* representational properties (for instance, some cubist paintings). Moreover, there are many works which have plastic properties as well as other representational properties, and where those plastic properties are aesthetically important considered in themselves.

2.4   Bell and Fry were rightly criticized for ignoring representation in painting, or playing down its importance. (Clement Greenberg's views are subtler.)[27] On the other hand, we should not overlook the fact that Bell and Fry were right to think that paintings *have* formal properties that are important. Bell wrote infamously:

> To appreciate a work of art we need bring with us nothing but a sense of form and color and a knowledge of three-dimensional space.[28]

This sentence has probably been the butt of more scorn than anything else written about aesthetics in the twentieth century. Yet only a minor emendation renders it respectable. Just delete the "nothing but":

> To appreciate a work of art we need to bring with us a sense of form and color and a knowledge of three-dimensional space.

This, I maintain, is almost always true! Without "a sense of form and color and a knowledge of three-dimensional space" we cannot appreciate a work of visual art.[29] If only Bell had put his point as a *necessary* condition rather than as a *sufficient* condition of appreciation.

It might be objected that conceptual art and other experimental work poses a difficulty for the moderate formalist view. But it is hard to see what the difficulty could be. Such art is alleged to have no aesthetic properties at

27. Bell's and Fry's view of the value of Cézanne's work is particularly implausible. They think that the value of Cézanne's paintings does not turn on what they represent (such as mountains, lake, trees). Greenberg also sees the *historical* significance of Cézanne in formal terms. We can distinguish what we might call "philosophical formalism," according to which nonformal aesthetic properties are impossible, from "substantive formalism", according to which nonformal aesthetic properties, though not impossible, are not very important when compared with formal properties. Substantive formalism can be historically restricted, so that the thesis is that formal properties are preeminent in some period. Bell and Fry are philosophical formalists, while Greenberg is a historically restricted substantive formalist.

28. Bell, *Art*, p. 37.

29. Translation: without an appreciation of the aesthetic properties determined by two-dimensional design and the representation of three-dimensional shapes, we cannot appreciate a work of visual art.

all—formal or nonformal. But formalism is a thesis about the aesthetic properties of works of art, *if they have any*. So conceptual art raises no difficulties—not even for the extreme formalist claim that all aesthetic properties are formal. Both moderate and the extreme formalists can concede that some works of art have no aesthetic properties at all. But such works are not relevant to our debate, which is about those works of art that have aesthetic properties.[30]

3 ARCHITECTURE

3.1   How formalist should we be about architecture? Consider an ancient Egyptian temple or a Seljuk mosque. An extreme formalist about architecture will say that the aesthetic character of the temple or mosque is internal to it and that its aesthetic character can be perceptually manifest to an observer who has no knowledge of the religious function of the building. Of course, to understand why a building has come into existence we need to know about its function as well as many other things about it. But the extreme formalist says that while that information may lead us to some kind of understanding of the building, it does not lead us to an enhanced *aesthetic* understanding. It cannot lead us to see that it is elegant or beautiful if we did not do so before. It may be that the architect intends to worship God *by* creating a work with certain formal virtues. Or it may be that a powerful ruler intends to display and reinforce his power *by* creating a work with certain formal virtues. There are all sorts of different causal histories that lead to the existence of a building and its specific aesthetic character. But once it exists, the hard-line formalist says that the building's aesthetic properties are independent of that history.

3.2   However, extreme formalism is not plausible as a complete account of aesthetic value in architecture. It is common to talk of the beauty of a building as an aesthetic expression or articulation of its function. The same goes for the beauty of parts of a building, such as doors and windows. In our ordinary aesthetic thought, the beauty of a building and the fulfilling of its functions are not two separable factors. Instead, they are intertwined.

---

30. It is a curious irony that so many of those who see themselves as conceptual artists persist in making objects, not only with aesthetic properties, but with formal aesthetic properties, even though they say that this is not their intention. Despite the official pledge of aesthetic celibacy they fail to resist the temptation to indulge in formal aesthetic sin. But even if there is some pure conceptual art with no aesthetic intent, it creates no difficulty for either extreme or moderate formalism.

(Again—multiplication rather than addition.)[31] Kant talked of the way a building is beautiful as a church or as an arsenal or as a palace, and he thought of such cases as *dependently* beautiful. Intuitively, a particular building might be beautiful as a mosque rather than as a post office, railway station, or library—not just because the building is beautiful *and* functions well (non-aesthetically) as a mosque, but because the building's aesthetically expresses or articulates the religious function of a mosque. This is what many of our actual aesthetic judgments about buildings are like. Intuitively, works of architecture should not be seen as oversized pieces of abstract sculpture. It is essential to a building that it is made to be used or inhabited by people, in more or less specific ways.[32] And there is a class of our aesthetic assessments of buildings that depends on our knowing these ways. Of course, common sense, or folk aesthetics, might be misguided here. Perhaps there is only free architectural beauty, on the one hand, and the fulfilling of function, on the other, and never a mixture of the two. But correcting our aesthetic thought so as to eradicate this error would be a radical undertaking, and it is difficult to see what could motivate it. So we should persist in thinking of the dependent beauty of works of architecture.

3.3   We must be careful not to take the emphasis on dependent architectural beauty too far. If we say that a building has certain aesthetic virtues as a building of a certain specific sort, why not go further and say that a mosque or station excels, not just as a mosque or station, but as a mosque or station of a certain sort? But then where should we stop? Maybe we should increase the specificity to infinity. Or, on the other hand, maybe we should be minimally specific, so a building is not beautiful as a mosque or station but rather beautiful merely as a *building* (a permanent structure designed for human occupation). Maybe we only have to see it as having the broad function of being some building or other, instead of having some narrower specific function—mosque, station, library, post office. How specific do we need to be about architectural function? This debate over the degree of specificity of function is not a purely philosophical concern but an issue of substance in the practice of architecture. The controversial question is: Which functions are, or should be, relevant to the dependent beauty of a work of architecture? What is important for us, however, is that buildings have *some* such dependent beauties.

31. Contrast the case where we use a sculpture to prop up a table.
32. See Roger Scruton, *The Aesthetics of Architecture* (London: Methuen, 1979), chap. 3. See also his entertaining discussion of 1960s Scandinavian "functional" cutlery (ibid., pp. 241–42).

3.4   Nevertheless, as Kant saw, things that have dependent beauty can also be assessed for their free beauty. There is indeed the beauty of a building considered as a building, and perhaps considered as a building with a certain specific function, but a building also has a free beauty, as pure abstract sculpture. Buildings, like many other artifacts, have many purposes and values. And their formal value is one value among others. That is not to say that it is always the most important value. Formal sculptural values are architectural values that have waxed and waned in perceived importance relative to other architectural values. But formal values should not be ignored altogether. An ancient Egyptian temple or a Seljuk mosque may have artistic values, including aesthetic values, which depend on its specific function. But they also have formal values that we can appreciate in blithe and perhaps blissful ignorance of the deeper meaning of what we see. An immaculately proportioned building delights the eye, immediately. Ignorant tourists can appreciate these values even when they have left their guidebooks behind.[33]

4   LITERATURE

4.1   What does the issue of formalism look like in literature? The simple answer is that it looks particularly complicated! Despite the complications, I think we must concede that it is unlikely that any interesting kind of formalism is defensible in literature.

Many notions of form are deployed in the writings of literary critics. I shall distinguish two main ones. The first is that of the formal properties that arise from the *purely sonic* properties of words. These properties are comfortably classified as formal from the point of view of my working definition. Purely sonic properties can generate aesthetic values which can be appreciated by someone who does not understand the language. We can think of this aspect of literature as we might absolute music. Some of the point of rhyme lies here.[34] However, there is another kind of sonic value that literature has which is not captured in this purely sonic idea. This is the value of words as the *apt sonic embodiment* or *expression* of their sense, which is a case of dependent beauty. Onomatopoeia is a simple example. Such dependent sonic values can be appreciated only by someone who knows the meaning of

33. The tour guide, who drones on about the marginally interesting history of some building, is often a distraction.

34. Monroe Beardsley discusses these properties in *Aesthetics* (Indianapolis: Hackett, 1958), pp. 230–37. Much of the pleasure we take in Lewis Carroll's "Jabberwocky" derives from relishing the sound of the words (*Through the Looking Glass* [London: Oxford University Press, 1971]).

the words. We might call this value "poetic" value, and it is usually of far greater importance in literature than purely sonic values. Listening to poetry in languages one does not understand has limited appeal. I suspect that almost all cases where we appreciate the sonic qualities of literature are of the dependent sort. Consider, for example, that there can be poetry that is beautifully expressed in languages that we might think ugly as pure sound.[35]

4.2   The issue over sonic form is relatively straightforward. What confuses the issue in literature is a profusion of senses of 'form' that rely on a contrast between *form* and *content*. In particular, there is a common use of the word "form" to refer to the *structure* of a literary work, in the sense of the relation between the parts of the work. There was a movement known as "formalism" in the theory of literature that originated in Russia early in the twentieth century. These "formalists" were partly interested in the close analysis of linguistic devices, such as meter, alliteration, and rhyme. These devices are tied to the sonic qualities of words, so in this respect the movement was well named from the point of view of the definition we have been working with. However, they were also interested in imagery and metaphor, which confuses the issue, for these devices are a matter of meaning as well of or instead of sound. Later in the century, those known as "structuralists" tended to go from this very close-up narrow focus to the other extreme of focusing on the overall structure of a work. These structuralists then came under attack from the "poststructuralists," who rightly criticized the structuralists' dichotomy of structure (or form) and content, since the structural properties of texts are just as much targets for creative interpretation as their other aspects.[36] The idea of structural form *as opposed to content* is plainly absurd. For literary structure is an *aspect of* content, not something opposed to it. However, the idea of the structure *of* a content is a useful one. Ring composition in Homer is a simple small-scale example. Some passages in Homer's *Iliad* have a ring structure, such as ABCDEDCBA. These features are stretched out in time; we understand them intellectually—they are not a rhythm we hear or see directly. We abstract them from the content of the work. And what we abstract is a structure that many different texts can share.[37] From the point of view of my working definition, it is unfortunate

35. I think that A. C. Bradley was reaching for the idea of the dependent beauty of the poetic expression of a content in particular words in his "Poetry for Poetry's Sake," in *Oxford Lectures on Poetry* (Oxford: Oxford University Press, 1909).

36. For a useful critical survey of this material see Stuart Sim, "Structuralism and Post-structuralism," in *Philosophical Aesthetics*, ed. Oswald Hanfling (Oxford: Blackwell, 1992).

37. Malcolm Willcock used to emphasize such structural features of the *Iliad* in his lectures at

that these structural properties have been called "formal," because literary structure is an aspect of content, which we have agreed is broadly determined. So this notion of form does not fit my working definition. There are structural properties of works of absolute music, which have been called "formal" by music critics. And there is clearly considerable commonality between the structure of absolute music and the structure of content in literature, even though the former is formal in my sense but the latter is not. But there is probably no way of showing that structural form in literature is intimately related to uncontroversially formal properties in the way that we found that we could connect plastic form in painting with sculptural form. I cannot see how to bring the notion of structural form into line with my general definition.[38]

4.3   Nevertheless we need not worry too much about the rogue use of the word "form" to mean literary structure. Let us generously admit two distinct notions of literary form: sonic and structural. Literary works *combine* a content with certain sonic and structural properties, so that the content is realized in sounds, with a particular structure. But the sonic and structural properties have little separable importance (if any). The pure sound of literary works is not usually admired in a topic-neutral, content-free way (although I do not deny that we may on occasion appreciate words as pure sound). Similarly, structure is of little or no value in itself; it is important only as the structure *of* a certain content. For example, the content of a novel or play typically involves a story, psychological portrayal, moral conundrums, and so on; and the structure of the novel or play has a role which is either subservient to that content, or which is at least intimately bound up with it. The situation is not at all parallel to the plastic properties of representational paintings, which can and often do determine aesthetic values by themselves. We can appreciate an interesting spatial arrangement of objects in a painting irrespective of further knowledge of what these objects are. But contemplating the pure structure of a literary work is uninteresting unless we know the content of the elements of the structure. So even if we

University College London. But he also drew attention to the way what seem to be purely structural features of the *Iliad* in fact turn out to be perfectly apt for its content.

38. Barbara Herrnstein Smith distinguishes 'form' from 'structure' and says that 'form' refers to the "physical nature of words, and include[s] such features as rhyme, alliteration, and syllabic meter" (Smith, *Poetic Closure* [Chicago: University of Chicago Press, 1968], p. 6). She uses 'structure' as a broader category that includes organizational properties arising from both form, in her sense, as well as theme. She stresses the analogies between literary and musical structure. What she calls "closure" in a poem is effected by both formal and thematic elements working in combination.

widen the notion of form to include structural form as well as sonic form, such properties are of no aesthetic significance.[39]

Literature is the least formal art because it involves content first and foremost. However, that does little to harm the *general* case for moderate formalism. The moderate formalist should tactically retreat, leaving most aspects of literature at the mercy of the anti-formalist hordes.

5 MUSIC

5.1   Eduard Hanslick advanced a powerful and sophisticated defense of musical formalism in his great work, *On the Beautiful in Music.*[40] Hanslick does not content himself with attacking erroneous theories of music which appeal to emotion; he also argues for absolute music. He writes:

> What kind of beauty is the beauty of a musical composition?
>
> It is a specifically musical kind of beauty. By this we understand a beauty that is self-contained and in need of no content from outside itself, that consists simply and solely of tones and their artistic combination.[41]

> Aesthetic inquiry does not and should not know anything about the personal circumstances and historical background of the composer; it hears only what the artwork itself has to say.[42]

These passages are extreme. Hanslick is ruling out nonformal aesthetic values in music.

Hanslick's view is that the beauty of music is *specifically musical*. He takes that to mean that musical beauty is inherent in tonal relationships and it involves no connection with anything extramusical, such as the emotions of a composer or listener. I prefer to describe Hanslick's view by saying that beauty in music is *determined* solely by tonal relationships, and it is not determined by anything extramusical. So music does not represent emotions, and it is not the purpose of music to express or evoke emotions. Music is a structured pattern of sound. And the value of a piece of music is determined

---

39. There is also a sense of 'form' in literature, which just means something like 'genre' or 'style'. Structure is *sometimes* an important aspect of genre or style, as with the Sonnet; but sometimes not. Again, such 'form' has little or no value that is independent of content.

40. Published under the title *On the Musically Beautiful* (Indianapolis: Hackett, 1986).

41. Ibid., p. 28.

42. Ibid., p. 39.

solely by its being a particular structured pattern of sound. Thus Hanslick has both a theory of the value of musical art as well as a theory about its nature. The two—healthily in my view—go hand in hand.[43]

5.2 Should we agree with Hanslick? It is common to distinguish absolute or instrumental music from its opposites—program music, music with a title, or music that accompanies some text or plot. We should understand the distinction between absolute and nonabsolute music in terms of the distinction between freely or formally beautiful music and dependently beautiful music. Absolute music is music that is only intended to have free or formal beauty, whereas nonabsolute music is intended to have a beauty that depends on some nonmusical purpose, such as marching, dancing, telling a story, meditating, or praying. Contrary to Hanslick's formalist evangelism, it seems that such music may be aesthetically valuable because of the *way* it serves those nonmusical purposes, just as a picture of a tree can be beautiful because of the precise way it represents it.[44] Music can *gain* by being mixed with the nonmusical. Nevertheless—as Peter Kivy quite rightly won't let us forget—we must not forget absolute music.[45]

43. Someone who was attracted to the view that the beauty of music is purely musical might not accept the strong thesis that the value of a piece of music is determined solely by *its* constituent tones. He might say that the musical significance of a piece of music is determined in part by the musical tradition of which it is a part. On this hybrid view, the beauty of a particular piece of music is partly determined by other pieces of music but not by some relation to emotion. A musical tradition is not extra-musical, unlike the emotions of a composer or listener. But it is clear that Hanslick is committed to the stronger formalist thesis and he would reject the hybrid view.

44. See Hanslick, *On the Musically Beautiful*, pp. 66–67. That Hanslick went too far in denigrating nonabsolute music does not in any way cast doubt on his powerful critique of emotion theories of music. Although I think that we should admit some dependent musical beauty, contrary to Hanslick, I do not think that arousing or expressing emotion could be a nonmusical function that music serves.

45. See for example Peter Kivy, "The Fine Art of Repetition," in *The Fine Art of Repetition* (Cambridge: Cambridge University Press, 1993). In his "Is Music an Art?" (also in The Fine Art of Repetition), Kivy claims that absolute music was not given the accolade of being high Art with a capital A rather than lowly "craft" before the middle of the eighteenth century. Before that it was considered more like a decorative art, while music that was used to set sacred texts was taken more seriously. The "Art" accolade was previously reserved for music that served the function of accompanying a text; and so absolute music lost out. He thinks that this damaging legacy lives on, and that aestheticians need to focus their minds somewhat more fixedly on the nature and value of absolute music. I heartily endorse this, of course. But we should note that the general distinction between free and dependent beauty does not align in any neat way with the Art/craft distinction. At different times and at different places different art forms and genres have been ranked differently by means of the evaluations implicit in the Art/craft distinction. And although these rankings have sometimes neatly coincided with the free/dependent distinction, at other times the combination has been different. I doubt that any generalization will stand up across the board.

Some music must be understood in its own terms. Moderate formalism is the right approach to music.[46]

5.3   This conclusion allows us to address a puzzle that Peter Kivy has posed. Although Kivy has some sympathy with Hanslick, there is a passage of *On the Beautiful in Music* that Kivy finds perplexing, and which he thinks reveals a general difficulty for Hanslick's view.[47]

The passage that perplexes Kivy is where Hanslick writes of Gluck's *Orfeo ed Euridice* that

> music certainly possesses far more specific tones for the expression of passionate grief.[48]

Kivy's question is: How can Hanslick say this if he thinks that music cannot express grief? Kivy thinks that Hanslick inconsistently helps himself to the idea, which he has officially eschewed, that some music expresses the emotion of grief. Kivy thinks that this passage reveals Hanslick lapsing into what he is officially denying, like a solipsist writing letters. Kivy suggests a couple of unconvincing ways of removing the tension, gives up, and then convicts Hanslick of inconsistency.

I think that Kivy's puzzle can be dissolved, however. It is crucial that Gluck's *Orfeo ed Euridice* is *not* a case of absolute music. At the relevant point in the story line of Gluck's opera, the *text* "expresses grief" in a nonaesthetic sense, in a quite straightforward way. (Let us write that "grief$_{NA}$.") But considered as absolute music, Gluck's music at the same point does not sound as full of grief as it might, in an aesthetic sense. (Let us write that "Grief$_A$.") That is why one will not serve the *purpose* of the other, so that the two fit together snugly. Notice the crucial but neglected word "for" in the quotation from Hanslick. He does *not* say "music certainly possesses far more specific tones that express grief." The word "for" denotes function or purpose. We are dealing here with a case of dependent beauty. We are thinking of the piece of music as serving a nonmusical *purpose*—one given by the text. So what

---

46. To deploy the terminology of note 27, it might be that Hanslick is a extreme "substantive" formalist but a moderate "philosophical" formalist.

47. Peter Kivy, "Something I've Always Wanted to Know about Hanslick," in *The Fine Art of Repetition*.

48. Hanslick, *On the Musically Beautiful*, p. 18. This passage occurs in chapter 2, where Hanslick is arguing primarily that music does not *represent* emotion. The first half of this chapter is concerned with instrumental or absolute music. The second half is concerned with program music, where music is combined with text. In chapter 1, he has argued that the purpose of music is not to *provoke* emotion. And in chapter 3, he will put forward his purist view of absolute musical beauty.

Hanslick is saying, quite consistently with his view, is that Gluck's music could be better *suited for* expressing grief$_{NA}$. But this is not the *musical* expression of emotion. It is only the words of the text which express grief, in the ordinary sense.

In an art that combines two media (music and poetry), each usually matches or fits the other so as to produce more than the sum of the two parts. Such a *multiplication* rather than an *addition* of parts is often an important artistic value. One part of the whole is not merely *added* to the others, but *combines* with them to yield a superadded emergent overall value. Not all works of art are like this. Symbolism is sometimes a purely *complementary* or *additional* value in visual art. Balinese kechak music sometimes contains apparently unrelated musical themes running in parallel. But it is more usual for the value of the different elements of works of art to combine to realize a greater overall value. What Hanslick is saying in the disputed passage is that Gluck's music fails to be as suitable as it might be for accompanying the text that literally expresses grief$_{NA}$. The words are what the music is appropriate *for*. Hanslick is presupposing that sad$_A$ music is appropriate for sad$_{NA}$ texts, although in general Hanslick is rather skeptical about the extent to which we worry about such appropriateness. But in the Gluck example, Hanslick's remark is to the effect that sadder$_A$ music would better serve the function of fitting words that express grief$_{NA}$.

If this interpretation is right, it means that Hanslick is indeed committed to the view that not all musical value is pure or absolute, in the sense that it has no reference to anything outside music. In this, *and in this respect only,* Hanslick has compromised a hard-line purist position. Music can serve extramusical purposes and attain new musical value as a result. But at no point has he committed himself to the view that music can express emotion. He has not compromised in *that* way. Hanslick never admits that music can express emotion, in a nonaesthetic sense. All he says is that sadder$_A$ music would be more appropriate *for* the sadness$_{NA}$ of Gluck's text.[49]

49. Kivy goes on to point out that, qua music critic, Hanslick used plenty of emotional descriptions. But this is not at all inconsistent with Hanslick's views. If we are to do justice to Hanslick, it is important to realize that his thesis does *not* imply that we should dispense with the *description* of music in emotional terms. What Hanslick is rightly against is hasty inferences from such descriptions. The descriptions themselves are innocent. For Hanslick, emotional descriptions describe something inherent in the relations between tones. Real emotion has nothing to do with it. It is a *metaphorical* description, using emotional terms, of something intrinsically musical. This point completely undercuts Malcolm Budd's main criticism of Hanslick in his *Music and the Emotions* (London: Routledge & Kegan Paul, 1985). Budd thinks that Hanslick is either out to ban emotional descriptions or else he seeks to translate them into nonemotional descriptions without loss of content. But Hanslick can happily admit that emotional descriptions may be quite irreplaceable as a way of describing purely musical characteristics. There is then an issue about why this is so. (I address that question in chapter 10.) But then the discussion takes a quite different turn,

There is no problem with Hanslick's text. And there is no problem with Hanslick's view, so long as he restricts himself to moderate formalism.[50]

CODA

Formalism has been unjustly maligned in the twentieth century. I have given what I hope is a serviceable account of what formalism is, and I tried to secure the truth in formalism. Moderate formalism recognizes both formal and nonformal aesthetic properties. Some works of art have only formal properties. Some works of art have only nonformal aesthetic properties. And some works of art have both. Formal aesthetic properties are important artistic properties that must not be ignored. I proposed an account of formal and nonformal aesthetic properties, and of the way that they combine together. In the light of that account, I explored the prospects for formalism in four art forms, and we saw that moderate formalism provides the best understanding of them.[51]

Bell and Fry were indeed naïve and extreme. But even so, there was something down-to-earth and refreshing about their approach to art. A moderate

---

and it is no longer simply a matter of pointing out an inconsistency in Hanslick, or an outrageous and impossible proscription on emotional descriptions.

50. It might be thought that a problem for musical formalism arises from the sort of cases that Edward Cone discusses, where a piece of music, as it were, points beyond its first and last notes ("The Picture and the Frame: The Nature of Musical Form," in *Musical Form and Musical Performance* [New York: Norton, 1968], pp. 18–22). For example, when we hear syncopation in blues or jazz, we often project back a rhythm that we hear as already in progress before the first note. Still, in projecting forward or backward in time we are responding to formal qualities of the music— qualities constrained within what he calls "the musical frame," within the first and last notes.

51. In case it should seem that what I defend lacks the gusto of extreme formalism—which at least made it an exciting doctrine—I shall mention a conjecture that I find attractive, but which I am not sure how to substantiate. I incline toward the view that free, formal beauty has a kind of priority, in the sense that we must be able to appreciate free, formal beauty if we are to appreciate dependent, nonformal beauty. For example, in the visual arts, the conjecture is that if we did not appreciate the free beauties of arrangements of colors and shapes, then we could not appreciate the more sophisticated dependent beauties of representational content. The claim is not that free, formal beauty *itself* is somehow prior to dependent, nonformal beauty. For there can be things which are dependently beautiful but not freely beautiful. The thesis is not a metaphysical one about aesthetic properties themselves, but about *us* and our appreciation of them. The priority claim is compatible with conceding that we can sustain an interest in the dependent beauty of particular works even if they are not formally beautiful. But that could only be against a background of the ability to appreciate other works which have formal beauty. As I say, I am not sure how to substantiate the truth of the priority thesis; and it faces special problems in the case of literature. But if the conjecture were true, it would mean that, in a garbled way, extreme formalism was onto something important.

formalist view of art chimes with most people's experience of art. And it is an approach that is well placed to make sense of the value that we place on art. That is more than can be said for the movements that have replaced formalism. It is time the pendulum swung in the other direction.

Appendix A   Defining Formal Properties

The simplest account of a formal property would be to take the formal properties of a work of art to be *those aesthetic properties that are determined solely by its intrinsic nonaesthetic properties.*[52] Nonformal aesthetic properties of a work of art would then be those aesthetic properties that are not just determined by its intrinsic nonaesthetic properties but also by its extrinsic nonaesthetic properties, such as its history of production.

Although such a definition is intuitive and not bad as a first approximation, it will not do if we are seeking to avoid needless controversy. If we define formal properties in this way, we will run into a trouble, or at least a complication, arising from certain response-dependent theories of both sensory and aesthetic properties. To assume that colors and sounds are intrinsic nonaesthetic properties of things would be to assume a disputable metaphysical view of their nature; for there are response-dependent views according to which colors and sounds are dispositions to produce experiences of a certain sort in perceivers of a certain sort.[53] And some (but not all) of those who think this assume that it means that colors and sounds are not intrinsic properties of things. (I am thinking of those who do *not* take the route suggested by Martin Davies and Lloyd Humberstone.[54] Davies and Humberstone suggested that a response-dependent account might "rigidly" specify that the relevant responses are like those that we *actually* have.) If we accept a nonrigid view, then the aesthetic properties of abstract paintings and absolute music would be determined by a certain kind of *relational* property. So they would not count as formal properties on this definition. A parallel issue arises over aesthetic properties themselves, irrespective of the nonaesthetic properties that determine them, since on some views, aesthetic properties are dispositions to provoke a certain kind of experience in a certain

52. On the general notion of an intrinsic property, see Rae Langton and David Lewis, "Intrinsic Properties," *Philosophy and Phenomenological Research*, vol. 58 (1998).

53. See, for example, Colin McGinn, *The Subjective View* (Oxford: Clarendon, 1982). See also his "Another Look at Color," *Journal of Philosophy*, vol. 93 (1996).

54. Martin Davies and Lloyd Humberstone, "Two Notions of Necessity," *Philosophical Studies*, vol. 37 (1980).

kind of perceiver.[55] For example, perhaps beauty is a disposition to produce pleasure in the right kind of perceiver. Such theorists would be banned from holding formalism given the account of formal properties in terms of intrinsic nonaesthetic properties. The definition would deem *all* aesthetic properties to be nonformal if a relational dispositional account of aesthetic properties turns out to be true. Thus the issue would be emptied of interesting content.

Another problem for the account in terms of intrinsic nonaesthetic properties is that we would only be able to characterize formal properties in terms of whether a *thing's* aesthetic properties are determined by its intrinsic nonaesthetic properties rather than in terms of whether a *work of art's* aesthetic properties are determined by its intrinsic nonaesthetic properties. For there is a sense in which the history of production of a work of art *is* an intrinsic property of *the work*, though not of the physical object or event in which it is realized. The relation between a work of art and its origins might be like the relation between an action and its intentional cause. It might be essential and thus intrinsic to a work of art's being the work of art it is that it has a certain history of production. If so, there would be a danger of trivializing the issue over formalism, since all aesthetic properties of a work of art would turn out to be formal even if they are determined in part by the history of production of the work.

My account is designed to be neutral between different theories of sensory and aesthetic properties, and thus it aims to avoid the problems besetting the intrinsic nonaesthetic property determination account. Although it might seem odd to use the word "narrow" to include dispositional relations to responses, on no sane response-dependent account do sensory or aesthetic properties essentially involve standing in a relation to *actual* responses. So on my account there is no danger that such relational dispositional theories of sensory or aesthetic properties will mean that we must deem intuitively formal aesthetic properties to be nonformal.

Appendix B   Formalism and the Intentional Fallacy

There is one other prevalent usage of "formalism" in this terminological jungle. There is a debate in which anti-formalists hold that the meaning of a text is fixed by the intentions of its author, whereas formalists see the text as having its own independent life. For example, Stephen Knapp discusses what

---

55. See, for example, Mary Mothersill, *Beauty Restored* (Oxford: Oxford University Press, 1984); and Alan Goldman, *Aesthetic Value* (Boulder, Colo.: Westview, 1995).

he calls "formalism" in his book *Literary Interest*, and he says that the formalist thinks that "the meaning of the work goes beyond what its author intended."[56] The issue in question is that surrounding the intentional fallacy. Wimsatt and Beardsley are formalists, in this sense, in their famous essay "The Intentional Fallacy,"[57] whereas anti-formalists hold that the intentional fallacy is not a fallacy since they think that the meaning of a text is fixed by its author's intentions.[58]

This debate is wholly about what fixes *meaning* and not at all about *aesthetic properties*. So nothing in this book requires me to take sides in this debate. However, my view is in fact that the author's intentions partly determine meaning, but not completely. On the one hand, words mean what they do irrespective of a particular person's intention to mean something specific by particular words. For example, one can misuse words. I used to misuse the word "enervating," thinking that it meant invigorating or energizing. On the other hand, we also intend to use words with their standard meanings in a certain speech community. We intend to use particular words with their standard meanings, but we can be wrong about what those standard meanings are. So I can say "enervating" and mean enervating even though I *intend*, but fail, to mean invigorating or energizing. In one sense, I do not intend to mean enervating by "enervating" because I have false beliefs about standard meanings. But there is also a sense in which I *do* intend to mean enervating by "enervating" since I intend to mean whatever the word "enervating" is standardly taken to mean. In such cases, I have conflicting intentions.

Meaning *does* depend on author's intentions. But some of these intentions may not be the intention to mean something specific by a word but rather the intention to use a word with its standard meaning. It is only because of my intention to use the word "enervating" with its standard meaning that I can get it wrong. Now, of course, such intentions do not *suffice* for meaning. Facts about what the standardly accepted meanings in fact are also play a role in determining what I mean, and those facts are non-authorial facts. But there are important limits to the *non*-authorial facts which determine meaning.[59]

56. Stephen Knapp, *Literary Interest* (Cambridge: Harvard University Press, 1993), p. 5.

57. Reprinted in *Essays, Moral, Political, Literary*, ed. Eugene Miller (Indianapolis: Liberty Classics, 1985).

58. See Stephen Knapp and Walter Michaels, "Against Theory," *Critical Enquiry*, vol. 9 (1982); and "Against Theory 2," *Critical Enquiry*, vol. 14 (1987).

59. *Metaphysically*, intentions anchor text meanings. But intentions are targets of interpretation just as much as texts or utterances. So for the interpreter, intentions are not *epistemologically* prior to texts (the "poststructuralists" were right there). As Donald Davidson emphasized, propositional attitudes and linguistic utterances must be interpreted in the light of each other. See Donald Davidson, *Essays on Truth and Interpretation* (Blackwell: Oxford, 1984).

What I say and mean by a text *is* entirely fixed by its history even though it is not entirely fixed by that *part* of its history which are the author's intentions. The meaning of a text is fixed by my actual historical intentions plus actual historical usage at the point of utterance. By contrast, what *cannot* play any role in determining meanings are the antics of future interpreters. Take a fanciful case: a totally alien Martian interpreter might, unbeknown to me, interpret my sounds to mean "My antennae are purple." But such an alien interpreter is interpreting my *sounds* not my *words*. And that interpretation is false, even if it is justified because they have reason to believe that I am trying to communicate in their Martian language. The same goes for future literary critics. Alien or future interpreters need humility: their job is to *understand* meaning, they play no part in *creating* it.

Knapp wants us to see works as the products of *authorial actions*. Actions, of course, can misfire. One can perform an action (such as starting First World War) which one did not intend, even though if something is an action, one must have intended some aspect of it.[60] If Knapp's comparison is apt, it is also true that texts need not mean what their authors intend them to mean, but if they have meaning then their authors must have intended them to mean something that they did succeed in meaning. (This may not be a consequence that Knapp would like.) Now there is *some* similarity between meaning and action. The similarity is that the meaning of a text is a *composite* of authorial intention plus other factors, just as an action is a composite of an intention plus (the right kind of) causal upshot. But there is a crucial difference. One can do something one did not at all intend (such as starting the First World War), but one cannot mean something which one did not at all intend to mean. (Remember that in the "enervating" example, I did have an intention which was essential to what I meant; moreover it was an intention that determined which social facts "completed" my meaning.) What one *does* can outrun all one's intentions, but what one *means* cannot. There is an important difference here. If meanings were like actions, Martian or future interpretations might set up new meanings unconstrained by any authorial intentions. But some authorial intentions *are* essential to meaning. The meaning of a text depends partly on the author's intention and partly on standardly accepted meanings—but not at all on what those outside my immediate speech community might make of my sounds. Alien or future critics have no meaning-creating power.

Author's intentions are *necessary* but not *sufficient* for meaning. Or rather they are *essential* to meaning, but they are not all that meaning *consists in*.

60. See Donald Davidson, *Essays on Actions and Events* (Oxford: Clarendon, 1980).

So—the truth lies between extreme formalism and anti-formalism. I would not object if this position were called moderate formalism. *Different categories?*

Appendix C   *Gendered Beauty?* (ch. 7) → can't be two must be 1 or dependent.

Is there such a thing as gendered beauty? That is, is there a specifically male or female beauty? Is there such a thing as beauty *as a man* or *as a woman*? Throughout history people have made gender-specific aesthetic evaluations. But recently academics who work on gender issues have tended to deny that this possible. The issue of gender specific beauty is controversial at present. In my view, in order to illuminate the issue, we need to reach for Kant's free/dependent beauty distinction. It can help in a neutral way. Human beauty is obviously not free or formal beauty. It is a case of dependent beauty—people are beautiful *as* human beings. The question is whether there is such a thing as beauty as a man or beauty as a woman. That question—the aesthetic question—depends on controversial general questions about gender. Are men and women different by nature? That is, do men and women have different natural functions? Suppose, as was traditionally thought, and as has resurfaced recently, the answer is yes. Then we would expect there to be different conceptions of beauty for each gender. Just as there is beauty as a human being, so there would also be beauty as a man or as a woman. On the other hand, suppose the answer is no, as the major trend in feminist thought held in the 1970s and 1980s. Then we would expect there to be more androgynous conceptions of human beauty. Such a correlation between views on gendered beauty and views on gender essentialism is surely what we do find. Those who believe that the sexes have different natural functions also believe in gendered beauty, while those who believe that they do not have different natural functions do not believe in gendered beauty. The aesthetic debate over gendered beauty lies downstream from the issue of gender essentialism.

Paper topic: pg. 81 + pg. 125

nothing substantial → only culture determines the difference between males & females
DIFFERENT DEPENDENT BEAUTY?
Way to avoid it → free beauty and dependent beauty but no other substantial difference

[Handwritten annotations at top of page:]

1. ^if T is true, then no thing found in tho dust on Mars have any aesthetic properties.
2. Some things found in the dust on Mars have aesthetic properties.
3. If T is false, then

T = Walton's theory: aesthetic properties depend on the categories it belongs to.

Categories = determined by the "art world" as well as the standard properties.

CHAPTER 5

In Defense of Moderate Aesthetic Formalism

[Handwritten:] ("Categories of Art" by: Kendall Walton)

Most of the debate for and against aesthetic formalism in the twentieth century has been little more than a sequence of assertions, on both sides. But there is one discussion that stands out for its argumentative subtlety and depth, and that is Kendall Walton's essay "Categories of Art."[1] In this chapter I shall defend a certain version of formalism against the anti-formalist arguments that Walton deploys. I want to show that while Walton's arguments do indeed create insurmountable difficulties for an extreme version of formalism, he has not shown that a moderate version is problematic or inadequate. In the previous chapter I put forward the positive case for moderate formalism. Here I shall *defend* moderate formalism, although some of its attractions will become apparent as a side effect.

1 FORMAL PROPERTIES AND FORMALISMS

1.1   Walton begins his essay by asking whether those who make aesthetic judgments should only be concerned with what can be *directly perceived* in works of art. The issue of formalism has often been described in these terms. But Walton rightly distances himself from setting up a debate in that way. He moves on to take as his target the view that

> Circumstances connected with a work's origin . . . have no essential bearing on an assessment of its aesthetic nature.[2]

1. Kendall Walton, "Categories of Art," *Philosophical Review*, vol. 79 (1970).
2. Walton, "Categories of Art," p. 334

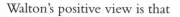

Walton's positive view is that

> (some) facts about the origins of works of art have an *essential* role in criticism, that aesthetic judgments rest on them in an absolutely fundamental way.[3]

In this statement of the issue, there is no idea that aesthetic judgments are connected with what can be directly perceived. Walton does well to distance himself from characterizing the issue in perceptual terms, because someone who thinks that matters of origin are aesthetically important could concede that the perception of works of art can be affected by knowledge of matters of origin. An anti-formalist need not deny that aesthetic properties are appreciated in perception. It is not as if he must say that we first perceive the work of art, next add our knowledge of its origin, and then deduce its aesthetic properties. He could say that *given* knowledge of the origin of a work of art, we perceive it differently, and we are thus able to appreciate its aesthetic properties in that transformed perception.[4] In general, the idea of direct perception is too slippery and problematic to help clarify the issue of formalism. It may be that there is something in the idea that aesthetic properties are directly perceivable. But whatever sense there is needs to be elucidated in other terms.

What Walton says is surely not enough, however. For the view he is opposing is not just that matters of origin are *not* aesthetically relevant. It is a view about what *is* aesthetically relevant. We need some idea of which the aesthetically relevant nonaesthetic properties are. Since we cannot isolate them as those that can be directly perceived, we need to find some other way of identifying them. This needs to be rectified. So to some extent I shall depart from Walton's way of characterizing the issue, although this will not make any substantive difference.

1.2   In order to finesse various difficulties, and to keep things as simple as possible, let us draw on the account I proposed in the previous chapter. I stipulated that the *narrow* properties of a work of art include both sensory properties (such as colors and sounds) and intrinsic and contemporaneous physical properties (such as being three feet across), as well as any dispositions to provoke responses that might be thought to be partly constitutive of sensory or aesthetic properties. The *broad* properties of a work of art include any

3. Ibid., p. 337.
4. Ibid., pp. 363–64.

other properties. In these terms, we can define *formal* properties as those aesthetic properties that are entirely determined by narrow nonaesthetic properties, whereas *nonformal* aesthetic properties are those that are partly determined by broad nonaesthetic properties.[5] The history of production of a work is always a broad property of it, since it is neither a sensory property, nor an intrinsic and contemporaneous physical property, nor some dispositional relation to our responses. So if the history of production of a work partly determines its aesthetic properties, then those aesthetic properties are nonformal. I gave the rationale for this characterization in the previous chapter.[6]

This definition of formal properties is controversial in some ways, but it gives us a way of characterizing the issue of formalism which will suffice for the purpose of discussing Walton. Although Walton never uses the word "formalism" in his essay, he opposes the formalist idea that what is aesthetically significant in a work of art is entirely determined by its narrow nonaesthetic properties. It is *because* the formalist holds this positive thesis that he thinks we can gain an aesthetic understanding of a painting or piece of music solely by looking at the painting, or listening to the music. And this is *why* he also holds the negative thesis (which is Walton's target) that the application of aesthetic concepts to a work of art can leave out of consideration facts about its origin.

1.3   Given the distinction between formal and nonformal properties, let us offer the following unqualified definitions, as a first approximation. An *extreme formalist* thinks that all works of art are purely formal works—where a work is purely formal if all its aesthetic properties are formal aesthetic properties.[7] An *anti-formalist* thinks that no works of art have formal aesthetic properties. A *moderate formalist* thinks, first, that all the aesthetic properties of works of art in a select class are formal, and second, that although many works of art outside that class have nonformal aesthetic properties, many of those works also have important formal aesthetic properties that must not be ignored.

The two moderate formalist claims are in principle independent. But let us stipulate that a moderate formalist believes both. One thesis focuses on

5. I assume that we have some kind of reliable distinction between aesthetic and nonaesthetic properties, so that 'beauty', 'daintiness', and 'elegance' and the like fall out as aesthetic properties. See chapter 2.

6. In that chapter I tackled a potential difficulty with this characterization which stems from the notions of plastic form in painting and of form as opposed to content in literature. But these potentially rogue notions do not fundamentally alter the dialectic with Walton because even given a conception of form which includes plastic form and literary form, Walton would still object that the aesthetic character of works of art cannot be understood solely in such terms.

7. An example would be Clive Bell, *Art* (London: Chatto and Windus, 1914).

works of art, the other on *aesthetic properties.* The two claims naturally go together, but it is possible to imagine someone who holds that although there are no purely formal works of art, nonetheless some aesthetic properties of works of art are formal. That would be a hybrid position. (The opposite combination is not possible—that works of art have no formal aesthetic properties but there are some purely formal works.) The problem with the hybrid position is that if some works of art have formal aesthetic properties then it is hard to see why there wouldn't be some works of art that have *only* formal aesthetic properties. The hybrid position seems an unstable and implausible compromise.

1.4   Walton focuses on the question of whether our aesthetic *judgments* about a work ought to turn on *information* about its history of production. He thinks that in order to make an aesthetic judgment about a work, we must see it under art-historical categories, such as "cubist" or "sonata." He then has a *separate* account of what makes a category the *correct* one—the one under which we *ought* to see the work. But I shall often directly address the issue of whether the aesthetic properties of a work are determined by its history of production. The issues are in fact the same because (a) aesthetic judgments ascribe aesthetic properties, (b) categories pick out art-historical properties, and (c) aesthetic properties are determined in part by art-historical properties (if Walton is right). For example, it is correct to judge that a work is elegant in the light of the category "cubist painting" because (a) it *is* elegant, (b) it *is* a cubist painting, and (c) its elegance *is* determined in part by its being a cubist painting. Nothing turns on this departure from Walton's focus.

Walton discusses the question of what makes a category correct in part 4 of his essay.[8] He considers four possibilities: (1) something has many of the standard features of paintings; (2) it is best seen as a painting; (3) the artist intended it to be a painting; and (4) it is widely recognized in society as a painting.[9] It seems to me that this list mixes up epistemological and constitutive matters. One's *grounds* for thinking that a work is a painting may include Walton's considerations 1, 2, and 4. But surely what *makes* something a painting is, in part, the artist's intention (consideration 3). Walton gives various

8. In a trivial sense, it is *correct* to see a work under the category of a painting only if it *is* a painting. But there is also a substantive question about what being a painting consists in, and thus there is a more substantive question about what the correctness of seeing a work under the category of a painting consists in. Being a painting is not a bare fundamental property of the universe. Something is a painting in virtue of certain features of it. Hence a work of art's having those features, whatever they are, would make it correct to deploy the category of a painting.

9. See Walton, "Categories of Art," pp. 357–58.

examples where considerations 1, 2, and 4 are outweighed, but he gives no
such case for the intentional consideration. I suspect that this is no accident.
(Note that he could have added biographical information about the artist's
intentions as another evidential consideration.)

1.5   Walton is not very explicit about the *strength* of his claims. He never
explicitly says that *absolutely all* works of art must be seen under categories.
But his claim is usually cast as one about "works of art," which looks universal, rather than a generalization about *most* works of art (see, for example, the
quotations that I gave in section 1.1). Moreover, as we shall see in section 3,
the thrust of his *guernica* argument seems to be universal, and thus, if it suc-
ceeds, would establish a universal conclusion. On the other hand, it is possible to read Walton as allowing that the ascription of *some* aesthetic properties
to works of art is *not* category-dependent. He may allow that some or even
all works of art have *some* formal aesthetic properties. However, I think that
Walton definitely does not allow that there are some works of art such that
all their aesthetic properties are formal. His position, I suspect, hovers
between the universal claim and the unstable hybrid one.[10]

The version of moderate formalism I want to defend is substantial. I think
that there is a large and significant class of works of art and aesthetic properties of works of art that are purely formal. In this chapter I shall assume
that moderate formalism is fairly substantial. So if Walton's thesis is just that
most aesthetic properties of *most* works of art are nonformal, then I also want
to resist that.

If it were thought too vague to speak of *most* works of art or *most* aesthetic properties, then we could stipulate that a moderate formalist is someone who resists a formal analysis of the works of art and aesthetic properties
that Walton discusses, and natural extensions of those examples to similar
cases.

1.6   Walton gives what he hopes are six kinds of counterexamples to
formalism. The first kind is of works of art which have representational
properties. In section 2, I argue that these are indeed genuine counterexamples, but they have limited application. I extend this pattern of argument to
what I call "contextual" art. In section 3, I consider Walton's very interesting
guernicas example, and I argue that, in spite of appearances, it does not have

10. Compare Walton's comment about his particular examples at p. 337, and his "most" at
p. 355, with his apparently universal claims at p. 338, 363, 364–65, and in the quotation I gave in
section 1.1.

to be interpreted as having anti-formalist consequences. Lastly, in section 4, I argue that Walton's four other examples are all resistible from a moderate formalist point of view: either the anti-formalist conclusion does not follow from the phenomena as Walton describes them, or else Walton's description of the phenomena is question-begging.

2 REPRESENTATION, CONTEXTUALITY, AND TACTICAL RETREAT

2.1   Here is the most memorable of Walton's examples of a work of art with representational properties:

> A marble bust of a Roman emperor seems to us to resemble a man with, say, an aquiline nose, a wrinkled brow, and an expression of grim determination, and we take it to represent a man with, or as having, those characteristics. But why don't we say that it resembles and represents a perpetually motionless man, of uniform (marble) color, who is severed at the chest?[11]

There is nothing in the object itself to say which of these it represents. To know what it represents, we need knowledge of extraneous matters. Understanding representational properties involves knowing about its origin.

This point seems undeniable because representational works of art have "derived" intentionality, in John Searle's terms.[12] Something with derived intentionality inherits its intentional content from the intentional content of something else. It has an extraneous source. Detecting derived intentionality requires knowledge of the extraneous source of the intentionality. Artistic representation is a case of derived intentionality since it requires representational conventions, or at least an artist's intention that certain aspects can be seen in the work, and we can only understand a representation if we understand the representational conventions or artist's intentions that are in play. But, as Walton's example shows, which representational conventions or aspect-intentions are in play is not a matter internal to the work that we can know just by scrutinizing its narrow properties. Nothing in Walton's bust could determine whether it represents a normal man or a motionless, gray, severed man.

How does this affect the issue over aesthetic properties? If representational properties just *are* a species of aesthetic properties, then we arrive at the anti-formalist conclusion very quickly. But if we are to avoid being accused of

11. Walton, "Categories of Art," p. 345.
12. John Searle, *Intentionality* (Cambridge: Cambridge University Press, 1983).

oversimplifying the issue, we should distinguish representational properties from aesthetic properties, even though both can be properties of works of art. Not every property of a work of art is an aesthetic property, and representational properties are possessed by things that are not works of art (such as road signs). The controversial question is then whether the representational properties of works of art are aesthetically relevant in that they are part of the nonaesthetic base that determines aesthetic properties. (If someone insisted on including representational properties within the class of aesthetic properties, we would then be interested in whether there is a determination relation *among* aesthetic properties; the controversial issue would be unaffected.)

We can now give the following two-premise argument. First, the representational properties of a work are determined in part by its history of production. Second, it is intuitive that the aesthetic properties of representational works of art are determined in part by what they represent—by their representational properties. For example, a painting might be beautiful *as* a representation of a tree, rather than beautiful *and* a representation of a tree. We can conclude from these two premises that the aesthetic properties of representational works of art are determined in part by their history of production, which means that such aesthetic properties are not formal. Walton seems to have an unstoppable point for representational works.[13]

2.2   However, anti-formalists seek a more general conclusion about all or at least most works of art, not merely about some subclass of them. And Walton's argument from representational properties does not have general application because many works have no representational properties. Many works are abstract. (By "abstract" I mean nonrepresentational, rather than a nonrealistic mode of representation.) Walton is clearly right about those works of art that have representational properties. But that is not enough for him to secure a general anti-formalist thesis. To do that, he needs to sustain the more general point about art-historical categories. If he is right only about representational properties, it could still be the case that many works of art—the abstract ones—have aesthetic properties that do not depend on their history of production. Formalism might yet be true of them. This is the strategy of tactical retreat.

(Some so-called abstract works of art involve the representation of colored

---

13. I considered and rebutted a rejoinder to this kind of argument in section 2.2 of the previous chapter.

volumes standing in spatial relation to each other and to the viewer. Many cubist works would be examples. Such works are not truly abstract in the sense I am using the term, since understanding them involves an awareness of depth. But there are works where this is not the case. Examples are mature Mondrians or Islamic decoration. In a mature Mondrian, the black lines do not lie *on top of* the white and colored rectangular areas, nor do they recede *behind* them. The black lines can be seen either way if we choose, just as we can see a face in a cloud. But the Mondrian does not represent the black line as being on top of the white and colored areas, or below them. Furthermore, it is not a deliberately ambiguous representation. It is not a representation at all.)

2.3   There is another range of cases where tactical retreat is in order. Some abstract works of art are intended to be seen *in the light of* or *juxtaposed against* other works of art, even though they do not *represent* anything. Such works exhibit a kind of self-consciousness of their art-historical context. We are *meant* to see them in the light of other works of art. For example, understanding the point of Duchamp's *Fountain* involves knowing the artistic norms he was flouting. Musical quotation is another example. And there are many more.

Let us label such art "contextual" art. Some contextual works (such as Duchamp's *Fountain*) have no significant aesthetic properties. But other contextual works may have aesthetic properties that depend on their context. In such works, the history of production that partly determines the work's aesthetic properties includes an artist's intention to refer to other works of art. So understanding such contextual art requires that we understand the artist's intentional references to other works of art.[14] Anti-formalism is once again unstoppable here. Such art cannot be understood in isolation from its art-historical context.

But even if we admit this, we still do not arrive at a general anti-formalist thesis. For much abstract art is not contextual in this sense. Of course, abstract art comes into existence in an art-historical context, and it is made by artists who are aware of that context. But that does not mean that the works themselves, as it were, *advert to* or *gesture toward* that context so that they can only be understood in terms of it. They may retain a dignified independence of the other works that surround them. It is not that such works only have a point if we see them against a background of other

14. I discuss contextual art and its relevance to the general theory of art in "The Creative Theory of Art," *American Philosophical Quarterly,* vol. 32 (1995), and "Are There Counterexamples to Aesthetic Theories of Art," *Journal of Aesthetics and Art Criticism,* vol. 60 (2002).

works of art. For example, this is not true of the tile-work of the Alhambra, nor, in my view, is it true of the works of the mature Mondrian. Such works make sense on their own.[15]

The fact that works of art are art-historically *situated* (with perhaps the exception of the very first Ur-art) does not mean that we must embrace the current anti-formalist consensus which says that the aesthetic properties of a work depend on its specific place in an artistic evolutionary process. We are not forced to admit that in order to make an adequate aesthetic assessment of a work we must see it in the light of its origins. Many works are not historically self-conscious—they are *situated* without being *contextual*.[16]

3   *GUERNICA* AND *GUERNICAS*

3.1   Let us now turn to Walton's argument that the art-historical categories into which a work of art falls are aesthetically relevant. (Henceforth I shall assume that the art-historical categories in question are the correct ones.) If Walton's argument from art-historical categories is successful, we cannot hold a moderate formalist position. For, unlike the argument from representational properties, the example generalizes to all (or nearly all) works of art, and to all (or nearly all) of their aesthetic properties. However, the argument from art-historical categories is more controversial than the argument from representational properties. It is not obvious that we can understand abstract works of art only if we subsume them under correct art-historical categories.

What does Walton understand by an art-historical category? For Walton, a category brings with it certain properties which are *typical* for works in the category, certain properties which are *atypical* for works in the category, and certain properties which are *neither typical nor atypical* for works in the category. Walton calls these "standard," "contra-standard," and "variable" features. For Walton, standard, contra-standard and variable features are constitutive of the category, and knowledge of the category involves knowledge of these features. Walton's thesis is that our belief that a work falls under a category affects our perception of it; we experience it differently when we experience

15. Similarly, Crispin Sartwell cites appropriated abstract art where a copy of a painting is exhibited under the copyist's name (so it is not a fake). See Crispin Sartwell, "Appropriation and Interpretation," *Journal of Value Inquiry*, vol. 28 (1994). But even if such works have contextually determined aesthetic properties (which is not obvious), all they show is that extreme formalism is inadequate. They fail to prove anything more general than that.

16. Jerrold Levinson's historical theory of art is inspired by the thought I am opposing here. See his "Defining Art Historically," in *Music, Art and Metaphysics* (Ithaca, N.Y.: Cornell University Press, 1990).

it in the light of the category. He concludes that understanding a work of art which falls under a category involves understanding the degree to which its features are standard, contra-standard, and variable with respect to that category.

Walton asks us to imagine a culture in which instead of paintings they make what he calls *guernicas*. These *guernicas* are just like Picasso's *Guernica* when viewed from directly above, but in fact they are all three-dimensional reliefs of varying dimensions of depth. They are all colored like Picasso's *Guernica* but they have differently sized and shaped bumps. So being flat is variable for a *guernica* but standard for a painting. And being in relief is contra-standard for a painting. Now one of the *guernicas* is an extreme case. It is flat. It is a physically indistinguishable duplicate of Picasso's *Guernica*, except of course that it cannot *be* Picasso's *Guernica*, since Picasso did not produce it and it is not a painting. (Picasso's *Guernica* has the essential properties of being produced by Picasso and of being a painting.) The two narrowly indistinguishable works of art have different art-historical properties. Walton then adds that members of this other culture somehow get to view Picasso's *Guernica*. He says that their different expectations

> would make for a profound difference between our aesthetic reaction to "Guernica" and theirs. It seems violent, dynamic, vital, disturbing to us. But I imagine that it would strike them as cold, stark, lifeless, or serene and restful, or perhaps bland, dull, boring—but in any case, *not* violent, dynamic, and vital.[17]

Walton's point here is that if the work is thought of as a *painting*, then it will be judged to be dynamic, whereas if it is thought of as a *guernica*, then it will be judged not to be dynamic. The *guernica* example is an "intuition pump," which Walton hopes will nudge us toward the conclusion that our judgments about the aesthetic character of works of art are dependent on the art-historical categories under which we subsume them.

In fact, the example would have been better if Walton had chosen an abstract painting. Picasso's *Guernica* represents various things; and, as we have seen, representation introduces a special and separable element. The sort of case we need to have in mind is one where intrinsically indistinguishable abstract and noncontextual works have different art-historical properties—for example, identical pieces of music or abstract visual designs. But for the sake of argument, we can treat *Guernica* and *guernicas* as if they were abstract.

Walton is arguing that we do not just judge that a work of art is elegant

17. Walton, "Categories of Art," p. 347.

and a painting or elegant *and* a *guernica*, but *elegant as a painting* or *elegant as a guernica*.[18] Moreover, a work might be an elegant painting but an inelegant *guernica*. Presumably Walton would also hold the same thesis about pure evaluations—something might be a good *painting* but a bad *guernica*. Walton thinks that aesthetic judgments are made in the light of a category which is thought to apply to the work.

How general is the conclusion of the argument? The *guernica* example is an example of narrowly identical counterparts, rather like Hilary Putnam's twin-earth example in the philosophy of mind.[19] The moral of Putnam's examples was general, within limits. It applied to intentional states but not to sensations. But Walton's argument seems to yield a conclusion about all works of art because it seems that for any aesthetic property of any work, we can imagine an example like Walton's *guernica* example. However, it does not matter if we interpret Walton as intending his argument only to apply to *most* aesthetic properties of *most* works of art.[20]

3.2   Should we believe what Walton says? An initial worry is that Walton's position seems to have the counterintuitive consequence that one cannot make aesthetic judgments about whole categories and that one cannot compare items in different categories. But someone might judge that Minoan art is (in general) more dynamic than Mycenean art or that a particular Minoan seal is more dynamic than a particular Mycenean seal.[21] How can the category-dependent view of aesthetic judgments account for such cross-category judgments?

Walton would presumably reply that we are widening our categories: we are forming a comparative aesthetic judgment about two categories, or about things in two different categories, but only in relation to some wider category. For example, when we say that Minoan art is (in general) more dynamic than Mycenean art, what we are saying is that this is how it is when we consider both sorts of works as belonging to the class of prehistoric Greek art. So it might, after all, be the case that aesthetic judgments are never category-free.

But why should we believe this story? It does not describe a psychological process that we are aware of when we make cross-category judgments. The

18. Ibid., p. 355.

19. Hilary Putnam, "The Meaning of Meaning," in *Mind, Language and Reality*, Philosophical Papers, vol. 2 (Cambridge: Cambridge University Press, 1975).

20. Compare his remarks about Martian works in "Categories of Art," p. 364, with what he says about natural objects on p. 355.

21. In the latter case, we are not just saying that the first seal is more dynamic as a Minoan seal than the second is as a Mycenean seal; it is an absolute comparison of the two seals. See section 3.4.

insistence that we are subconsciously operating with some more embracing category, even though we are not aware of it, seems to be an artifact of the anti-formalist theory that there is no independent reason to believe. If aesthetic judgments are category-dependent, we would expect speakers and thinkers to be aware of it. But phenomenological reflection does not support the category-dependent view.

We can imagine Walton replying that our aesthetic judgments have a "deep structure" which is not apparent to those who make the judgments.[22] But we need special evidence for this. The evidence would have to be some aspect of our inferential behavior that we become aware of only on reflection or after prompting. The trouble is that our inferential behavior does not point decisively in Walton's favor. Consider transitivity. Transitivity may fail where we are deploying categories which serve to alert us to the fact that the works have aesthetically significant representational or contextual properties: x could be more elegant than y considered as an abstract painting; y could be more elegant than z considered as an abstract painting; but z could be more elegant than x considered as a representation of a tree. But where we are *not* dealing with categories which alert us to representation or contextuality, our ordinary pre-theoretic aesthetic thought seems to include a requirement to respect transitivity.[23]

3.3   It is true that we often *say* that something is "elegant for a C" or "an elegant C." But this does not prove Walton's point that aesthetic judgments are category-dependent. There is an alternative *pragmatic* way of construing what is going on when we say this. Questions of goodness and elegance are matters of degree, and we often make ascriptions that make reference to a comparison class because this is a quicker and easier way of communicating questions of degree. But the formalist will say that the precise degree of some C thing's elegance does not involve the elegance of other existing C things. Being a matter of degree is quite different from being category-dependent.

For example, suppose we think that Minoan seals as a class are more

22. Compare Donald Davidson's theory of events in *Essays on Actions and Events* (Oxford: Clarendon, 1980).

23. An empirical approach would be to consider whether people who accept 'x is more elegant than y' and 'y is more elegant than z' also tend to infer that 'x is more elegant than z'. Assuming rationality, the extreme formalist would predict that there is such a general tendency, whereas Walton should predict that there is not, since there would be an equivocation when different categories are selected in the different judgments. The moderate formalist would predict a general tendency only for judgments about abstract and noncontextual art.

dynamic than Mycenean seals. Then we might want to say of a particular seal, which we know to be a Mycenean seal, that it is dynamic for a Mycenean seal. And we would want to say of a particular seal that we know to be a Minoan seal that it is not dynamic for a Minoan seal. This can be the case even though, if we were to compare the two, we might judge that the Minoan seal is the more dynamic of the two.[24] We would assert that although the Mycenean seal is dynamic compared to most other Mycenean seals, it is not all that dynamic considered by itself. So although *ascriptions* of dynamism are often qualified by a category, this is because dynamism is a matter of degree, not because it is category-dependent. For a formalist, the reference to a comparison class is a matter of pragmatic convenience: it is a way of expressing questions of degree in an effective and accessible way.

Although aesthetic judgments often take a category-dependent form, we can also make category-neutral aesthetic judgments. And, for the formalist, these category-neutral judgments are fundamental: category-dependent judgments are only possible because of category-neutral ones. We can make judgments about the intrinsic aesthetic nature of things without knowing about their relational properties. Unless we did so, we would have no basis for comparisons. At least, that is what the formalist will say, and Walton has not shown that it is not the case.

3.4   What then, in the light of this, should we say about the *guernicas* example? We should grasp the nettle! It is appropriate to say that a flat *guernica* is "lifeless" because it is less lively than most *guernicas*. But this whole class of artworks is an exceptionally lively one. Picasso's *Guernica* is appropriately said to be vital because it is more vital than most *paintings*, which, considered as a class, are not particularly lively. There is nothing inconsistent about the thought that the flat *guernica*, which is less lively than most *guernicas*, is just as lively as Picasso's *Guernica*, which is more lively than most paintings. The two might be equivalent in terms of degree of liveliness and also equivalent with respect to other aesthetic properties.

We can refuse to have our intuitions pumped in the direction Walton wants. We can stubbornly maintain that the two narrowly indistinguishable things are aesthetically indistinguishable, so long as they are both abstract and noncontextual works. Some will not share the intuition that we can say this. Some will persist in having the intuition that Walton wants to evoke. That's

---

24. Plato jokes that true beliefs are like the works of Daedelus in that they have a tendency to run away unless they are tied down (*Meno* 97d). I presume that Plato's joke plays on the notable dynamic qualities of Minoan art and also on the fact that they were notoriously subject to theft.

okay. So long as there are a fair number with the formalist intuition, we can insist that a non-question-begging argument has not been provided.

The same response can be given to a similar argument of E. H. Gombrich's. In *Art and Illusion*, Gombrich wrote:

> In most of us the name of Mondrian conjures up the expectation of severity, of an art of straight lines and a few primary colors in carefully balanced rectangles. Seen against this background, [*Broadway Boogie-Woogie*] gives indeed the impression of gay abandon. . . . [T]his impression is in fact grounded on our knowledge of the restricted choice open to the artist within his self-imposed discipline. Let us imagine for a moment that we were told the painting is by Severini, who is known for his futurist paintings that try to capture the rhythm of dance music in works of brilliant chaos.[25]

Again, the formalist can grasp the nettle. Gombrich asks us to imagine a painting exactly like *Broadway Boogie-Woogie* but painted by Severini. (This is in fact somewhat hard to imagine, but let us put that aside.) Mondrian's *Broadway Boogie-Woogie* is more gaily abandoned than most of his other works, and a similar painting by Severini would be more restrained than Severini's other works. But—unless Severini's painting was meant to be seen as a deliberate contrast with his other works—it could be maintained that it would be just as gaily abandoned or restrained as Mondrian's painting. At least, that is the formalist's intuition, and it is one that many would share. Let us counterpose Gombrich's willfully historical description to Clement Greenberg's more formal description of Mondrian's similar painting *New York Boogie-Woogie:*

> The checkered lines of [red] squares produce a staccato rhythm—signifying jazz—too easily contained by the square pattern and white ground of the picture. At hardly any point does the rhythm threaten to break out of and unbalance this pattern enough to justify the latter's final triumph. There is resolution, but of an easy struggle.[26]

There is no sense here that this description is beholden to Mondrian's other works. Given this more formal description, Greenberg then goes on to con-

---

25. E. H. Gombrich, *Art and Illusion* (London: Phaidon, 1959), p. 313.

26. Clement Greenberg, "Review of Mondrian's *New York Boogie-Woogie* and Other New Acquisitions at the Museum of Modern Art," in *Clement Greenberg: The Collected Essays and Criticism,* ed. John O'Brian, vol. 1 (Chicago: University of Chicago Press, 1986), p. 153. I have assimilated Greenberg's rectification of his misdescription of the red squares as orange (p. 154).

trast the work with Mondrian's earlier works, and he speculates about what Mondrian was attempting to do in the picture. But he *begins* from a formal description. For a formalist, that is the right way round.[27]

4 WALTON'S OTHER EXAMPLES

4.1   Having dealt with Walton's ingenious *guernicas* example, we can deal more briskly with his other examples.

Walton's third group of examples comprises cases where we hear something as belonging to a category:

> Proceeding along the lines of sonata-allegro form seems *right* to us; to our ears that is how sonatas are *supposed* to behave. We feel that we know where we are and where we are going throughout the work—more so, I suggest, than we would if we were not familiar with sonata-allegro form, if following the strictures of that form were variable rather than standard for us.[28]

It is true that we can hear a sonata as correctly exemplifying sonata form. We often hear music with a sense of its appropriateness. Walton argues that we could not do so unless we think of the music as conforming to a category.

There is indeed the phenomenon of listening with a sense of appropriateness for a category. For example, if we are listening to a twelve-bar blues, we will certainly feel the sort of familiarity that Walton describes. But it is not obvious that this sense of familiarity is aesthetically significant. For it might be that to hear a twelve-bar blues *as* a twelve-bar blues just involves hearing it as possessing certain familiar formal aesthetic properties.

The formalist can be content with a benign dilemma: either the music is blues in virtue of formal characteristics that we can directly hear in the music, or else being an instance of the blues genre is aesthetically irrelevant. That is, either 'blues' is a formalist category and thus the experience of hear-

27. Michael Baxandall writes: "[Picasso] changed forever the way we can see Cézanne (and African sculpture), whom we *must* see partly diffracted through Picasso's idiosyncratic reading" (*Patterns of Intention* [Yale University Press, 1985], p. 61, my emphasis). This goes too far, in my view. We are not so subject to the vicissitudes of history. There is an innocent formal eye! Some years ago there was exhibition of Cycladic sculpture at the British Museum, which was prefaced—and defaced in my view—by a large sculpture by Henry Moore. Cycladic sculpture needs no such apology.

28. Walton, "Categories of Art," p. 348.

ing music as a blues does not describe anything over and above hearing its
narrowly determined aesthetic properties, or else hearing music as correct
for some genre may be an interesting intellectual exercise but it is a separate
matter from the aesthetic experience of the music.[29] Similarly, a writer or
composer may strive to create works which artfully conform to certain
established forms—such as the sonata or sonnet. But the artist's achievement
is either an aesthetic achievement that is immediately manifest in the work,
considered on its own, or else it is an intellectual achievement that is not aesthetically relevant. (Such an intellectual achievement may of course be relevant to the overall *artistic* value of the work, where its artistic value is broader
than its aesthetic value.)

At any rate, Walton's appeal to the sense of familiarity does not show that
in order to ascribe *aesthetic* properties to a work we need to hear it as partak-
ing in a genre which subsumes other things.[30]

4.2   An example of Walton's fourth kind is this:

A piano passage that sounds lyrical or *cantabile* to us is one in which the individual tones are *relatively* sustained, given the capabilities of the instrument.
Such a passage sounds lyrical only because piano music is limited as it is, and we
hear it as piano music; that is, the limitations are standard properties for us. The
character of the passage is determined not merely by the "absolute" nature of
the sounds, but by that in relation to the standard property of what piano tones
can be like.[31]

Walton thinks that this can solve the problem of how piano music can be
lyrical when individual piano sounds are sharp and percussive. Walton also
worries about how violin music can sound fast and brilliant when fast electronic music sounds neither. He notices

the lack of energy and brilliance that we sometimes find even in very fast passages of electronic music.

29. To take another example—if subsuming a work under the category "cubist" does not
essentially involve attributing a certain history of production to it but is made solely on the basis of
the work's visual face, then "cubist" is a formal category and there is no problem.

30. For an insightful discussion of this issue with respect to the category of the sonnet, see
Barbara Herrnstein Smith, *Poetic Closure* (Chicago: University of Chicago Press, 1968), pp. 50–56.
She concludes: "although the reader's sense of closure at the end of a highly conventional form
will be increased by his familiarity with that form, it does not depend exclusively upon it" (p. 54).

31. Walton, "Categories of Art," p. 350. Hereafter cited by page number in the text.

And he concludes that

> the energy and brilliance of a fast violin or piano passage derives not merely
> from the absolute speed of the music . . . but from the fact that it is fast *for that
> particular medium*. (p. 350)

Walton thinks that piano music sounds lyrical only because we know that it
is lyrical *for* a piano, and the violin or piano sounds fast, unlike electronic
music, only because we know the limitations which are imposed by the
instrument. So we know which properties are standard, contra-standard, and
variable within the category corresponding to the instrument.

However, these examples do not show this and are best interpreted otherwise. The phenomena to which Walton appeals can be explained differently.
An organized complex whole of individual piano or violin sounds may have
aesthetic properties which the parts lack. That is, a series of sounds may have
aesthetic properties that the individual sounds lack, considered in themselves. A concatenation of percussive and unlyrical piano notes can sound
lyrical as a whole; and a concatenation of many short electronic notes can
sound less fast than a concatenation of fewer longer violin or piano notes. So
there is no need to appeal to categories under which anyone might listen to
the piano and violin passages. There is a perfectly satisfactory formalist
explanation.

Indeed, the formalist explanation is not just a rival—it is more plausible
than the category-dependent explanation, since we *do* ascribe properties
such as lyrical and fast to music even when we do not know what instrument we are listening to. But if Walton were right, we should be at a loss in
such cases. Walton's line is too intellectualist.

4.3   Walton's fifth kind of example is a near relation of his third kind. He
writes:

> Suppose also that while [a] sonata is in C-sharp there are signs that, given other
> rules of sonata form, indicate that the recapitulation is imminent (motivic
> hints of the return, an emotional climax, a cadenza). Listeners who hear it as a
> work in sonata form are likely to have distinct feeling of unease, tension,
> uncertainty, as the time for recapitulation approaches. If the composer with a
> stroke of ingenuity accomplishes the necessary modulation quickly, efficiently,
> and naturally, this will give them a feeling of relief—one might say of deliver-
> ance. (p. 351)

It is true that our expectations will produce feelings of tension and relief. But—contrary to Walton—this might not be because we are hearing the music under a category, but because the tension and resolution inheres in the sounds themselves. The tension and resolution is a formal tension and resolution. Walton too briskly overlooks this. (There would be something comic about a person who was mostly preoccupied with how a piece of music was to end, given certain rules.)

However, soon after the above quotation, Walton provides an argument:

> suppose that the rule for sonatas were that the recapitulation must be *either* in the original key or in the key one half step below it. . . . This possibility removes the sense of tension from the occurrence of C-sharp major in the development section . . . [and] there would also be no special *release* of tension when the modulation to G is effected, there being no tension to be released. (pp. 351–52)

Walton asks us to suppose that the rules of sonata resolution are quite different. As things actually are, we experience certain modulations as producing a tension in need of release. Hypothetically, with different rules of sonata formation, and with the sounds unchanged, Walton says that we would hear those sounds differently. But one cannot innocently assume this. For one thing, perhaps sonatas *must* have most of the rules they have. And second, waiving such essentialism, it is likely that what we might call *schmonatas*—which are just like sonatas but with the alternative rule—would create tension with no sense of release. For example, many traditional tangos end by descending to the dominant key never to return to the tonic. The effect is a pleasing tension. The tension does not go away just because it is variable for a tango. And I think the same would be true in Walton's sonata/schmonata case. At any rate, that is *my* intuition. Maybe it is a bad formalist intuition. But in that case, at most, we have a standoff.

4.4   Lastly, of the sixth group of examples, Walton writes:

> I now turn to features which are contra-standard for us—ones which have a tendency to disqualify a work from a category in which we nevertheless perceive it. We are likely to find such features shocking, or disconcerting, or startling, or upsetting, just because such features are contra-standard for us." (p. 352)

These are cases where a work has an unusual property which we find shocking. It has a contra-standard property; but it is not so contra-standard that it completely removes the thing from that category. Walton's examples are paintings with three-dimensional objects stuck to them, or monochromatic canvases. Walton says that these are misfits within a category.

But—once again—the matter can be differently described. One avenue is to say that shock is not an aesthetic reaction. If a work is unusual, it still has whatever formal characteristics it has. We may be surprised that a work of art has certain properties, but surprise at those properties need not lead us to make an aesthetic judgment.

This is one line of argument. But maybe we cannot always dismiss shock value like this. Perhaps we are *meant* to see the work as an aberrant painting. If so, it seems to me that we should simply concede Walton's point in these cases. We are then dealing with contextual art—and the thing to do is to tactically retreat. So long as *all* art does not suffer from such contextuality, moderate formalism is secure.

4.5   Fundamental to my approach is a certain caution with the notion of an art-historical category. We should not assume that art-historical categories always pick out aesthetically relevant properties of works of art. Such categories may be a convenient way of classifying art, artists, and art movements. But not every such classification is as significant as every other. For example, one can classify artists or works of art by putting their names in alphabetical order. Maybe some art-historical categories are similar in that they do not pick out aesthetically relevant properties.

The moderate formalist insists on a benign dilemma, in at least some cases: either the properties to which the category refers are narrow properties that are aesthetically relevant or else they are broad properties that are not aesthetically relevant. That is, either categories group works of art by narrow properties which are aesthetically relevant (in which case such categories would be formal categories) or else categories group works of art by their history of production, or by some other broad matter (in which case such properties are not aesthetically relevant, even though they might be interesting in their own right). I exploited this dilemma in all Walton's cases, together with the strategy of tactical retreat. I conceded that some works of art are representational and that some works of art are contextual. In those cases the benign dilemma fails to hold because there are broad properties which *are* aesthetically relevant. But much art is neither representational nor contextual, and for such art the benign dilemma holds.

CODA

Moderate formalism can be defended against Walton's arguments. His counterexamples can be finessed. Many works of art are purely formal works—all their aesthetic properties are formal aesthetic properties. For example, abstract painting and absolute music are purely formal arts—assuming that we are not dealing with contextual works. At the other extreme, it is true that many works of art have *no* formal aesthetic properties. These works divide into those that have nonformal aesthetic properties and those that have no aesthetic properties at all (such as some of the more "conceptual" works of the twentieth century). But many works of art—including most representational and contextual works—fall between these extremes, having both formal and nonformal aesthetic properties. The purpose of tactical retreat is to protect a privileged core of purely formal works of art. But that allows that many other works outside the stockade sport both formal and nonformal aesthetic properties. The strategy of tactical retreat is not a scorched-earth policy.

Moderate formalism allows that many works of art only have formal aesthetic properties, that many works of art have nonformal aesthetic properties, and that many works of art have both formal and nonformal aesthetic properties. Only moderate formalism recognizes that all three possibilities are generously populated. Extreme formalism does violence in one direction and anti-formalism does violence in the other. Only moderate formalism allows us to articulate the variety of kinds of aesthetic properties that different works of art have.

CHAPTER 6

Defusing Anti-Formalist Arguments

Anti-formalism has become the consensus in aesthetics. But in my view anti-formalism is not true to our aesthetic experience; it gives a revisionary account of the aesthetic properties that we think we find in works of art. The thesis I think we should hold is not extreme formalism—the view that all or almost all aesthetic properties are formal—but the moderate thesis that many are. This view has not been given its due because so many aestheticians have been convinced by anti-formalist arguments. In this short chapter, I propose a systematic method for resisting anti-formalist arguments. The method is to apply one of three strategies. These strategies are repeatable archetypes. I shall show these neutralizing strategies at work with seven objections to formalism.

For these purposes, we can take a formal aesthetic property to be an aesthetic property of a work of art that does not depend (at all) on the history of production of the work. By contrast, a nonformal aesthetic property does depend (in part) on its history of production. So, for example, the formal aesthetic properties of a visual work of art, if there are any such properties, depend solely on nonhistorical properties such as the colors and shapes on its surface. There is more to be said about the distinction between formal and nonformal aesthetic properties. This way of dividing them is problematic in some respects.[1] But it will do for the purpose of this chapter. In these terms,

1. In chapter 4, I considered notions of form that figure in writings about painting and literature that do not obviously fit this kind of characterization: in particular, the notion of plastic form in painting, which is a matter of the representation of colored physical objects which stand in spatial relations to one another, and the notion of form as opposed to content in literature, which is a matter of the structure of a literary work. It would be surprising if a characterization fitted all uses

we can say: anti-formalists believe that all the aesthetic properties of works of art are nonformal; extreme formalists believe that all their aesthetic properties are formal; and moderate formalists believe that some of their aesthetic properties are formal and some are not. Alternatively, given that those of an anti-formalist persuasion sometimes concede that some works have insignificant formal properties, and given that a formalist might concede that some works have insignificant nonformal aesthetic properties, we can say: anti-formalists believe that all or almost all of the aesthetic properties of works of art are nonformal; extreme formalists believe that all or almost all of their aesthetic properties are formal; and moderate formalists believe that many of their aesthetic properties are formal and many are not.[2]

1 TACTICAL RETREAT

The first strategy is that of tactical retreat. We can see it at work in defusing the following objection to formalism.

Objection 1:   What about the aesthetic properties of representational works of art? Typically their aesthetic properties depend on what those works represent. But what they represent depends on the history of production of those works—since what they represent depends (in part) on what the artist intended them to represent. So the aesthetic properties of representational works depend on the history of production of those works. A similar case is that of the aesthetic properties of contextual works of art— works that are meant to be seen in the light of other works or that have a point only in relation to other works. Typically their aesthetic properties depend on the context in which they are intended to be seen. But which context is intended depends on the history of production of those works. So the aesthetic properties of contextual works depend on their history of production.[3]

[handwritten: portraits have representational aesthetic properties that not depend on the painter's intentions]

---

of the term "form," given the proliferation of uses. But I argue that we can be happy enough if our characterization enables us to make sense of the most common uses. We can then see the unusual rogue notions as variations on the central theme or as different in various ways. Either way, they need not take center stage.

2. Examples of anti-formalists are Kendall Walton, "Categories of Art," *Philosophical Review*, vol. 79 (1970); and Jerrold Levinson, "What a Musical Work Is," in *Music, Art, and Metaphysics* (Ithaca, N.Y.: Cornell University Press, 1990). An example of an extreme formalist is Clive Bell, *Art* (London: Chatto & Windus, 1914).

3. This first objection figures in Walton, "Categories of Art," pp. 343–47. In chapter 5, I examined this first objection in greater depth as well as the many other objections that can be found in

[handwritten margin: non-formal aesthetic properties]

[handwritten bottom: Thus, formalism is false.]

Reply: It is true that both these sorts of cases create insurmountable diffi-culties for the *extreme* formalist. But the *moderate* formalist can retreat in both cases. Aesthetic properties that depend on a work's representational or contex-tual properties are indeed nonformal. But that does not entail that there are not many abstract and noncontextual works of art which nonetheless have significant aesthetic properties, or indeed that many representational or con-textual works do not have *other* aesthetic properties that are formal. Accumu-lating some or even many cases of works with nonformal aesthetic properties does not show that there are not some or even many works all of whose aes-thetic properties are formal. Moreover, many representational or contextual works have aesthetic properties that are formal. What we need but do not get is a claim about all or even most works of art or about all or even most aes-thetic properties of works of art. The sin of faulty generalization plagues dis-cussions of formalism. Many arguments against formalism have this incomplete character. The moderate formalist concedes that *many* works of art cannot be fully understood in purely formalist terms, but he persists in maintaining, first, that there is a significant residual class of works of art that *can* be so understood, and second, that there are many works that have both formal and nonformal aesthetic properties.[4]

2 IRRELEVANCE

The second defensive strategy is to charge the proffered case with irrele-vance to the formal or nonformal status of the aesthetic properties of a work. This strategy can be effectively deployed against the following two objections.

Objection 2:   Even in the case of abstract and noncontextual art, we always bring previous knowledge and expectations to our experience of par-ticular works. So we always experience and judge a work of art in the light

---

Walton's essay. Apart from this first objection, none of the anti-formalist arguments I consider in this chapter figure in Walton's essay.

4. The following are three prima facie examples of mixed works, with both formal and non-formal aesthetic properties. First, a number of Egyptian wall paintings from the Valley of the Nobles represent groups of mourning women (Tomb of Userhet, in particular); the position of the women's arms makes for an elegant spiraling movement in the composition, and that is a for-mal value. Second, many of Jenny Saville's paintings of women have strength and solidity; whatever other values those paintings have, they also work on a formal level. Third, many of I. M. Pei's buildings combine a tension between the parts with a certain serenity of the whole; for example, the Bank of China in Hong Kong and the east wing of the National Gallery in Washington, D.C.

(comparing)   THUS CANT BE FORMAL.

of our knowledge of other works. So the aesthetic properties of a work cannot be considered in isolation from other works.   → bringing in more
knowledge

Reply: It is true that our experience of a work of art is often affected by
previous aesthetic judgments about other works of art. But that does not
show that the aesthetic properties of a particular work of art depend on those
other works of art. It just shows that being in a position to *ascribe* or *know* its
aesthetic properties often involves knowing about other works. Knowing
about radioactivity involves knowing about matters external to the radioactivity. For example, we need to know about Geiger counters. But that does not
make Geiger counters constitutive of radioactivity. Similarly, it might be that
what is appreciated by someone armed with knowledge of other works
depends on the immediate, nonhistorical properties of the work. One's ability to judge that certain formal properties are instantiated may depend on
one's previous experience of the formal properties of other works. One
might need considerable acquaintance with works of an unfamiliar genre in
order to ascribe formal aesthetic properties to a work in that genre. But *what*
one ascribes, given previous experience, is independent of those other works.

Objection 3:   The strategy of tactical retreat cannot save any kind of formalism because we *always* need information about the history of production
when considering abstract and noncontextual works of art, since we need to
know that such works *lack* representational and contextual properties.[5]

Initial reply: Although we need historical information to *know* whether a
work is abstract or noncontextual, this does not mean that the aesthetic
properties of an abstract and noncontextual work themselves depend on its
history of production. It just means that *knowing* that a work's formal properties exhaust all its aesthetic properties depends on *knowing* about its history
of production. So the point is merely an epistemological one which has no
metaphysical anti-formalist consequences. Similarly, we may need to *know*
that a work is *not* a contextual work in order to make an adequate aesthetic
assessment of it; but that does not show that its aesthetic properties are determined by the negative property of not being a contextual work.

Follow-up objection: This is beside the point, for aesthetic properties of
abstract and noncontextual works are *negatively* determined by the *lack* of
certain historical properties, and this is not a merely epistemological point.

5. Jerrold Levinson put this objection to me.

Follow up reply: A full treatment of this problem would require a lengthy excursion into the metaphysics of negative properties. I incline toward the view that the aesthetic properties of an abstract and noncontextual work of art are determined by the conjunction of its *positive* nonaesthetic properties, and not, in any interesting sense, by *negative* nonaesthetic properties, such as *not* being a representation of Napoleon or even *not* being identical with the number seven. But this is a controversial matter. Fortunately, the issue does not matter much for our concerns, since what anti-formalists maintain is not that aesthetic properties depend on certain negative historical properties but that they depend on *positive* historical properties. The history of production of a work is a matter of a positive causal relation in which the work stands. Anti-formalism was never meant to be the trivial doctrine that the negative determination argument would make it.

3 BENIGN DILEMMA

The third strategy is that of *benign dilemma*. This strategy does not try to duck potentially problematic examples of valuable properties of works of art but seizes hold of them by posing a dilemma. The dilemma is: either the proffered property is an aesthetic property and it is formal, or else it is not aesthetic at all. Works of art have many interesting and valuable properties besides aesthetic properties. Formalism is secure so long as the *aesthetic* properties do not depend on the history of production of the work. Other valuable and interesting properties may depend on the history of production without threatening formalism. This strategy is effective against the following four objections, although sometimes it needs to be deployed in combination with one of the other strategies.

Objection 4:   To understand a work of art we always need to know an artist's *reasons* for creating his works.[6] But these reasons are a matter of the history of production of a work. *Need to know BROAD Properties*

This [crossed out] isn't just determined by Formalist, narrow, properties.

Reply: One can make a distinction among reasons. On the one hand, some reasons are formal reasons. The artist may desire to create certain formal aesthetic properties, and that may cause those formal aesthetic properties to be instantiated. On the other hand, many reasons for creating works of art

---

6. See, for example, Crispin Sartwell, "Appropriation and Interpretation," *Journal of Value Inquiry* (1994): 337–38.

REALIST = artist intentions are irrelevate.

are not relevant to the work's aesthetic properties. For example, money or fame are probably significant motives in many cases. All sorts of motives are causally efficacious without having any direct bearing on the resulting work's aesthetic properties. Now, the idea that we must understand art by appealing to the artist's reasons is close to the idea that we must see art in terms of problem solving. It is often said that artists set themselves problems and then try to solve them, so understanding art involves reconstructing what problems are being addressed and seeing how far they are solved. Art historians such as Erwin Panofsky, E. H. Gombrich, and Michael Baxandall have taken this approach.[7] Again, there is a benign dilemma. On the one hand, some problems and solutions are formal problems and solutions. And, assuming some degree of success in solving formal problems, formal success is manifest in the work. The fact that the artist was concerned with certain formal problems drops out as aesthetically irrelevant except insofar as it played a causal role in generating the formal properties of the work. On the other hand, some problems and solutions are not formal problems and solutions, and they are not aesthetically relevant. Earning a living is a problem, and making and selling art is a solution. Such causes may be interesting in their own right. But they do not necessarily manifest themselves in the resulting work's aesthetic nature. Where an artist's reasons and problems concern something represented, or the mode of representation, or the art-historical context, then the dilemma will fail to hold, and tactical retreat will be appropriate. But not all reasons and problems are of this sort.

Objection 5: Works of art can possess or lack the property of *originality* (in the sense of doing something new rather than not being a fake). But the property of originality is not something internal to a particular work that we can detect just by looking at it, at a particular time; and this is because being original, or not being unoriginal, is a historical matter.[8]

Reply: Here the formalist should insist on the second horn of the dilemma: originality is not an *aesthetic* property, although it is an important property of works of art. Originality is a relation between what determines

[right margin, handwritten:] works of art can be expressions of an artist's intention.

7. Erwin Panofsky, "The History of Art as a Humanistic Discipline," in *Meaning in the Visual Arts* (New York: Doubleday, 1955), esp. pp. 20–22; E. H. Gombrich, *Art and Illusion* (London: Phaidon, 1959), esp. p. 313; and Michael Baxandall, *Patterns of Intention* (New Haven: Yale University Press, 1985).

8. See Jerrold Levinson, "What a Musical Work Is," in *Music, Art and Metaphysics* (Ithaca, N.Y.: Cornell University Press, 1990), p. 70. The other examples in Levinson's paper (pp. 70–71) are more or less in the same terrain as those in Walton's "Categories of Art," which I excavate in chapter 5.

the valuable properties of a work (aesthetic or nonaesthetic) and what determines the valuable properties of other works. In particular it is a certain distance between what determines a work's valuable properties and what determines the valuable properties of *preceding* works. A very early cubist painting may have more originality than an otherwise similar painting created five years later. Originality is an *artistic* value, not an *aesthetic* value—which is a matter of beauty, elegance, delicacy, and so on. At this point, I am, of course, helping myself to the distinction between aesthetic and nonaesthetic properties and to the idea that beauty, elegance, and delicacy are instances of the former, and originality of the latter. My view is that this is relatively unproblematic.[9] Of course one can imagine someone querying this. But then the moderate formalist position is still secure. For originality would then be just one aesthetic property among many, and we could tactically retreat. Originality might be a nonformal aesthetic property, while there are plenty of other formal aesthetic properties remaining.

Objection 6:   What can a formalist say about fakes? A fake of some particular work, or of works in the style of an artist or genre, differs only in historical respects from an original. It might be argued that our aesthetic judgments about *all* works of art would be affected by the knowledge that they are fakes. That seems to show that assumptions about the origins of works of art are *always* tacitly involved in aesthetic judgments about them, since we normally assume that the works of art we consider are *not* fakes. If so, the strategy of tactical retreat will not work since it threatens to leave the moderate formalist holding no ground at all.

Reply: The debate over fakes tends to be set up in terms of whether being a fake makes an aesthetic difference.[10] But this is oversimplistic. A moderate formalist *can* concede that it makes an aesthetic difference in *some* cases. If a work involves representation or contextuality then an indistinguishable fake might not share those features and so might differ aesthetically.[11] So the moderate formalist can beat a tactical retreat to abstract and

9. See chapter 2.

10. See Alfred Lessing, "What Is Wrong with a Forgery?" *Journal of Aesthetics and Art Criticism*, vol. 23 (1965); Nelson Goodman, *Languages of Art* (Oxford: Oxford University Press, 1969), chap. 3; and Dennis Dutton, "Artistic Crimes," *British Journal of Aesthetics*, vol. 19 (1979). Dutton appeals to the Panofskian/Gombrichean idea of art as "problem-solving." But as we saw when dealing with objection 4, this does not have the anti-formalist consequences that many suppose.

11. Although this *might* be so, it should not be taken for granted in any particular case that these historical differences *will* make an aesthetic difference. For example, a fake might share representational properties with an original, and if so, there might be no aesthetic difference.

noncontextual art. The moderate formalist concedes that learning that a work of abstract and noncontextual art is a fake might force us to revise our *artistic* assessment of it, say, with respect to its originality, but it does not force us to revise our assessment of its *aesthetic* merits. (This is the second horn of the benign dilemma.) So no difficulty for the moderate formalist arises from fakes: being a fake makes no difference to formal properties, and if the work is abstract and noncontextual, it makes no difference to any aesthetic properties. At least, that is what the moderate formalist will say. What one thinks about fakes depends on one's attitude to formalism. The extreme formalist is bound to say that whether a thing is a fake is always or almost always aesthetically irrelevant. The extreme anti-formalist is bound to say that being a fake is always or almost always aesthetically relevant. And the moderate formalist is bound to say that it is often relevant and often not. So the appeal to fakes supplies no dialectical pressure.[12]

Objection 7:   We often describe music in historical terms; and some even say that we *hear* music in historical terms. For example, Jerrold Levinson writes:

> We hear passages as *sighing*, as *chirping*, as *sawing*, as *hammering*, as *crashing*, as *booming*, and so on, all of which make implicit reference to a kind of action connected to the passage's sonic face as its presumed source.[13]

He thinks either that such descriptions directly invoke the history of production of these sounds ("sawing," "hammering," etc.), so that a specific history is attributed, or else that these sounds are like sounds that have such histories. Therefore the aesthetic properties of these passages of music are nonformal.

Reply: The formalist should deny Levinson's analysis of the phenomena. Instead the formalist should say that terms like "sawing" and "hammering" are used to make metaphorical descriptions of formal aesthetic properties and our experience of them. It is not at all obvious, or indeed plausible, that it is part of what it is to hear music as sawing or as hammering that the

12. For example, Clive Bell writes: "To those who have and hold a sense of the significance of form what does it matter whether the forms that move them were created in Paris the day before yesterday or in Babylon fifty centuries ago?" (*Art*, pp. 45–46). On the extreme anti-formalist wing, Mark Sagoff merely asserts the contrary view of fakes in "On the Aesthetic Value of Forgeries," *Journal of Aesthetics and Art Criticism*, vol. 37 (1978).

13. Jerrold Levinson, "Authentic Performance and Authentic Means," in *Music, Art and Metaphysics*, p. 397.

hearer thinks that someone is *literally* sawing or hammering something, or that the hearer thinks that what he hears is like sounds that are typically produced in such ways.[14] The hearer might also happen to *believe* either of these things, but this is not part of the *content* of what he hears, just as this would not be what he *meant* if he were to describe the music in these historical ways. Rather, the description is a special way of drawing attention to the immediately heard sonic face of the music. In a nice contrast with Levinson, Scruton writes:

> The middle C that we hear does not strike us as the effect of someone blowing on a clarinet; rather it is a response to the B that preceded it, and calls in turn for the E that follows.[15]

This analysis is formalistically acceptable, unlike Levinson's. A formalist can agree that the clarinet tones sound *as if* someone is blowing something, while remaining formalistically kosher. For that might be a description of what we can immediately hear in the music. It is only when our description makes reference to *actual history* that it oversteps the formal, and if the formalist is right, courts aesthetic irrelevance. I do not take myself to have shown that Levinson's reading of the situation is incorrect. All I want to point out is that there is a happy formalist reading and that Levinson has not provided an argument against it. (Recall that my purpose in this chapter is primarily defensive.) Thus, in the case of what is described in these historical terms, the formalist can grasp the first horn of the dilemma; the properties in question are in fact formal properties.

Coda

Potential counterexamples to moderate formalism can be dealt with by the strategies tactical retreat, irrelevance or benign dilemma. For example, when dealing with representational and contextual properties, we should tactically retreat; with the other works, knowledge of which we must have in order to make an aesthetic judgment, we should claim irrelevance; and with originality and fakes, we should insist on the benign dilemma. The dilemma holds only when we are dealing with nonrepresentational and noncontextual

14. See Roger Scruton, "Understanding Music," in *The Aesthetic Understanding* (London: Carcanet, 1983).

15. Roger Scruton, *An Intelligent Person's Guide to Philosophy* (London: Duckworth, 1996), p. 144.

art—a significant concession. But within that circumscribed range, all aesthetic properties are formal. Moderate formalism can be defended against the anti-formalist arguments that we have encountered. And I predict that unencountered anti-formalist arguments can be neutralized by the same means. Formalism, of a moderate sort, can then be given the consideration I believe it deserves.

CHAPTER 7

Formal Natural Beauty

[handwritten: In order to see natural beauty you need to understand nature.]

1 VARIETIES OF ANTI-FORMALISM AND THE QUA THESIS

Some things have *dependent beauty*, in Kant's sense. Things that have dependent beauty have a function, and their beauty expresses or articulates that function. If we are accurately to judge the dependent beauty of a thing, we must subsume it under a category that picks out the function it has. But not all beauty is dependent beauty. Some beauty does not express a function but depends entirely on how the thing is considered in itself. That beauty is *free* or *formal* beauty (see chapter 4). Dependent beauty is nonformal beauty. Extreme formalism says that all beauty is formal beauty. Anti-formalism says that all beauty is nonformal beauty. Moderate aesthetic formalism says that there is much beauty of both sorts.

In my view, moderate formalism is true of both art and nature. Both art and nature include things that have dependent beauty, and both art and nature include things that have free beauty. In the previous three chapters, however, I have argued this only in the case of art. Perhaps nature is different?

Allen Carlson is a staunch anti-formalist about the aesthetics of nature. He thinks that we must *always* subsume natural things under correct historical and functional categories if we are to ascribe aesthetic properties to them.[1] One demanding form that such anti-formalism might take would be to hold that the correct aesthetic appreciation of nature depends on a scientific understanding of it. But a less demanding thesis would be merely that we

---

1. See his essays collected in Allen Carlson, *Aesthetics and the Environment* (London: Routledge, 2000).

[handwritten: Qua Thesis: something in nature is beautiful qua (as) in its category.]

must appreciate natural things as the *kinds* of things they are, where these kinds can be commonsense natural kinds. On the commonsense kind view, we must appreciate things *as* things of their kinds, but we need not have a *scientific* understanding of those kinds. On either view, however, the natural kinds under which things fall fix the categories under which we should perceive them if we are to appreciate their aesthetic properties.[2]

The question we have to consider is: Do natural things have their aesthetic properties *qua* the natural kinds they are members of?

We can distinguish weak and strong versions of this "Qua thesis." According to the strong version, we must subsume things under either the correct scientific or the correct commonsense natural categories. We must appreciate a natural thing as the *particular kind* of natural thing it is. But all the weak Qua thesis holds is that one need only appreciate a natural thing as *a* natural thing. Malcolm Budd expresses the weak thesis when he writes:

> Just as the aesthetic appreciation of art is the aesthetic appreciation of art *as art*, so the aesthetic appreciation of nature is the aesthetic appreciation of nature *as nature.*[3]

Carlson defends the strong thesis. Budd only endorses the weak thesis. But in my view, *both* theses should be resisted. What is unacceptable about both the weak and strong theses is their generality. But these theses are not so far from a thesis which I think *is* acceptable. What I think is acceptable is the thesis that in *many* cases we must appreciate a thing as the particular natural kind it is. But this is a different matter from a quite general thesis that we must *always* appreciate a thing as art or as nature or as the particular natural kind it is.[4]

Carlson developed his view from a critique of some remarks of Kendall Walton's on the aesthetics of nature in his essay "Categories of Art." Walton's general thesis is that aesthetic judgments should be made in the light of some category. But he also thinks that art and nature differ in that there are correct

2. One person who has attacked the scientific thesis is Noel Carroll. He thinks that we can be moved by nature without erudite scientific understanding (Carroll, "On Being Moved by Nature," in *Landscape, Natural Beauty, and the Arts,* ed. S. Kemal and I. Gaskell [Cambridge: Cambridge University Press, 1993]). I agree with that. But, as Carlson said in reply to Carroll, that leaves in place the commonsense thesis, which I also want to question (Allen Carlson, "Nature, Aesthetic Appreciation, and Knowledge," *Journal of Aesthetics and Art Criticism,* vol 53 [1996]).

3. Malcolm Budd, "The Aesthetics of Nature," *Proceedings of the Aristotelian Society* 74 (2000): 138. See also his "The Aesthetic Appreciation of Nature," *British Journal of Aesthetics,* vol. 35 (1996).

4. We can reject Budd's thesis while agreeing with him that it is a mistake to think that we (have to) experience nature as art.

depend on the category of nature?

and incorrect categories under which we should think of works of art, whereas this not the case for nature.[5] Walton thinks that both sorts of aesthetic judgments are *category-dependent,* but only aesthetic judgments about nature are *category-relative.* So a natural thing can be beautiful relative to C1 and not beautiful relative to C2, where C1 and C2 have equal validity or lack of validity. Like Walton, Carlson *accepts* the category-*dependent* thesis about both judgments about art and nature, but by contrast with Walton, he *rejects* the category-*relative* thesis about the aesthetics of nature. For Carlson holds that there *are* correct categories under which we should perceive natural things.[6] By contrast with both Walton and Carlson, my view is that we should reject the category-dependent thesis as a quite general thesis about both art and nature. I think Carlson is right to reject Walton's category-relative view of nature. But I think that he should do that without accepting Walton's general category-dependent thesis about aesthetic judgments.

There is something suspicious about the way anti-formalists like Carlson set up the debate. Having been persuaded by Walton's general category-dependence thesis, they accept the conditional that *if* aesthetic judgments about nature were not category-dependent *then* they would have no claim to objectivity or correctness. If this fear is motivating Carlson and others, it is baseless. Aesthetic judgments about nature might claim objective correctness despite being category-independent. The trouble is that many of the participants in the debate over natural beauty accept Walton's category-dependent view of aesthetic judgments about *art.* This is, I think, why they accept the conditional that I say we should reject. According to moderate formalism, however, many aesthetic judgments about art are not category-dependent.

As a moderate formalist, I partly agree with Carlson about biological nature. It sometimes matters aesthetically what kind of creature we are appreciating, or what part of a creature we are appreciating. If so, we have cases of dependent beauty. But I think that nature also has purposeless beauty. And about inorganic or nonbiological nature, I do not agree at all. Inorganic nature, I say, has *only* formal aesthetic properties. I shall defend these views after one preliminary matter.

all aesthetic properties of nature of dependent on it → anti-formalist.

5. Kendall Walton, "Categories of Art," *Philosophical Review* 79 (1970): 355.

6. See his essays "Appreciation and the Natural Environment," *Journal of Aesthetics and Art Criticism,* vol. 38 (1979), and "Nature, Aesthetic Judgment, and Objectivity," *Journal of Aesthetics and Art Criticism,* vol. 40 (1981), both reprinted in his *Aesthetics and the Environment.*

2 METHODOLOGICAL REFLECTIONS

In philosophy, we often argue by appealing to examples, actual or imaginary. In particular, we often appeal to indiscernible counterparts. But those who do so often manage to convince themselves more speedily than their opponents. For their opponents often refuse to agree with the proffered interpretation of the examples. In the aesthetics of nature, I am tempted to offer arguments like the following.

(1) Consider very good quality plastic or silk flowers (and suppose that they have also been augmented with the right fragrance and texture). Do they differ aesthetically from real flowers? I think not. To be sure, part of one's pleasure in flowers is from the thought that they are or were living things. But that might be a nonaesthetic pleasure. *[margin: FORMAL-IST]*

(2) Suppose we find out that the fjords were artificially constructed (just as some lakes are artificial). For a while, after the revelation, wandering around the fjords, one's experience would perhaps be different and perhaps disturbed. But after a while, would it not revert to what it was previously? *[margin: FORMAL-IST.]*

(3) For the theist, nature *is* art. (As the hymn goes: "All things bright and beautiful, the Lord God made them all.") But is the theist's aesthetic experience of nature so different from that of the atheist's? I think not. Suppose someone loses his faith, or indeed gains it. Does his aesthetic experience of nature alter (in the long term)? Again, I think not.

Such examples *may* persuade those who are undecided to come over to the formalist camp. But those who have already signed up with anti-formalism are unlikely to be impressed. The examples probably serve only to elucidate *my* intuitions about cases, which are probably infected by my commitment to moderate formalism, whereas I expect that anti-formalists like Carlson will have different intuitions. Such examples of indiscernibles will cut little dialectical ice with those with implacably different intuitions. Nevertheless, the effectiveness of examples is audience-relative. If we can find examples that our audience agrees with, or has a tendency to agree with, then one can use that fact as a dialectical fulcrum to gain some leverage on their more theoretical views. I shall try to put examples that appeal to the waverers, and also to hidden repressed formalist sympathies buried deep in the breasts of those who are publicly and consciously committed to anti-formalism.

[right margin handwritten: adjusting your theories, over the time you intuitions change]

[handwritten notes at bottom:]

(1) Has the same aesthetic properties as the real ones.

(2) Realize that one fake think it is meant, then it goes back to normal.

(3) Confused for a little, but NOT IN THE LONG RUN.

3 QUALESS BIOLOGICAL BEAUTY

Let us first consider biological, living things—things that have teleological natures. Since I am a moderate formalist, I leave room for the idea that biological things are beautiful qua the biological kind they are.[7] But I also leave open the possibility that these things also have *qualess* beauty. That is, I think that biological things have aesthetic properties that are *not* dependent on their biological kind.[8]

An obvious example to think about is that of the whale. Does it make a difference to its beauty that it is a mammal and not a fish? Is a giant shark beautiful in quite a different way from the way that a whale is beautiful, since it is a fish and not a mammal? I think not. But this is inconsistent with the strong Qua thesis. However, Carlson does not agree with me about whales. Our intuitions clash. So there is a problem making dialectical progress here.

I want to set more store by the following example. Consider the elegant and somewhat dainty beauty of a polar bear swimming underwater.[10] Surely, we need not consider its beauty as the specific type of animal that it is. If so, the strong Qua thesis is wrong.

This example also puts pressure on the weak Qua thesis as well as the strong one. Need one consider the underwater-swimming polar bear as a beautiful *living* thing or a beautiful *natural* thing or just as a beautiful *thing*? I think this last will do. It is a formally extraordinary *phenomenon*. It might even turn out to be an artfully choreographed swimmer dressed in a polar bear suit. No matter. It is still a beautiful *spectacle*. It has a free, formal beauty. Similarly, consider the extraordinary beauty of the way an octopus moves underwater. That beauty would remain even if the octopus some-

THIS happens in ART and NATURE.

----

7. However, this idea is far from straightforward. In particular, things fall under many natural kinds. What determines which kind is relevant? Is a leopard beautiful as a leopard *and* as a member of the cat family *and* as a mammal *and* as a land animal *and* as a living thing?

8. The Qua thesis is most plausible if we consider *parts* of a creature. The beauty of a part of a creature is plausibly a beauty which is relative to its function. One may have to know what the part does—that is, we may have to know its function with respect to the whole organism—in order to see, not just its free, formal beauty (if it has any), but also its dependent, nonformal beauty. The part is beautiful as a thing with its function. But *whole organisms*, and the way they move, in my view, often have a free, formal beauty.

9. Carlson writes: "The rorqual whale is a graceful and majestic mammal. However, were it perceived as a fish, it would appear lumbering, somewhat oafish, perhaps even a bit clumsy (maybe somewhat like the basking shark)" ("Nature and Positive Aesthetics," *Environmental Ethics* 6 [1984]: 25). This essay is reprinted in his *Aesthetics and the Environment*, where the quotation is on p. 89.

10. Some zoos, such as those in Washington, D.C., and San Diego, have a glass panel that enables one to see this.

how turned out to be a fish, or a mammal, or even if it were somehow an artifact.

Hence I reject even the weak Qua thesis as a general thesis. We need not judge nature *as* nature in order to ascribe aesthetic properties to it. Carlson may be right that *many* aesthetic properties are revealed to us only when we conceptualize nature in the right way. What I resist is the thought that we *must* conceptualize nature according to its natural kinds in order to appreciate it aesthetically.[11] Nature has formal aesthetic properties as well as dependent aesthetic properties.

Now perhaps Carlson will try to reject what I have just said about underwater polar bears and octopuses, just as he rejects my intuition about whales. So let me draw attention to an aspect of the polar bear example, in order to forestall this intransigent reply.

The striking thing about the beauty of the underwater polar bear is that it comes as a *surprise* in the light of the limited amount that most of us know about these animals. That beauty was the last thing we expected. Our surprise shows that it is *not* a beauty that we took to be dependent in some way upon our grasp of its polar-bearness. We did not find it elegant *as* a polar bear. It has a category-free beauty. The underwater polar bear is a beautiful *thing* in beautiful motion, just as a swimming octopus is a beautiful thing in beautiful motion. The underwater polar bear is surprisingly beautiful in the sense that it has a formal beauty that is surprising given that we know that it is a polar bear and our limited knowledge of typical bear activities. It does not have the kind of formal beauty that we expect polar bears to have. Moreover, if polar bears were to have dependent beauty, a beauty that they have qua polar bears, then it would surely not be like this! For, amazingly enough, the underwater polar bear was *dainty*. Whatever next? A dainty polar bear! Given our background beliefs about polar bears, that is not at all how we would have thought that a polar bear would look underwater. We think of its aesthetic character as strong and lumbering. And if the polar bear were to have aesthetic properties qua polar bear, we would expect it to have *those* aesthetic properties or similar ones. Not *daintiness*. In fact, its aesthetic character had nothing to do with its being a polar bear.[12] I cannot see how Carlson can account for this.

---

11. I use *appreciation* to mean "appropriate appreciation" or "appreciation of the aesthetic properties that the thing really has."

12. Suppose there were a creature physiologically like the polar bear—a "schmolar bear"—which swims under water just like the polar bear but which was also very graceful on land. Is the schmolar bear *less* graceful under water than the polar bear? Surely not.

There is something important that Carlson and those who follow him have missed in the aesthetics of nature, which is simply that *nature is full of surprises*. In particular, it is full of things that have an *incongruous beauty*. Many natural things have a beauty that seems incongruous to us given what we know of the natural kind categories into which they fall. Sea horses or sea cucumbers are further examples. Their beauty has nothing to do with the natural categories into which they fall, and if anything their beauty preposterously flouts those categories. They are not beautiful *by* flouting those categories. Their beauty, gloriously, *has nothing to do with them*.

Carlson's Qua thesis cannot give due recognition to the incongruousness of much natural beauty. For Carlson, natural things are to be categorically *tamed*. He thinks that the beauty of natural things is constrained by their natural categories. But in fact their natural beauty is often quite at odds with their natural kind categories. The beauty of nature is often categorically anarchic, anomalous. Only moderate formalism can account for this prevalent aspect of the aesthetics of nature.[13]

4 Inorganic Natural Beauty

Extreme formalism about inorganic nature seems obvious to me. Surely, where a natural thing has no purpose, we need only consider what we can immediately perceive, and we need not know about its origin. The beauty of an inorganic natural thing at a time is surely determined just by its narrow nonaesthetic properties at that time. Anything else may be interesting, but it does not (or should not) affect aesthetic appreciation. Or so one would naturally think. However, Ronald Hepburn's superb example of a wide expanse of sand and mud creates a difficulty. In 1965, he wrote, famously:

> Suppose I am walking over a wide expanse of sand and mud. The quality of the scene is perhaps that of wild, glad emptiness. But suppose I bring to bear upon the scene my knowledge that this is a tidal basin, the tide being out. The realization is not aesthetically irrelevant. I see myself now as walking on what is for half the day sea-bed. The wild glad emptiness may be tempered by a disturbing weirdness.[14]

13. The extraordinary film *Microcosmos* celebrates the extraordinary and surprising beauty of nature. The snail sex scene is particularly notable.

14. Ronald Hepburn, "Contemporary Aesthetics and the Neglect of Natural Beauty," in *Wonder and Others Essays* (Edinburgh: Edinburgh University Press, 1984), p. 19.

Considered as a beach, the stretch of sand and mud seems to have certain aesthetic properties ("wild, glad emptiness"), but considered as the seabed of a tidal basin, it seems to have other aesthetic properties ("disturbing weirdness"). This example is rather like Walton's *guernicas* example.[15] It is a case of narrow indiscernibles which seem to have different aesthetic properties depending on their broad context. The conclusion is that the aesthetic properties that natural things seem to have are not independent of our beliefs about their history and context. We need to know a natural thing's history and context in order to make an aesthetic judgment about it. Thus the aesthetic properties of inorganic natural things are dependent in part on their history and context as well as their perceivable properties.

In the years following the appearance of Hepburn's example, no one challenged his analysis, and therefore anti-formalism about natural beauty became the default position. I want to dispute Hepburn's anti-formalist analysis. He is obviously on to something interesting in the example. But I see nothing that is incompatible with an extreme formalist analysis.

In Hepburn's example, there is the flat area of sand and mud at the time. Call it *A*. It has the aesthetic properties it has in virtue of its narrow non-aesthetic properties. But this area can also be considered as part of a wider whole, in this case the wider temporal whole in which this area is submerged at a later time. (Note that it is crucial to Hepburn's example that one *imagines* the empty area later submerged, while looking at the expanse of mud and sand.) Call the later submerged area *B*. We may consider the aesthetic properties of A alone, those of B alone, and also those of A + B. Now it may be that considered in itself, A has certain aesthetic properties (wild, glad emptiness), but that A has other aesthetic properties in the light of the whole, A + B (disturbing weirdness). This is like the way that a brief jolly passage sounds strange in a funeral march. Or again, it is like the way a delicate ornament can be out of place in a triumphal arch. Considered in itself, a thing might be jolly or delicate. But as part of a funeral march or triumphal arch it is strange or inappropriate. There is nothing anti-formalist about this phenomenon. Considered as part of a larger whole which has certain aesthetic properties, the part may not have the same aesthetic properties that it has considered in itself. There is no threat to formalism here so long as the thing still retains its own aesthetic properties and these are not annihilated by the wider whole. The stretch of mud and sand does indeed have a wild, glad emptiness considered in itself, but it is *also* disturbingly weird considered as part of a wider whole. It was not a *mistake* to judge that

15. Walton, "Categories of Art."

"Things can be beautfl when you consider them in a BIGGER CONTEXT → that can be free beauty.

it had a wild, glad emptiness; that judgment need not be *replaced* by the judgment that it is disturbingly weird. It can be both. One and the same thing can have intrinsic aesthetic properties and relational aesthetic properties.

So Hepburn's example can be dealt with by means of general principles governing the organic combination of the aesthetic properties of parts and wholes. Things can retain their own aesthetic identities despite their contribution to a wider aesthetic whole and despite their aesthetic properties in the light of the wider whole. Hepburn's example can thus be given a satisfactory formalist analysis, which accounts for the peculiar features that tempted us to interpret it anti-formalistically.[16]

5 THE FRAME PROBLEM

The most pressing problem for moderate formalism about natural aesthetics, in my view, is the frame problem.[17] The problem is over the boundaries of natural things. Works of art are relatively discrete. They are physically bounded. Or else they at least have beginnings and endings. By and large, it is clear what is part of the work and what is not. (Perhaps there are *some* aspects which are neither clearly part of the work nor clearly not part of it; but many aspects are clearly part of it, or clearly not part of it.) These boundaries are by and large fixed by the artist's intention. Consider an art gallery with several ordinary paintings displayed. We typically know that we are to consider each work in isolation from the others. In unusual cases, some of them are supposed to form a group, such as triptychs, or Poussin's *Seven*

16. Here are two other examples in the literature. First, Hepburn has the following rock-face example: "As we look at the rock face in nature, we may realize imaginatively the geological processes and turmoils that produced its pattern. The realizing of these need not be a piece of extra-aesthetic reflection" ("Contemporary Aesthetics and Neglect," p. 25). *Merely imagining* the geological processes and *really believing* them to have taken place are different. Let us suppose that the latter is required. (The former would have little bearing on our debate.) Then what if the geological theories in question are wrong? Would our experience then be worthless? Surely not. Secondly, Carroll gives the example of the beauty of a thundering waterfall ("On Being Moved by Nature," p. 253). Carroll seems to deny that even a commonsense understanding of the waterfall is necessary. Carlson seems to respond that he thinks that it is ("Nature, Aesthetic Appreciation, and Knowledge," p. 399). The exchange between Carroll and Carlson over this example is somewhat inconclusive. But I think I side with Carroll. Imagine a substance—"twater"—which is just like water in perceivable respects but which is differently composed. (See Hilary Putnam, "The Meaning of Meaning," in *Mind, Language and Reality* [Cambridge: Cambridge University Press, 1978].) Does it matter aesthetically whether something is a waterfall or a twaterfall? Carlson must say yes; but I say no, and I think I have intuitive plausibility on my side.

17. Hepburn draws attention to this phenomenon in "Contemporary Aesthetics and Neglect," pp. 13–15.

Sacraments in the Edinburgh National Gallery. In these special cases, we are supposed to consider the paintings together. By contrast, with a copse of trees, one is free to consider each tree in isolation, and also the whole aesthetic value of the combination of trees. But apart from rather unusual cases, it would be odd to consider the aesthetic value of a combination of paintings in this way. There is no interesting emergent aesthetic value of a combination of paintings in the way that the aesthetic value of one painting is usually an emergent property of the combination of its parts. But why assess the copse as a unit? Is this not arbitrary? Why not assess the copse of trees plus the lake two hundred yards away? What we select as a unit of evaluation in nature seems arbitrary—unlike our evaluation of art.[18] So it might seem that the idea that nature possesses mind-independent aesthetic properties is rendered dubious.

One reply would be to concede that the frame problem reveals a kind of volatility in the beauty of nature, so that as one modifies the frame, the beauty of the whole which is framed fluctuates wildly.[19] This is possible, I suppose. But it is not my experience. Of course, conjoining a car park to a copse would be aesthetically bad news. But that is because the car park itself is ugly. (Assume that this is standard British car park; there are attractive car parks elsewhere.) We are adding a beautiful thing to an ugly thing. But if we add some extra daffodils adjacent to the copse, which are in themselves beautiful, or the nearby beautiful lake, then it is likely that the combination—copse plus daffodils or lake—will also be beautiful. This optimism would be reinforced by a weak version of what is called "positive aesthetics," which is a thesis to the effect that nature is by and large beautiful. I do not believe that there are radical fluctuations in beauty as we modify the frame of nature.

But what about *substantive* aesthetic properties? Two differently framed natural complexes might be beautiful in virtue of very different substantive aesthetic properties. These surely *do* vary as the frame varies. Many individually *delicate* things might be *magnificently powerful* in concert (such as a hillside covered in flowering gorse.)[20] Here I think we must simply accept that nature is *aesthetically complex*. This can be seen to be unproblematic as follows. Sup-

18. We should note that by itself the freedom in framing point is clearly quite distinct from the Qua thesis, and provides absolutely no support for it.

19. Let us not overlook the fact that quite ordinary properties, such as mass and color, also vary as one varies the frame, without that supplying the slightest temptation to think that these properties are mind-dependent.

20. See Allen Carlson, "Formal Qualities in the Natural Environment," *Journal of Aesthetic Education* 13 (1984): 109–10 (*Aesthetics and the Environment*, pp. 36–37); and Hepburn, "Contemporary Aesthetics and Neglect," pp. 12–13.

pose we consider a complex whole—for example, copse plus lake plus daffodils (C + L + D). Then we would have no qualms about accepting an internal complexity to this organic whole. So C + L might have one substantive aesthetic property while C + D has some other incompatible substantive aesthetic property, while L + D has yet another. All these substantive aesthetic properties can then organically combine to generate a substantive property of the whole. (Of course, internal complexity is usually far greater than this.) But now, if that is acceptable, then it should also be acceptable to consider C + L + D as part of some larger whole, or as a part of an indefinite number of larger wholes. If *internal* aesthetic complexity is unproblematic, then so is this kind of frameless complexity.

Perhaps it is not that the aesthetic of nature is frameless so much as that it is indefinitely framed. Nature *has* the aesthetic properties that it is has in all the frames that there are. Is there somehow some mysterious limit on the *number* of aesthetic properties that nature can have? Aesthetic properties which are relative to a frame can nevertheless be genuine mind-independent features of the world. Frame-dependence is not mind-dependence, for the frames are not mind-dependent. Certain combinations of things exist whether or not we choose to isolate those combinations in our thought. And if those combinations exist, then so do the aesthetic properties they determine. In a sense, nature has contradictory properties, but not in the same place and the same time. That is, one combination of things does not have contradictory properties, but different combinations can do so. There is nothing mysterious about that.

6 The Magnification Problem

Beauty, in my view, must be manifest to particular modes of sensory perception. It is not independent of sensory experiences. Hence *our* judgments of taste are universally valid, but only for all *human* beings, not for all *rational* beings. The beauty that human beings are aware of, I think, has particularly to do with colors, sounds, and spatiotemporal appearances as human beings perceive them (see chapters 8 and 11). In this sense, our aesthetic judgments have a peculiarly *human* limitation that moral judgments lack. Morality applies to angels and to other possible life-forms and intelligences. But in a sense beauty is relative to kinds of sensory experiences.

Although beauty is relative to the *sensibility* that confronts it, I think that it is not limited by the human scale. The enormous and the minute, which the telescope and microscope have revealed to us, can both be beautiful so long as those things are colored and appear to have spatiotemporal properties.

But perhaps there is a problem here. Malcolm Budd argues that this threatens the idea that nature has aesthetic properties independently of us.[21] In the case of art, there is a prescribed way of perceiving a work, set by the maker's intentions. But in the case of nature, there is no such control. Budd gives the Blakean example of a grain of sand, and he asks at what level of magnification we should view it. The argument is that it is arbitrary or indeterminate at what level of magnification we should view a grain of sand, and if so, what aesthetic properties it has is also arbitrary or indeterminate. So there is here a threat to aesthetic realism about nature. However, I do not think that the magnification problem has the relativist consequences that Budd draws.[22]

In reply, I think we need a notion of the total aesthetic nature of a thing, which is the sum of all the aesthetic properties that it possesses. We can view a thing at a number of different levels of magnification. At any particular level, many of its aesthetic properties are revealed. And so long as we can sum the aesthetic properties revealed at all levels, there is no difficulty.

Someone might argue as follows. Suppose that nature possesses an infinite number of levels. And suppose that it is beautiful at the N level but ugly at the N + 1 level, beautiful at the N + 2 level, ugly at the N + 3 level, and so on. If so, it would be indeterminate whether the thing is beautiful.

One reply would be to appeal to positive aesthetics. On such a view, we can be confident that there are positive aesthetic properties on all levels or at least on most levels.[23] But even if this is true, things might be beautiful in different ways on different levels. That is, there might be conflicting *substantive* aesthetic properties at different levels. The appeal to positive aesthetics would not solve this problem.

What we said about the frame problem also applies here. It is simply that nature turns out to be enormously complicated and aesthetically varied. We can admit this without compromising the idea that nature has aesthetic properties independently of us. A thing might be elegant at a high level of magnification and not elegant at a lower level, just as the top left-hand corner of a painting might be elegant but not delicate while its bottom right-hand corner might be delicate but not elegant. Just move to the top left-hand cor-

21. Budd, "The Aesthetics of Nature," pp. 154–56.
22. The magnification problem *may* turn out to be a version of the frame problem. But I shall assume not for the sake of argument.
23. Carlson, "Nature and Positive Aesthetics."

ner and you will see the elegance, and just move to the bottom right-hand corner and you will see the delicacy. Similarly, look at nature at one magnification and you will see certain aesthetic properties; look at it at another, and you will see others. It would be arrogant to make the aesthetic properties thus revealed relative to us. It is just that if we place ourselves differently, different aesthetic properties of nature become available to us. It is quite unproblematic that one part of something can have a property that another part lacks. And the same goes for different levels of magnification. For example, things can be differently colored at different levels of magnification. And something might have a rectilinear design at one level of magnification and a spiral design at another. So even if things do possess conflicting aesthetic substantive properties on different levels, there is no problem for aesthetic realism.

7 ACTIVE APPRECIATION

Lastly, and briefly, Carlson has another argument against formalism (derived from Hepburn), which is that our appreciation has an active aspect to it. It is not purely contemplative, as he thinks a formalist would require. One is *immersed* in nature, part of it, not distanced from it, as formalism seems to require.[24]

I agree with this. But I think that Carlson has succumbed to the error he elegantly diagnoses in the first half of his essay, which is the error of thinking that we appreciate landscape the way we appreciate landscape painting. He calls this the "landscape cult." But what possesses aesthetic properties, indeed formal aesthetic properties, are natural things, not views of natural things. In this sense, our aesthetic appreciation of nature is indeed frameless. We do not appreciate landscape as we appreciate a landscape painting, which is as a two-dimensional representation of a three-dimensional reality. Our movement through and around natural things may help us to wallow in, and fully savor, the many three-dimensional formal properties that natural things possess, independently of us. Being active and immersed in nature might be the best way to appreciate its three-dimensional formal aesthetic properties, just as the best way to appreciate such properties of works of sculpture or architecture might be to walk around such works.

I suspect that Carlson's overemphasis on two-dimensional formal aesthetic

24. Carlson, "Formal Qualities in the Natural Environment," pp. 109–10 (*Aesthetics and the Environment,* p. 37); Hepburn, "Contemporary Aesthetics and Neglect," pp. 12–13.

properties in his definition of formal properties loads the dice unfairly against formalism about natural beauty.[25] Three-dimensional spatial relations between objects can generate formal aesthetic properties. Of course, three-dimensional plastic properties of *paintings* give rise to special problems, given that ways of representing such spatial arrangements are intention-dependent. Nature cannot have such properties. But it can have three-dimensional formal properties, which are best appreciated in an active way.

In sum, moderate formalism about the aesthetics of nature is not only unproblematic but also attractive. And extreme formalism is plausible about inorganic nature. Anti-formalists want us to appreciate nature with the eyes of a connoisseur. But I think that childlike wonder is often more appropriate.

Appendix   One Beauty: Art and Nature

(1 notion and 1 property)

I believe that there is a single *notion* of beauty applicable to both art and nature and that there is a single *property* of beauty that both possess.

Someone who has questioned this "unitarian" thesis is Christopher Janaway. His target is the claim that "the term 'beauty' stands for a single, generic concept of aesthetic value, which has application both to natural objects and to art."[26] He doubts that there is a univocal concept of beauty that applies to art and nature. Presumably he also doubts whether the beauty that nature possesses is the same property as the beauty that art possesses.

Janaway argues by appealing to the possibility of indiscernible counterparts of works of art. He takes Mary Mothersill's *Beauty Restored* as his target. Mothersill claimed, as a quite general thesis, that perceptually indiscernible things have the same aesthetic properties. But Janaway argues, following Arthur Danto, that there can be indiscernible works of art that have different aesthetic properties. One might be beautiful while the other is not. So Janaway thinks that Mothersill was wrong in her general claim.

I agree with Janaway about this. I would put this point by saying that Mothersill has not seen that the aesthetic properties of a work of art may have a *wide* supervenience base, so that *narrowly* indiscernible (or "perceptually indiscernible" in Mothersill's terms) works of art can differ with respect to their beauty or other aesthetic properties.

25. See Carlson, "Formal Qualities in the Natural Environment," pp. 99–100 (*Aesthetics and the Environment*, p. 28).

26. Christopher Janaway, "Beauty in Nature, Beauty in Art," *British Journal of Aesthetics* 33 (1993): 321.

However, Janaway thinks that it follows that Mothersill was wrong to think that the concept of beauty is univocal as applied to nature and to art. But this does not follow. Here I think Mothersill is right and Janaway wrong. For one thing, there are narrowly indiscernible counterparts with different aesthetic properties in nature as well as art. The beauty of a natural thing can have a wide supervenience base where we have a case of *dependent* natural beauty. In such cases, the thing is beautiful *as* a thing with a certain natural purpose. A thing's purpose is not a narrow property of it, but a matter of its history. For example, a part of a fish, such as a fin, might be beautiful only *as* a fish's fin, which is a thing that has a certain function. But an indiscernible counterpart of the fin, considered as a part of a land animal, such as a human being, might not be beautiful at all.

Moreover, even if Janaway were right to think that only in art are there narrowly indiscernible counterparts with different aesthetic properties, it still would not establish his thesis. It would just show that works of art have both free and dependent beauty whereas natural things only have free beauty. We would then need an argument to the effect that these free and dependent beauties are not all instances of the same property of beauty. Such an argument will be hard to come by. For on most theories, it turns out that free and dependent beauty are both species of the same general kind. For example, the account I endorsed in chapter 2, according to which aesthetic judgments have subjective universality or are closely related to such judgments, allows that we make one kind of judgment—aesthetic judgments—about both nature and art, whether those are judgments of free or dependent beauty.

Perhaps it is true that there is a sense in which artistic and natural beauty cannot be compared. But then in that sense it is also true that different sorts of artistic beauty cannot be compared and that different sorts of natural beauty cannot be compared.

Both art and nature have free, formal beauty, and both have dependent beauty.[27] On the unitarian view, neither art nor nature has aesthetic priority. Neither aspires to be like the other, and neither imitates the other. Beauty is one, though variously realized.

---

27. It might be that only works of art can have a beauty that depends on *meaning*. But perhaps natural things can have a beauty that depends on what Paul Grice called "natural meaning." A cloud might be beautiful *as* a harbinger of rain. This would I think be like Hepburn's beach example, which I discuss in section 4 of this chapter.

CHAPTER 8

Aesthetic/Sensory Dependence

Is the aesthetic tied to the sensory? Are lovers of beauty "lovers of sights and sounds"?

In this chapter I shall defend a *weak dependence* thesis:

> Aesthetic properties depend in part on sensory properties, such as colors and sounds.

Just as something has moral properties only if it has mental properties, so, according to the weak dependence thesis, aesthetic properties are properties that something has only if it has sensory properties.

When we think of certain paradigm cases, this thesis seems plausible. For example, it is obvious that beautiful abstract paintings would not be beautiful unless they consisted of certain arrangements of colors on surfaces; and delicate performances of pieces of music would not be delicate unless they consisted of certain temporal arrangements of sounds. The thesis is not that an abstract painting is beautiful *entirely* because of a certain arrangement of colors on a surface, or that a performance of a piece of music is delicate *only* because of a certain temporal arrangement of sounds. The thesis is not the *strong* thesis that the aesthetic properties of a thing depend *only* on its sensory properties. The thesis is that sensory properties are *necessary* for aesthetic properties, not that they are *sufficient*. Accepting a weak dependence thesis is compatible with admitting that other factors are also necessary. But the weak thesis does entail that without sensory properties, there would be no aesthetic properties.

I shall argue that this thesis is a lot more plausible than is usually supposed.

127

I will show how many apparently nonsensory cases in fact conform to the weak dependence thesis. I shall discuss architecture, painting, literature, and an assortment of less usual cases.

1 ARCHITECTURE

One source of worry with aesthetic/sensory dependence arises from the aesthetic properties of architecture. What I say in this section also applies to abstract sculpture. Representational sculptures can be considered along with representational paintings, which I discuss in section 2.

Architecture is peculiar in that it is tempting to think that the aesthetic properties of buildings depend only on their physical properties; so their sensory properties are irrelevant. Many critics and architects have said or implied that this is so. We might put the view by saying that what is aesthetically important in architecture is *pure spatial form*. The expression "spatial form" is intended in a nonaesthetic sense, according to which it picks out the a certain physically describable spatial arrangement of walls, roofs, ceilings, doors, and windows. (The phrase is sometimes intended in an aesthetic sense according to which it picks out aesthetic properties which depend on such spatial properties and relations; but I shall not follow that use.) Let us call "spatial purism" the extreme position that only spatial form is aesthetically relevant.

Ranged against spatial purism, is what we might call "sensualism." According to sensualism, the aesthetic properties of buildings depend only on their sensory properties—preeminently the pattern of colors on the surface of buildings. (The shadows cast on the surface of buildings, and the sounds that can be heard when buildings are in use, may sometimes be important; but I shall ignore this.) On the sensualist view, the spatial form of buildings is aesthetically irrelevant in itself. Spatial form functions only to determine sensory properties, and it is these sensory properties alone that determine aesthetic properties. So a mock facade on a building would do just as well as something constructed with more three-dimensional "integrity," so long as nobody ever saw the other side. I do not know if anyone has ever held this position.

A somewhat intermediate view is that the aesthetic properties of buildings depend on perspectival appearances of their spatial properties. So what matters in our appreciation of architecture is the perception of spatial form from various perspectives. For example, a building might have the property of having a southern elevation which looks rectangular from a certain position. On this view, spatial properties themselves function only to determine a range of appearances of these spatial properties, and it is these appearances which are of aesthetic significance. Let us call this view "spatial perspectivism."

A more complex or "organic" view would be that the aesthetic properties of buildings depend on a combination of two or more of the above three kinds of properties. Perhaps there is a mutual dependence between spatial properties, appearances of spatial properties and sensory properties in generating the aesthetic properties of the whole work of architecture. Let us call this complex view the "complex view." I will say more about it in a moment.

What about architectural functionalism, which says that the aesthetic properties of a building depend on how well the building "expresses" or "articulates" its function—such as being a library, station or mosque? This view does not map directly onto either spatial purism, spatial perspectivism, sensualism, or the complex view, and it does not affect our issue. It may be true that the aesthetic excellence of many buildings depends on their functions. But what generates aesthetic excellence is the *expression* or *articulation* of those functions *in particular spatial and sensory properties*. So the issue of function is irrelevant to our concerns, unless we are dealing with what we might call "eliminativist functionalism," according to which aesthetic properties are irrelevant and function is all.

It is true that we cannot *know* about spatial properties without knowing about appearances of spatial properties, and we cannot know about appearances of spatial properties unless we know about sensory properties. Only by perceiving the color of the surface of a building, plus the shadows cast on it, can we discern its spatial form. But this is merely an epistemological point. It tells us nothing about the properties on which aesthetic properties depend.

I shall give two arguments to the effect that spatial purism is false: the aesthetic properties of buildings do not depend only on their spatial properties. I then extend the second argument, so that it also shows that spatial perspectivism is false. I conclude that the aesthetic role of sensory properties, such as colors and sounds, is ineliminable.

The first argument against spatial purism is this. If spatial form were all that mattered in a work of architecture, then it would be better appreciated from a God's-eye point of view—that is, from no point of view at all. But it is essential to our experience of a work of architecture that we confront it from various perspectives, allowing the building to present certain visual aspects to us. And it is essential to our experience of a work of architecture that we move around and appreciate the work from many different angles. But the consequence of this is not that we abstract away from all such viewpoints and form an intellectual conception of the work as a pure spatial structure, as God would know it, dispensing with its various appearances. Rather, we come to a better appreciation of its total appearance as presented to us in perception from different viewpoints.[1] Spatial purism is untrue to the phenomenology of our experience of architecture. This argument makes trouble for spatial purism, but not spatial perspectivism.

The second argument is perhaps rather far-fetched and difficult to imagine as applied to architecture, and it works better with abstract sculpture. Imagine a counterpart of a sculpture which is of exactly the same shape as the original, and so has the same spatial form, but which is made of completely transparent, nonreflecting, nonrefractive Perspex and thus has no color at all. Imagine the counterpart to be completely invisible—like glass except more so. The boundary of such a counterpart could only be *felt* and not *seen*; its spatial form could be detected only by touch. The two might share tactile properties (assuming they have the same texture), and thus they might share any aesthetic properties which depend on tactile properties. To some extent the spatial form might be appreciable by touch. But it is clear that the invisible counterpart would not have the visual impact or visual appeal of the opaque, colored original. There is something we appreciate *visually* in our experience of a sculpture. How it *looks* is aesthetically important. So the invisible counterpart lacks aesthetic properties which depend on the original's visual impact. For those who find this thought-experiment too outré, we can note that our situation with respect to the invisible counterpart is the one a blind or blindfolded person would be in with respect to the opaque original. What the invisible counterpart lacks is what a blind or blindfolded person would fail to appreciate in the opaque original—even if he is aware of its spatial form by another sense modality. The counterpart has many different aesthetic properties from the opaque original because of how they *look*. And the blind or blindfolded person misses out on that look in the opaque original. That difference generates an aesthetic difference between the original and the invisible counterpart. The argument is a *modus tollens*. If what is aesthetically important were only a matter of pure spatial form, then all aesthetic properties ought to be shared between the opaque original and the invisible counterpart. But they are not. Therefore spatial form is not all that is aesthetically important.

Again, this argument makes trouble for spatial purism but leaves open the spatial perspectivist view that what is aesthetically important are *visual* appearances of spatial properties. But a slight modification of the example

1. Roger Scruton describes this phenomenon illuminatingly in *The Aesthetics of Architecture* (London: Methuen, 1979), chap. 4.

makes it threaten spatial perspectivism. Instead of a transparent counterpart, we can imagine an absurdly colored counterpart. Imagine a building exactly like the Pantheon, except pink—the Pink Pantheon. The perspectival appearance of spatial properties produced by the Pink Pantheon and by the normal Pantheon would be the same. But there would be a significant aesthetic difference. This seems to show that sensory properties are aesthetically important.

Now, by itself, this appeal to differently colored counterparts is not decisive. It does not show that *all* aesthetic properties depend on sensory properties. For the argument does not exclude the possibility that there are *some* residual aesthetic properties which depend only on spatial properties, or appearances of spatial properties, and which owe nothing to sensory properties. Perhaps the building is balanced or unified solely in virtue of its spatial properties or appearances of spatial properties.

But how plausible is this? Surely the aesthetic properties of a building do not partition into two distinct sets—on the one hand, those depending on spatial properties and their appearances and, on the other hand, those depending on sensory properties. It is not that certain shapes and colors just *happen* to be combined in a work of architecture. Of course, the two sorts of properties are independent of each other in the sense that each could have obtained without the other. But in any actual work of architecture, spatial and color properties are combined together in a way that is essential to that work. It is true that there is usually a range of sensory properties which *could* be combined in an acceptable way with a certain spatial structure. And such aesthetic flexibility is part of the architectural vision. But that flexibility is limited, as the Pink Pantheon example shows. It is essential to a particular work of architecture that spatial properties are combined with a limited range of color properties. And the aesthetic properties of a particular work of architecture depend on the specific combination of the two factors of spatial and color properties. (For example, despite their concern with spatial structure, both Adolf Loos and Le Corbusier display a strong aesthetic preference for white surfaces.) So the aesthetic properties of a building depend on *colored masses* or *appearances of colored masses* (perhaps which realize some function—a matter we have been ignoring for the sake of simplicity), where the italicized phrases denote a complex that cannot be broken up. It is not just that if we separate the elements of the complex there is then an aesthetic loss in the whole, but that the spatial properties determine aesthetic properties only when clothed in some sensory garb. Hence there are no aesthetic properties of buildings which depend solely on their spatial properties or spatial appearances. Spatial properties or their appearances do not generate aesthetic properties quite independently of sensory properties. Sensory properties are essential to the aesthetic properties of the work of architecture. And that means that spatial perspectivism is false. The role of sensory properties in architecture is ineliminable.

This is not just a theoretical conclusion. It has first-order aesthetic consequences. In much modernist rhetoric, the importance of color is underplayed. Many who followed Adolf Loos in his dictum that "ornament is crime" have thought of color as a dispensable ornament by contrast with spatial structure.[2] But this attitude is founded on a mistake. The color of a building is not a dispensable trimming or an inessential addition. It is not mere ornament. Treating it this way is unfortunate, for it encourages architects to neglect an essential part of their art. The modernist tradtion, which in ideology or practice concentrates exclusively on pure spatial structure or on the appearance of spatial structure, rests on an error about the metaphysics of architecture.

The opposite error is an extreme sensualism according to which the aesthetic properties of a building depend merely on a kind of kaleidoscope of flat, two-dimensional color images which the building presents from different viewpoints. But we should not lurch from Scylla to Charybdis. Color has aesthetic significance in architecture for the way it *attaches* to spatial form, and not merely as a two-dimensional pattern. A false facade would *not* do just as well. So it is not true to say that physical properties function merely to determine sensory properties, which do all the aesthetic work. The matter is more complex than extreme sensualism allows. The right view is the complex view: it is sensory properties in a certain three-dimensional spatial context which have aesthetic significance in architecture. We should reject spatial purism and spatial perspectivism without accepting extreme sensualism. The complex truth is that the aesthetic properties of a work of architecture depend on *both* spatial *and* sensory properties in a mutually dependent fashion. Both are necessary, neither is sufficient. The only asymmetry is that the importance of sensory properties, unlike that of spatial form, has been underrated in the writings of critics and practitioners in the twentieth century. Color and spatial form have a reciprocal importance; each plays its role only in combination with the other. An analogy: Descartes might have shown that we are essentially thinking beings; but as Antoine Arnauld pointed out, that does not show that we are not essentially physical beings as well. Similarly, although it is true that the aesthetic properties of

2. Adolf Loos, "Ornament and Crime," in *The Architecture of Adolf Loos* (London: Art's Council, 1985).

works of architecture are necessarily tied to their spatial properties and appearances of spatial properties, that does not show that they are not necessarily tied to sensory properties as well.

2 VISUAL REPRESENTATION

Another source of worry with the weak dependence thesis stems from the representational, symbolic, and narrative properties of works of visual art.

The aesthetic properties of paintings often depend on their representational properties. A painting of a tree, for example, may be beautiful because of the *way* the tree is represented. And this beauty is something over and above the beauty of the two-dimensional abstract pattern. Indeed, the tree-representation may not be at all beautiful considered as a two-dimensional abstract pattern; it may only be beautiful considered as a tree-representation. (Try squinting at a representational work of art; an interesting representation is often transformed into an ugly, abstract, shapeless blot.) In my view, the beauty of a representation as a representation is a case of what Kant calls *dependent* beauty as opposed to *free* beauty. It is essential to the beauty of these things that they have a representational *function*, and this beauty is not merely conjoined with that function but is an expression or articulation of it.[3]

However, the existence of such dependent representational beauty does not threaten our weak dependence thesis. Although, in these cases, the representational properties are essential for the realization of the aesthetic properties, sensory properties are also essential. Sensory properties are a necessary constituent of that on which aesthetic properties depend because the beauty lies in the precise aesthetically appropriate sensory realization of those representational properties. So sensory properties are *necessary* for the beauty of a representation, even though they are not *sufficient*. Aesthetic properties that depend on representational properties also depend on sensory properties, and are nothing without them.

This move also allows us to sidestep someone who argues that the aesthetic properties of some works of art do not depend on sensory properties

3. See chapter 4, and section 16 of Kant's *Critique of Judgement*, trans. James Meredith (Oxford: Oxford University Press, 1928). See also Eva Schaper, *Studies in Kant's Aesthetics* (Edinburgh: Edinburgh University Press, 1979), chap. 4, for a sympathetic reconstruction of Kant's notion of dependent beauty. We should deploy this idea to understand the aesthetic role of function in architecture. It is unfortunate that we have to use the word "dependent" in "dependent beauty" when we are already talking of aesthetic/sensory "dependence"; but there should be no confusion.

because they depend on their art-historical context.[4] We can concede that in some cases, the aesthetic properties of a work of art depend *partly* on its context; but that does not mean that its aesthetic properties do not *also* depend partly on its sensory properties.

We should distinguish representation from symbolism. I follow Richard Wollheim in thinking that if something is a representation of something then there is a requirement that we can experience it *as* that thing or that we can experience the thing *in* the representation. For example, if a picture is a picture of a tree, it must be possible to see it *as* a tree, or to see a tree *in* the picture.[5] By contrast, purely symbolic properties—for example, a dove's symbolizing peace—cannot be experienced in the same way. Purely symbolic properties of paintings seem not to depend on sensory properties.

Another category, which seems to lie somewhat between symbolic and representational properties, is that of narrative properties. A painting might represent a historical, mythological, religious, or purely imaginary event. It might represent the coronation of Napoleon, Paris choosing Aphrodite, the parting of the Red Sea, or a pastoral scene in Arcadia. But it is not clear whether we can see such content *in* a picture or see a picture *as* depicting such a scene. So it is not clear that Wollheim's account extends this far. The matter is a delicate one, and it may be a matter of degree. But to be on the safe side let us assume that there are narrative properties that do not count as representational properties, as Wollheim construes these.

I return to symbolic and narrative properties in a moment. Let us refer to both as "pictorial meaning."

3 MULTIPLY INSTANTIABLE WORKS

I shall briefly mention in passing a worry which might be thought to arise from multiply instantiable works of art, such as symphonies and poems. It might be argued that these are abstract objects; and the aesthetic properties of abstract objects cannot depend on sensory properties because abstract objects have no sensory properties. But this objection is too strong. The aesthetic properties of multiply instantiable works of art must be somehow related to sensory properties. Consider composed pieces of music, so as to avoid the

4. Kendall Walton argued that the aesthetic properties of works of art depend on their context in "Categories of Art," *Philosophical Review*, vol. 79 (1970). But I am not suggesting that Walton has in mind an argument like the one I mention.

5. See Richard Wollheim, "Seeing-as and Seeing-in, and Pictorial Representation," in *Art and its Objects*, 2d ed. (Cambridge: Cambridge University Press, 1980).

extra semantic complications in the case of literature. It would be implausible to suggest that Beethoven's Fifth Symphony has nothing at all to do with sounds, even though it does not involve any local and particular manifestation of sounds. The exact relation between Beethoven's Fifth Symphony and particular sounds is complex and controversial; but it is clear that there is some indirect connection. What I think we should say is that both musical works and their performances involve sounds: performances of a work involve particular sounds, whereas the work itself involves types of sounds. We can then say that the aesthetic properties of performances of works depends on particular sounds, and the aesthetic properties of the work itself depends on types of sound.

4 LITERARY CONTENT AND PICTORIAL MEANING

Let us now turn to literature—which is the most problematic case for the weak sensory dependence thesis.

There are two ways that sound can be important in literature. First, there are some aesthetic properties which depend on the "music" of words, as pure sound. And second, the choice of certain words with certain sonic properties to express certain thoughts may be aesthetically appropriate. (This is another case of dependent beauty.) The sonic aspect of words is an important part of literary art.[6] It is one reason why there is a special problem about translating literary works—especially poetry. In this respect, literature seems to be like representational painting, since aesthetic properties depend on semantic properties *as well as* sonic properties.

But many people say that works of literature have aesthetic properties that do not depend at all on the sensory properties of words. They say that many aesthetic properties of literature depend on the semantic properties of words. What is aesthetically significant is what the work means, the story it tells, the characters it portrays, the emotions it evokes, the ideas it involves, and so on. Let us call all this the *content* of a work of literature. It seems that some contents are elegant, some clumsy, some beautiful, some ugly. Such aesthetic properties of the content of a literary work seem to be independent of the sensory properties of the words in which that content is realized.

So we have two residual cases where aesthetic properties seem not to depend on sensory properties: pictorial meaning and literary content. In

6. See Monroe Beardsley, *Aesthetics* (Indianapolis: Hackett, 1958), pp. 228–37.

these cases it seems that nonsensory properties bear all the responsibility. We saw that no problem arose from the aesthetic properties of representational paintings because, although these aesthetic properties depend *in part* on representational properties, sensory properties were also essential. So they were caught in the weak dependency thesis. But pictorial meaning and literary content seem not to be like this, since they do not depend on specific sensory properties. Many sorts of quite differently painted doves can symbolize peace, the same event can be quite differently portrayed, and one story can be told in quite different words. The aesthetic value of pictorial representations and some aspects of literature depends on their precise sensory manifestation, but the aesthetic value of pictorial meaning and literary content does not.

One unpromising line of defense would be to argue that the residual cases can be tamed by saying that although it is true that pictorial meaning and literary content do not depend on any *specific* sensory properties, they do depend on *some* sensory manifestation. Although differently painted doves can symbolize peace, the dove must be painted somehow or other. And although all sorts of different words can tell the same story, the story must be told in some words or other. So such properties are ultimately dependent on sensory properties, in that without sensory properties there would be no pictorial meaning and no literary content. Pictorial meaning and literary content are aesthetically significant properties which can float free of specific sensory properties, but at least some sensory manifestation is required. So a work must have sensory properties if it has meaning or content properties. However, this response will not do because the sense of dependence in question is too weak to be interesting. Aesthetic/sensory dependence implies that if a thing had very different sensory properties then it would have different aesthetic properties.[7] For example, the aesthetic properties of a representational painting depends on the precise arrangement of colors of its surface. Nonnegligible differences in the arrangement of colors yield differences in aesthetic properties. But pictorial meaning and literary content can be realized in a wide variety of very different sensory properties. A thing could have had quite different sensory properties but the same meaning or content properties. So it seems that it is not the case that if such a thing had very different sensory properties it would have lacked its aesthetic properties. And that means that the aesthetic properties of pictorial meaning and literary content do not depend on sensory properties.

7. Here I mean its total aesthetic character, the conjunction of all its aesthetic properties. See chapter 3.

I shall pursue a different line that I think is more promising. This is simply to deny that meaning and content properties have *aesthetic* significance. Pictorial meanings and literary contents may be clever, inspiring, moving, or interesting, but not beautiful or elegant. What we find valuable in a work when we are moved or inspired by a scene or story is not its *aesthetic* value.

Artistic value is a broad category which includes aesthetic value as one element. Just because we value works of literature does not mean that all the properties we value in them are aesthetic values. Some artistic values are aesthetic and some are not.

The view I am proposing is that if a literary work has aesthetic properties, they derive from the particular choice of words, because of the way they sound, either in themselves or as the sonically apt expression of a particular meaning; and if a literary work has values which are not linked in one of these ways to the sonic properties of words, then they are not aesthetic values. The same is true of pictorial meaning: if a pictorial representation has aesthetic properties, they derive from the particular pattern of colors, because of the way they look, either in themselves or as the visually apt portrayal of a particular scene; and if a picture has values which are not linked in one of these ways to patterns of color, then they are not aesthetic values. A benign dilemma holds: if the valuable properties are aesthetic, then they depend on sensory properties, and if they are not aesthetic, then they don't.[8]

5 FURTHER REMARKS ON LITERARY CONTENT AND PICTORIAL MEANING

Thus far I have merely asserted that the benign dilemma holds. I shall now make some remarks in support of it, which will also serve to protect it against overhasty criticism.

Remark 1:   The word "aesthetic" is one in fairly ordinary usage. The dictionary definition firmly links the word with the concept of beauty. I think

---

8. I note with some unease that what I say here departs from Kant's views in his *Critique of Judgement*. There is a presumed authorial duty to present one's claims as if one believed them with complete conviction. However, I confess that I am not sure of the weak dependence thesis as regards literature. I feel considerable inclination toward it, but sometimes I have doubts. I have found that others I have polled divide roughly equally: about half agree with me that the value of pictorial meaning or literary content is nonaesthetic, and about half go the other way. Having registered an element of doubt, I shall henceforth ignore it.

this is right. Beauty and ugliness are the preeminent aesthetic concepts, not merely two among many with no privileged position.[9] If we take the use of the word "beauty" to be a mark of the aesthetic, then intuition, I think, is on my side. It has often been noted that although *Guernica* is a great painting, it would be inappropriate to call it "beautiful." Similarly for the play *King Lear*. What this shows is not that beauty and ugliness are not the preeminent aesthetic concepts, but that these works of art have important nonaesthetic values. What is important about these works is their moral, political, or psychological content, and their emotional appeal. There are aspects of *Guernica* and *King Lear* which are indeed beautiful—matters of pictorial composition or the use of language. But these are not what people find most interesting and impressive in those works. We should look to see whether we express judgments in terms of the words "beauty" or "ugly." We will soon see that this linguistic criterion of aesthetic judgment is defeasible. But we can rely on it in the absence of the special sort of defeater that we will examine.

Remark 2:   Aesthetic properties are necessarily *hierarchically structured*. This is reflected in our aesthetic concepts, and to some extent in our aesthetic terms. Substantive aesthetic judgments, such as judgments of elegance, daintiness, dumpiness, and delicacy, function to describe what beauty or ugliness depends on. So if, on some occasion, a description does *not* function that way, then it is not a substantive aesthetic description, even if the words in question are ones which on other occasions are used in substantive aesthetic descriptions. For example, when we admire a play and call it "elegant," "balanced," or "powerful," it is for the way these properties contribute to the *value* of the work. But if that value is not *beauty* then the contributing properties which we call "elegant," "balanced," or "powerful" do not describe substantive aesthetic properties.[10] Since it is not appropriate to call *King Lear* "beautiful," the power of *King Lear* is not aesthetic power. It contributes toward the moral, political, psychological, or emotional greatness of the play, not its beauty.

Remark 3:   Visual art often has narrative properties which are aesthetically irrelevant. For example, the Bayeaux tapestry and *Guernica* depict certain historical events. And countless paintings depict mythological or religious

9. See chapters 1 and 2.

10. See chapter 10 for the view that the metaphorical use of terms like "delicate," "balanced," and "powerful" can sometimes serve to describe aesthetic properties. The present case, however, is the reverse, when they don't. I say more about the metaphorical use of terms like "elegant" in section 6 of this chapter.

scenes which are aesthetically irrelevant, although they are interesting in other ways. That a man or a tree is depicted is usually aesthetically relevant, but not that the man is supposed to be Jesus or Zeus, or that the tree has some mythological or religious significance. Those who reject the moral, political, or religious values presupposed or presented in a picture are usually able to appreciate the aesthetic nature of the picture. Indeed, rejecting the values implicit in a work often helps one to appreciate it aesthetically. (Few great historians of Renaissance art have been believing Christians.) I suspect that this independence from ideology is essential to aesthetic value.[11] It is significant that it is otherwise with the values of the narrative properties of paintings and the values of the content of literary works. Someone who thought the Basques had it coming or that filial duty is an erroneous value would quite reasonably find less value than most of us in *Guernica* or *King Lear*. What we value in the narrative properties of paintings and the content of literary works is altogether too tied in with other things we care about—our moral, political, and religious values and our emotional lives—to be comfortably categorized as aesthetic value.

Remark 4:   We might say or think, "That was beautiful" after reading or listening to a literary work. But what is the referent of "that"? If the word is functioning transparently, then what is thought to be beautiful is what is represented in the work. "That" does not refer to the work itself, as a set of words. What we find beautiful is the scene conjured up in our imagination. Some descriptions of gardens and palaces in the *Thousand and One Nights* and some passages of pastoral poetry evoke such a response. But this is unusual. Often when we say or think, "That is beautiful," we are thinking of the work itself, and then, if the dilemma holds, we are responding to their sonic excellence, either as pure music, or as the sonically appropriate way of embodying a certain content.

Remark 5:   Contents have purely structural properties. The *Odyssey*, for example, has a harmoniously proportioned overall construction. And the *Iliad* makes impressive use of ring composition. It might be suggested that we can appreciate such structures in themselves, in the way that we appreciate the temporal structure of a piece of music or the visual structure of an abstract

11. Many cannot bear to listen to the Wagner's music because of its Nazi associations. I suspect that it is irrational to form a negative aesthetic judgment about a piece of absolute music because one associates it with matters external to it—though that may sometimes be an understandable and even morally admirable failure of rationality. But the situation is different if we object to operas which have a dubious content; for in that case our objection is not an aesthetic objection.

pattern. Perhaps this literary structure can be an object of aesthetic appreciation even though it does not depend on sensory properties. However, we only appreciate literary structure for the way it is appropriate for the content in question. It does not have a value which is independent of content. When we value structural properties of content, it is because of its role in the presentation of a story which has an independent moral, political, religious, or emotional appeal. So if we use words like "beautiful" and "elegant" to describe properties of plot, that use is metaphorical.

Remark 6:   There may be some visual works of art for which pictorial meaning is the *only* thing of importance, and no value at all attaches to the visual pattern. Many conceptual artists have said that they aimed at this, but they rarely succeed in adhering to their stated aim. Visual interest refuses to go away, despite the artist's conscious denial. William Craig-Martin may put a glass of water on a shelf and call it Tree, but the glass, shelf, and room look remarkably Bauhaus, and that is no accident. And those who indulge in "happenings," such as burying things and then digging them up again, always succumb to the temptation to document these happenings in elegant photographs. It is pleasing to see conceptual puritanism succumbing to the temptations of the senses. But perhaps there are some conceptual works which are not like this, where the artist did not succumb to sensory temptation. It certainly seems as if there could be. However, even if there are, or could be, such puritanical works, they are not counterexamples to the dependency thesis; for in such cases, we also have a rejection of the aesthetic. It is not that there are some aesthetic properties which do not depend on sensory properties.

6 PROOFS, THEORIES, CHESS, MACHINES, GOALS, PLATO'S FORMS, DEATH

It may help to cast light on literary content and pictorial meaning to consider some other disputes over the boundaries of the aesthetic. It is often said that mathematical and logical proofs, scientific theories, and chess moves can be beautiful or elegant. Unlike pictorial meaning, proofs, theories, and chess moves do not necessarily have any sensory embodiment or manifestation. One can consider a proof, theory, or chess move in one's head. And many say that we can appreciate their beauty in purely intellectual contemplation.

But why should we agree that the properties we appreciate here are *aesthetic* ones? There are *intellectual* pleasures, of course, but that should not encourage us to deem these pleasures *aesthetic* pleasures. We could put such cases in the same bag that we put purely conceptual art, pictorial meaning, and literary content.

It is true that we sometimes *call* a theory or proof "elegant" or "beautiful," but such a description might be metaphorical, like calling a company takeover "elegant," a hand of cards "beautiful," or a mood "ugly." The use of these terms is *defeasible* evidence for the aesthetic nature of a judgment. But that evidence is not decisive since their use is sometimes metaphorical. Company takeovers, hands of cards, proofs, theories, and chess moves may all be things to admire or even marvel at. But that does not mean that we are admiring or marveling at their aesthetic properties.

What could motivate us to go one way or the other over the question of whether our application of aesthetic terms to abstract objects, like proofs, theories, or chess moves is metaphorical? One argument for saying that they are applied metaphorically is that in all these cases, the abstract entity has a *purpose*. The point of a mathematical or logical proof is to demonstrate a truth on the basis of other truths. The point of a scientific theory is to explain the data. And the point of a chess move is to win. Our admiration of a good proof, theory, or chess move turns solely on its effectiveness in attaining these ends, or else on its having properties which make attaining these ends likely. Could a proof be elegant even though it was invalid or did not possess properties which tend to make proofs valid? Could a scientific theory be beautiful even though it did not explain much of the data? And could a chess move be elegant or beautiful even though it was an obviously disastrous losing strategy? Surely not.

It might be replied that a proof, theory, or chess move could be beautiful in the *way* it fulfilled its function.[12] However, the situation is not like the dependent beauty of architecture or the beauty of a representational painting where a building is beautiful *as* a thing with a certain function or a painting is beautiful *as* a representation of something. For in such cases, the aesthetic expression or articulation of function and the actual fulfilling of it can come apart. A building might aesthetically express the function of being a library but not actually function well as a library. It may even have no potential to function well as a library. Roger Scruton gives the wonderful example of Scandinavian cutlery which is functional in an aesthetic sense— it expresses a functional aesthetic—but in fact, for the reasons Scruton painstakingly catalogues, it actually functions as cutlery far worse than its

12. Peter Kivy may envisage this when he suggests that we take the beauty of scientific theories to be a case of the beauty of a realistic representational art. See his "Science and Aesthetic Appreciation," *Midwest Studies in Philosophy*, vol. 16 (1991).

classical cousins.[13] Similarly, a painting of an animal may capture something aesthetically important even though it is biologically inaccurate.[14] By contrast, the beauty of a proof, theory, or chess move necessarily involves actually fulfilling the function in question or at least having properties which usually contribute toward fulfilling that function. There cannot be proofs, theories, or chess moves which are dysfunctional yet beautiful or elegant. So what we are appreciating in these cases is not dependent beauty or elegance but the mere technical achievement of finding a very effective means to an end. It is not genuine aesthetic appreciation. So aesthetic terms are metaphorically applied in these cases.

Compare our admiration of proofs, theories, and chess moves with our admiration of machines—for example, the piston engine of an old paddle steamer. Of course, we may aesthetically appreciate the visual elegance of the motion of the pistons, but put that to one side. We might also marvel at the feat of engineering—at a cleverly constructed means to an end. Or we might admire the human ingenuity that went into making it. But none of that is aesthetic appreciation. The machine is merely a technological achievement—a clever and effective means to an end. The pleasure we take in a proof, theory or chess move is similar.

Consider so-called beautiful goals in football.[15] There is, I suppose, the beauty of football as a kind of ballet. This is the purely visual aesthetic of movements which could be appreciated by someone who knew nothing about football. But a "beautiful goal," as these words are usually used, is something which can only be appreciated by someone who understands football. One might admire the ingenuity, subtlety, speed, or panache of the maneuver that led to the goal. But this is not, I maintain, genuine aesthetic appreciation. As with proofs, theories, and chess moves, a beautiful goal is not the aesthetic expression of the purpose of scoring goals, just as a beautiful machine is not beautiful as something which executes a certain task. For beauty and function cannot come apart. Although there can be beautiful maneuvers which do not result in a goal, it cannot be that a maneuver is beautiful even though it does not have any properties which are goal-conducive. Similarly, if a machine is a beautiful engineering solution, it might not actually work, but it must have properties which are usually conducive to

13. Scruton, *Aesthetics of Architecture*, pp. 241–42.

14. Géricault's paintings of racing horses captures their speed and power far better than those paintings which attempted to be accurate in the light of Muybridge's photographs of horses in action.

15. For example, Gascoigne's goal for England against Scotland in the 1996 European Cup championship.

effectiveness. But if a beautiful goal or machine were the aesthetic expression of a function or purpose, then something could be beautiful without fulfilling its function or purpose, and without any tendency to fulfill it.

Another rogue case of beauty is Plato's claim that the form of the beautiful is itself beautiful. But that is an odd enough claim not to provide an uncontroversial example of nonsensory beauty.

Perhaps the most puzzling candidate for nonsensory beauty is the description of deaths as "beautiful." People do call deaths "beautiful"—usually when a person dies peacefully, surrounded by a loving family, with everything resolved. A different kind of death which might be called "beautiful" is a heroic sacrifice for a noble cause. And someone might also call a whole life "beautiful"—or just an evening spent with someone special. Again, my inclination is to cry metaphor in these cases. But there seems to be nothing akin to the means-end phenomena that we unearthed in the case of proofs, theories, chess moves, machines, and goals. Nevertheless, there is something odd and unusual about the idea of a beautiful death, life, or evening. Why might we make such descriptions? A beautiful death might involve emotional closeness, strength, and dignity by all as the end approached. A beautiful life might involve an evolving development of desirable concerns and pursuits. A beautiful evening might involve an evolving rapport between people. It seems that we speak of beauty in these cases because of the significance of a certain temporal structure. The point of the ascription of aesthetic terms to events like deaths is to draw attention to the way a value of a sequence of events depends on the temporal relations between the important events in that sequence—and this is rather like the way that structure can be important in literature or music. But it seems to me that this is *all* we mean. If so, these cases are not literal ascriptions of beauty and elegance. They are extended usages of these notions. There is no aesthetics of death.

The rogue cases that we have considered can all be tamed. So they do not cast doubt on our diagnosis of literature. In both literature and our rogue cases, once we move away from the sensory, we move away from the aesthetic. And where we use aesthetic terms beyond the sensory, that use is metaphorical.

7 CONCLUSION

I argued that the weak aesthetic/sensory dependence thesis can be pushed a lot further than is usually supposed. Aesthetic/sensory dependence obviously holds in the cases of abstract painting and music. Whether it can be maintained as an absolutely general thesis depends on what we say about the aesthetic properties of a range of potentially problematic examples. I argued that the weak dependence thesis holds for architecture, representational painting, and the sonic aspects of literature. And I argued that it holds even in the cases of pictorial meaning, literary content, and a motley assortment of other cases.

As the etymological origins of the word "aesthetic" suggest, aesthetic properties are those that we appreciate in perception. Lovers of beauty are indeed lovers of sights and sounds.

Appendix   Intuitions and the Concept of the Aesthetic

In many cases, I defended a certain view about the properties on which aesthetic properties depend. I did so by appealing to our intuitions. These intuitions have their source in our concept of the aesthetic—they have their source in our grasp of the kind of properties that aesthetic properties are. I exposed and pumped these intuitions in various ways, including using thought experiments, phenomenological reflection on our aesthetic experience, and reflection on our typical modes of aesthetic description. Our concept of the aesthetic delivers a clear and uncontroversial verdict that most aesthetic properties depend on sensory properties. But in the case of literary content, and some other cases, pumped and reflective intuition was less decisive than in the uncontroversial cases. In the controversial cases, I had to cajole intuition to make it point in the direction I wanted.

In appealing to intuition, I tacitly operated with a methodology of "reflective equilibrium." (See Nelson Goodman, *Fact, Fiction and Forecast* [Cambridge: Harvard University Press, 1965], pp. 66–67.) And so it might be thought that the appeal to intuition shares all the shortcomings of that methodology. (See Shelley Kagan, *The Limits of Morality* [Oxford: Oxford University Press, 1989], chap. 1; Stephen Stich, *The Fragmentation of Reason* [Cambridge: MIT Press, 1993].) It might be objected that even where the appeal to intuition does deliver a clear verdict about the sort of properties on which aesthetic properties depend, this does not establish anything. For the appeal to intuition merely elicits what is built into our concept of the aesthetic. But we need some reason to suppose that our concept is not defective. Perhaps our concept of the aesthetic should go the way of the concept of phlogiston or ether. This is what countless sociologically minded theorists have urged. (We should distinguish between theories according to which there is merely a faulty construal of our aesthetic lives by theorists and the view that ordinary folk are operating with a corrupt category; it is the latter which is threatening.) If the category of the aesthetic turns out to be corrupt, then we would be making a mistake if we relied on intuitions which have that concept as their source even in the uncontroversial cases. Surely we cannot accept the deliverances of intuition until we have seen some reason to have faith in our ordinary concept of the aesthetic.

On the other hand, the issue over aesthetic/sensory dependence presupposes that the concept of the aesthetic is in order. It could not be that the concept of the aesthetic is perfectly legitimate but that our intuitions about dependence are wildly erroneous—so that the aesthetic properties of abstract paintings do not after all depend on colors on surfaces and the aesthetic properties of music do not after all depend on sounds. Too much doctrine denied here changes the subject. So it is all right to deploy intuitions about dependence in uncontroversial cases. Insofar as those intuitions are decisive, we can rely on them, given that we are not questioning the overarching assumption that the concept of the aesthetic is respectable.

PART THREE

REALISM

CHAPTER 9

Hume, Taste, and Teleology

1 HUME'S PROBLEM

Realism vs. Anti·realism

1.1 Sentimentalism *(version of anti·realism)*

In his essay "Of the Standard of Taste,"[1] Hume set himself a problem. He takes off from a "sentimentalist" view of taste, according to which

> beauty and deformity ... are not qualities in objects, but belong entirely to the sentiments. (p. 235)

(feelings/emotions)

Such a sentimentalist view stands in opposition to a view according to which judgments of taste or beauty are "determinations of the understanding" which represent qualities of beauty and deformity.

What is this distinction between 'understanding' and 'sentiment', which is so fundamental for Hume? He writes:

> All determinations of the understanding ... have a reference to something beyond themselves, to wit, real matter of fact. (p. 230)

Hume is here talking about what philosophers nowadays call a "belief" or a "cognitive state": a belief represents a state of affairs, and when it is true, it is true in virtue of the fact or state of affairs which it represents. What is a sentiment? It is a felt reaction to a belief or perception—paradigmatically a

→ The ~~facts~~ truths and falsity in something.

---

1. Page references cited in the text and notes are to Hume, "Of the Standard of Taste," in *Essays, Moral, Political, Literary*, ed. Eugene Miller (Indianapolis: LibertyClassics, 1985).

What is the most peticular pauts of aesthetic judgements? ~~You need Seperates it from~~ It is subjechvely universal.

150   Realism

aesthetic judgements links humans to the World.

pleasure or displeasure. It is what philosophers nowadays call a "noncognitive" state.

It is often objected that noncognitive states also represent real matters of fact, just like cognitive states. We are pleased *about* things; we are proud *of* things. If so, wherein lies the difference between understanding and sentiment, or between cognitive and noncognitive states? Hume seems not to have given us a satisfactory account of the distinction. Many have taken Hume to be making a simple blunder when he writes: "sentiment has a reference to nothing beyond itself" and "no sentiment represents what is in the object" (p. 230). But the blunder lies in the uncharitable interpretation of Hume, not in Hume himself. For Hume does not mean to deny that sentiments have content; he is not denying the obvious truths that we are pleased *at* or *by* various things. The point is just that the sentiment does not represent any distinctive quality of objects over and above what is represented in the belief or perceptual experience to which it is a reaction. This is why the sentimentalist view is bound up with the metaphysical claim that "Beauty is no quality in things themselves" (p. 230). Since there is no genuine property of beauty, there are no facts or states of affairs which consist in things possessing this property. Sentimentalism means that there is no aesthetic reality.[2]

Involves believes (REPRESENTATION) non-cognithist involus emotions.

1.2 Normativity

the problem w. anti-realists

Unlike many who wish to avoid a cognitivist and realist position in aesthetics, Hume is sensible enough to recognize that it is essential that he avoid the view that "All sentiment is right" or that "every individual ought to acquiesce in his own sentiment, without pretending to regulate those of others" (p. 230). The trouble with this is that

Whoever would assert an equality of genius and elegance between OGILBY and MILTON, or BUNYAN and ADDISON, would be thought to defend no less an extravagance, than if he maintained a mole-hill to be as high as TENERIFFE, or a pond as extensive as the ocean. Though there may be found persons, who give the preference to the former authors; no one pays any attention to such a taste; and we pronounce without scruple the sentiment of these

2. By contrast with his works on moral philosophy, Hume spends no time arguing against such an opponent in "Of the Standard of Taste." He thinks that the sentimentalist view is "certain" (p. 235). He does not have quite the same confidence in his belief that moral judgments belong to the sentiments rather than to the understanding. He employs several arguments to try and show this; and in the *Enquiry concerning the Principles of Morals* he expresses uncertainty as to the result. But it is not difficult to imagine how Hume would have redeployed similar arguments in aesthetics.

pretended critics to be absurd and ridiculous. The principle of the natural equality of tastes is then totally forgot. (pp. 230–31)

What Hume describes here is one major aspect of the normativity which is involved in our practice of making aesthetic judgments. (Other aspects are 'mind-independence' and consistency, but I shall not discuss these here.) Our thought and talk in aesthetics has much in common with our thought and talk about things in the physical world, such as molehills, Teneriffe, and ponds and oceans. What gives this impression is that we think that our sentiments can be more or less *appropriate*; and we think that in at least some cases, an aesthetic judgment and its opposite cannot both be *correct*. Hume's point here is qualified later in the essay, when he admits that there are *some* cases where it is all right to think that neither side in a dispute is correct (pp. 243–45). Preferences which stem from "the different humours of particular men" (Ovid or Tacitus) or from "the particular manners of our age or country" result in differences which are quite "blameless on both sides" (p. 243). But for the most part, Hume is interested in cases where this is not so.

1.3 The Problem

The overriding problem for the sentimentalist (or noncognitivist) in aesthetics is this: if aesthetic judgment and experience does not represent aesthetic reality, then why isn't any sentiment as good as any other? On Hume's theory, why should we not have any sentiments we please? The dialectical state of play is that if Hume wants to be able to respect the normative claims of our aesthetic thought, he is going to have to do some hard work. He needs to *earn* such claims.

To his credit, Hume attempts to do this. He writes:

It is sufficient for our present purpose, if we have proved, that the taste of all individuals is not on an equal footing. (p. 242)

This is the problem he sets himself. Hume seeks a "standard of taste," which is, he says:

a rule, by which the various sentiments of men may be reconciled; at least, a decision, afforded, confirming one sentiment, and condemning another. (p. 229)

This may look at first sight as if it reveals a tendency on Hume's part to seek some *law* or *principle* of taste by reference to which we can make reliable aesthetic judgments. It is not clear that he should be interested in anything so strong. All Hume needs is the more primitive idea that some sentiments can be better than others, that not all sentiments are right, and that some may be defective. This is presupposed by the stronger law idea. But if he could achieve the stronger idea, he would have achieved his purpose.[3]

2 HUME'S SOLUTION

2.1 The Underlying Idea

What I shall call Hume's *underlying* idea is the idea that the normativity of aesthetic judgment is constructed from the virtues and vices of aesthetic sensibilities. As he says:

> In each creature, there is a sound and a defective state; and the former alone can be supposed to afford us a true standard of taste and sentiment. (pp. 233–34)

A good critic is someone whose sensibility is in a sound state. Hume gives an account of what it is to be a good critic, and from there he derives the idea of correctness in judgment, not vice versa. A good critic is not someone who makes correct judgments; rather, correct judgments are those made by the good critic.

Hume's second idea, which builds on the underlying idea, is the idea that our sensibility is a delicate mechanism which is prone to being upset and distorted by internal and external influences. For Hume, an aesthetic sensibility is a psychological function from an input of ordinary belief or perception (of physical, sensory, or semantic properties) to aesthetic reaction. But this function can be more or less healthy in itself and it can be more or less independent of extraneous influences. Call this the *mechanism* idea. Hume writes:

> Those finer emotions of the mind are of a very tender and delicate nature, and require the concurrence of many favourable circumstances to make them

---

3. Hume's project is recognizably the same as that which his twentieth-century reincarnation, Simon Blackburn, pursues in moral philosophy. (See for example, chapters 5 and 6 of his *Spreading the Word* [Oxford: Clarendon, 1984].) Like Hume, Blackburn attempts to explain the realistic-looking feature of moral thought on a noncognitivist basis. He calls this project "quasi-realism," and he often cites Hume's "Of the Standard of Taste" as a source of inspiration.

play with facility and exactness, according to their general and established principles. The least hindrance to such small springs, or the least internal disorder, disturbs their motion, and confounds the operation of the whole machine. (p. 232)

As we shall see, Hume has various suggestions about what these internal disorders and external and hindrances are. It is these suggestions that are supposed to amount to "principles of taste" (p. 241), in the sense that they are principles in accordance with which we ought to judge.

These are the two pillars of Hume's answer.

Hume several times draws an analogy between "mental taste" (that of moral and aesthetic judgment), and "bodily taste" (that of secondary qualities such as colors, sounds, tastes, and smells). Of color he writes

The appearance of objects in day-light, to the eye of a man in health, is denominated their true and real colour, even while colour is allowed to be merely a phantasm of the senses. (p. 234)

Judgments of color do not represent real qualities of objects, but even so, those with a fever or with jaundice make defective color judgments. This is no more than an analogy, and Hume could have omitted it. But its dialectical role is to get us to see the error in a *principled* objection that where there are no matters of fact, all judgment is right. The secondary quality analogy functions to dissuade those who think they know that Hume's project must fail, so they need not bother to look at the details.

2.2 Hume's Suggestions

My plan will be first to glance at Hume's various suggestions concerning what makes for an good critic; then I will consider what I think underpins the idea. Here is the passage where he sums up his various suggestions after having described each one in more detail:

When the critic has no delicacy, he judges without any distinction, and is only affected by the grosser and more palpable qualities of the object: The finer touches pass unnoticed and disregarded. Where he is not aided by practice, his verdict is attended with confusion and hesitation. Where no comparison has been employed, the most frivolous beauties, such as rather merit the name of defects, are the objects of his admiration. Where he lies under the influence of prejudice, all his natural sentiments are perverted. Where good sense is wanting, he is not qualified to discern the beauties of design and reasoning, which are the highest and most excellent. Under some or other of these imperfections, the generality of men labour; and hence a true judge in the fine arts is observed, even during the most polished ages, to be so rare a character: Strong sense, united to delicate sentiment, improved by practice, perfected by comparison, and cleared of all prejudice, can alone entitle critics to this valuable character; and the joint verdict of such, wherever they are to be found, is the true standard of taste and beauty. (p. 241)

Let us separate the five suggestions in this passages.

(1) There is what he calls the "delicacy" of taste, which he has earlier illustrated with the much discussed wine-tasting example from Don Quixote (pp. 234–37). Our experience, and the judgment we base upon it, can have more or less fine-grained discriminative power.

(2) We need practice in judgment. It is good to have a well-exercised sensibility (pp. 237–38).

(3) A broad experience is important, for it gives us scope to make comparisons. A narrow range of comparisons leads to crude and naive judgment (p. 238).

(4) There is sheer prejudice. We must remove obstructions to true appreciation, such as any jealousy or affection we might feel toward the author; and we must not blindly follow fashion (pp. 240–41).

(5) We need what Hume calls "good sense," which is the operation of our normal cognitive faculties. We need good sense for many purposes: to keep our prejudices in check; to understand and compare the parts of a work; to assess a work with respect to its purposes; to understand and assess the plot and characters in a work of literature; and to understand the representational features of visual works of art (pp. 240–41).

Before he embarks on all this, Hume merely mentions in passing another possible failing in a sensibility which does seem to fit into any of the previous five categories.

A perfect serenity of mind, a recollection of thought, a due attention to the object; if any of these circumstances be wanting, our experiment will be fallacious, and we will be unable to judge of the catholic and universal beauty. (pp. 232–33)

That is, we need to be in the right mood and paying attention to the object. These are the resources with which Hume hopes to construct aesthetic normativity. They constitute his answer to the problem that he originally set himself.

2.3 Sensibilities and Judgments

At first sight, there is something wonderfully commonsensical about Hume's suggestions. But this appearance is deceptive. It is no doubt true that our aesthetic sensibilities often suffer from the defects which Hume catalogues. Any theory of aesthetic judgment, including a cognitivist one, needs to admit the possibility of such defects. But we should separate the uncontroversial nature of Hume's suggestions, considered in themselves, from the question of whether the appeal to such defects can suffice for the Herculean task of capturing the normative aspirations of our aesthetic judgments. That is far more controversial.

One way to highlight the problem is to employ the method of appealing to a comparison of judgments of beauty and ugliness with judgments of niceness and nastiness as applied to food and drink; for these contrast with judgments of beauty and ugliness in an important respect. Like judgments of beauty and ugliness, judgments of niceness and nastiness are based on sentiments of pleasure and displeasure. But they lack the normative aspirations of judgments of beauty and ugliness. As far as judgments of niceness and nastiness are concerned, anything goes. If you do not like smoked salmon, you are not lacking in the way that you are if you do not appreciate the beauty of the Alhambra. To think that there is an equality of niceness between smoked salmon and baked beans is not like thinking that there is "an equality of genius between OGILBY and MILTON, or BUNYAN and ADDISON." The trouble is that all of the virtues and vices that Hume cites apply equally to our capacity to experience pleasure in food and drink. As far as food and drink go, we can be more or less finely discriminating, more or less well practiced, more or less widely experienced, more or less prejudiced, more or less possessed of good sense, and in better or worse moods. So it seems dubious whether any of these virtues and vices can do the job of earning normativity in the case of the sensibility whose products are judgments of beauty and ugliness. The contrast with judgments of the nice and nasty serves to remind us of exactly how much needs to be achieved for judgments of beauty and ugliness. This objection may not be definitive. There are possible responses which could mitigate its force. But there seems to be a prima facie worry with Hume's suggestions. However, I do not want to be too concerned with the *details* of Hume's account, so whether this objection is right is not of great importance.

2.4 Natural Aptness (~~Husora~~ Illusionary theory)

Most commentators get no further than examining the details of Hume's suggestions. I want to bypass such discussion. It will be more worthwhile to see what lies beneath the details. It is true that on the face of it, Hume's suggestions seem to be inadequate to the task of capturing normativity, however commonsensical they are considered in themselves. This can be brought out by the method of contrast with the nice and nasty. Other critics of Hume have had other worries. But in fact, Hume's techniques all presuppose a certain thesis, which, if correct, would underwrite them all. There is an aspect of Hume's account which the commentators have missed. And in missing it, they have missed what is most interesting and powerful in Hume's account.

Hume writes:

There are certain qualities in objects which are fitted by nature to produce those particular feelings. (p. 235)

Some particular forms or qualities, from their original structure of the internal fabric, are calculated to please, and others to displease; and if they fail of their effect in any particular instance, it is from some apparent defect or imperfection in the organ. (p. 232)

Though some objects, by the structure of the mind, be naturally calculated to give pleasure, it is not to be expected, that in every individual the pleasure will be equally felt. (p. 234)

This idea is obviously important to Hume, since he returns to it again and again. Let us call it the doctrine of *natural aptness*, since the idea is that certain things are somehow apt by nature for pleasurable contemplation. But what nature? The nature of the object or our nature? What does natural aptness amount to? What might it mean to say that anything is fitted by nature for anything else?

I suggest that Hume is offering us some kind of *teleological* account of aesthetics. Just as legs are for walking and eyes are for seeing and the heart is for pumping blood, so our sensibility is for responding with pleasure to flowers and to Homer. The function of the heart is to pump blood, and it can function better or worse in this respect, and similarly, the function of our sensibility is to yield pleasure when confronted with certain things, and it too can function better or worse in this respect.[4]

4. I do not find the same teleological approach in Hume's earlier essay "The Sceptic."

Hume's account would be most naturally supplemented by an evolution-ary account. No one would have been more excited by the discovery of evolution than Hume; and he would have been eager to press it into the service of his science of human nature. It is not immediately clear why con-templative pleasures in art and nature should be adaptive. But Hume only requires that there is *some* teleological relation. A teleological account does depend on there being some account of that in virtue of which something has the function in question. But the account itself could be neutral on such further details. Perhaps God designed our aesthetic sensibilities with a certain intention. If Hume's account is to be vindicated in the long run, an evolu-tionary account must presumably be forthcoming. But Hume need not be criticized for not providing that account.

2.5 Optimism

Hume is not just doing abstract speculative philosophy. He wants to sup-ply us with a means of recognizing when our critical faculties are function-ing well. Hume wants his essay to make us better critics.

The practical problem is to spot the natural relation, in view of all the dis-tortions which a sensibility may suffer. Hume's answer is the test of time. The test of time is evidence for the existence of a natural relation between form and sentiment:

We shall be able to ascertain [the] influence [of the relation, which nature has placed between form and sentiment] not so much from the operation of each particular beauty, as from the durable admiration which attends these works, that have survived all the caprices of mode and fashion, all the mistakes of ignorance and envy. (p. 233)

He continues:

The same HOMER, who pleased at ATHENS and ROME two thousand years ago, is still admired at PARIS and LONDON. All the changes of climate, government, religion, and language, have not been able to obscure his glory. Authority or prejudice may give a temporary vogue to a bad poet or orator; but his reputation will never be durable or general. . . . On the contrary, a real genius, the longer his works endure, and the more wide they are spread, the more sincere is the admiration which he meets with. Envy and jealousy have too much place in a narrow circle. . . . But when these obstructions are removed, the beauties, which are naturally fitted to excite agreeable sentiments, immedi-ately display their energy; and while the world endures, they maintain their authority over the minds of men. (p. 233)

Here we see Hume's faith in the convergence of judgments of taste under ideal conditions. Let us call this Hume's *optimism*.[5] Hume's natural aptness doctrine is bound up with his optimism about our convergence on judgments of taste. It is not clear whether convergence in judgment (the test of time) is looked upon as evidence for the natural aptness doctrine in general, or as evidence for the correctness of particular judgments. At any rate, Hume needs there to be convergence. Without convergence, the natural aptness doctrine would be idle; and without natural aptness, there would be no reason to expect convergence.

Confirmation of this view of the role of Hume's optimism is his willingness to abandon normativity where no defect can be found in each of two conflicting sensibilities.[6] For where there is "such diversity as is blameless on both sides," Hume concedes that there is no right answer to be had. Both the judgment giving preference to Ovid over Tacitus, or its opposite, are defective. The normativity of aesthetic judgment in general would not collapse unless most or all cases were of the Ovid/Tacitus sort rather than the Ogilby/Milton sort.

The test of time weeds out impediments and biases because various impediments and biases operate more or less randomly: some biases make us judge a thing positively whereas others make us judge it negatively. By contrast, the pure underlying natural disposition will operate in the same way—militating toward one judgment. Hence if our judgments converge on a certain judgment, despite prejudices and biases pulling us one way or the other, the judgment probably derives from an underlying response which is pure and uncorrupted.

Hume assumes a universal species-wide disposition to take pleasure in certain objects. If only we can remove impediments, then universal agreement on correct judgment will prevail. In a sense, agreement decides what is beautiful (pp. 233–34). This has a Wittgensteinian ring to it. But the agreement is between those whose organs are in a "sound state."

---

5. By contrast, I suspect that the cognitivist will be more pessimistic about convergence—which is, of course, ironic in view of a certain standard view in the philosophy of science. It is the *sentimentalist* who sees our aesthetic judgments as "tracking the truth," with causal deviance brought in to explain error! And I would argue that the cognitivist about aesthetics ought to eschew any such theory; but we need not pursue this.

6. The Ovid/Tacitus passage (pp. 243–45), which Blackburn sometimes mentions, is the point at which Hume abandons the attempt to capture normativity. See for example, Blackburn, *Spreading the Word*, pp. 199–200.

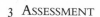

3 ASSESSMENT

3.1 The Naturalistic Fallacy?

It might be objected that Hume is committing a naturalistic fallacy: the standard of taste is a normative matter, but what pleases is a matter of psychological and sociological fact. So how can he derive the one from the other?

However, most philosophers have come to doubt whether there ever was a naturalistic fallacy, so long as the naturalistic theory is not one about meanings but about properties. Hume can be construed as providing a naturalistic reductionist account of aesthetic normativity in terms of a certain natural function. Hume's project of naturalizing aesthetic normativity is in some ways analogous to the "biosemantic" approach to the theory of meaning pioneered by Ruth Millikan.[7] Biosemantics is the project of reducing semantic normativity to the normativity associated with biological function (a "good wing"; a "well-functioning" liver). Similarly, for Hume, the sense in which we ought to judge in certain ways derives from, or is explained by, a teleological *ought*. We ought to appreciate Shakespeare and Homer in the same sense that eyes are what we ought to see with. Certain things are fitted for our sensibilities just as bodily organs are fitted for certain tasks. And—since Darwin—we know that this teleological ought has an evolutionary basis. Hume's aesthetic theory can be construed as a form of biological naturalism; and there would be no reason for him to be ashamed of that.

3.2 Evolutionary Underpinnings?

NATURAL REACTIONS TO THE WORLD.

Another problem is about the availability of the evolutionary underpinning that Hume requires in the long run. We can give some evolutionary explanation of why people do not like to drink urine and eat excrement. These things are not naturally apt for pleasurable consumption because eating and drinking these things is unhealthy and thus nonadaptive. Mother Nature tends to conjoin pleasure and healthy activity. If you do not like smoked salmon you are likely to deprive your body of excellent nourishment. That's why it tastes so good.

The irony is that an explanation of the limited normativity that constrains judgments of the niceness and nastiness of food and drink seems easier to come by than an explanation of the more substantial normativity of judg-

---

7. Ruth Millikan, *Language, Thought and Other Biological Categories* (Cambridge: MIT Press, 1984); Millikan, *White Queen Psychology and Other Essays for Alice* (Cambridge: MIT Press, 1993).

ments of beauty and ugliness. It is difficult to see how we could even begin to give an evolutionary explanation of why Milton might be more naturally apt for pleasurable contemplation than Ogilby. An evolutionary explanation of our aesthetic life seems hard to come by because it is not obviously adaptive. Spotting the color and shape of a berry may be useful because it might enable us to avoid those which are poisonous. But responding to its color and shape with pleasure seems to be useless. Hume's teleological approach needs to be underpinned by an evolutionary story; but it is difficult to see how it would go.

It is true that an evolutionary account of the normativity of aesthetic judgment is problematic given Hume's picture. But Hume can reply that things are no easier for his opponent. He can point out that if cognitivism is true, an evolutionary account is no more easily forthcoming, since even if we cognized real aesthetic properties, sensitivity to such real aesthetic properties would not be adaptive. There are problems all round. And anyway, even though it is difficult to see where the evolutionary story would begin, it is certainly not obviously the case that such a story could never be told. Most likely, our aesthetic life would have to be explained as a by-product of some other trait which is adaptive. There is more work to be done on Hume's behalf. But there is no reason to think that it cannot be done.

3.3 Question-Begging?

I distinguished various sorts of defectiveness in a sensibility. Some are the corruption and perversion of our sentiments from outside, whereas others are the weakness and ineptness of our sentiments themselves. Hume supposes that a well-functioning faculty of taste will, if left alone, produce appropriate reactions and hence ground correct judgments of taste. But it might be objected that this is exactly what Hume needs to show if he is to construct normativity. It is not what he can use to construct it. What threatens Hume, then, is that in his optimism and his doctrine of natural aptness, he is simply helping himself to what he wants. Hume does not just think that we have a species-wide disposition to converge in judgment; he also thinks that we have a species-wide disposition to converge on *correct* judgment. And the objection is that he has no right to start from that point. Hume seems to be begging the question.

The reply to this question-begging objection is that *it* is question-begging. It begs the question against the teleological account. On the teleological account, an excellent sensibility is ultimately just a well-functioning or healthy sensibility. This entails that the response of the normally functioning sensibility determines the correctness of responses. The obligation to judge in one way rather than another derives from an obligation to feel in one way rather than another, which in turn derives from a natural relation of fit between object and feeling. Therefore the convergence of the judgments of healthy sensibilities would have to be the convergence on correct judgments. This is just part of the teleological approach.

3.4 Too Relativist?

It might be objected that, given a teleological account, it is quite contingent that certain things are apt for pleasurable contemplation. Hume thinks that normativity is in the last resort merely statistical, since it is just a question of what most human beings find beautiful over the long term. So Hume is a relativist of a sort: beauty, for Hume, is species-relative.

Hume can brush aside this relativist argument as question-begging. Once one is a sentimentalist, he might say, a broadly statistical conception of normativity is acceptable. At one point Hume argues in passing that any rules of composition must be derived from what generally pleases (p. 231). So if something generally pleases, which flouts certain critical canons, it is the critical canons which must be revised rather than the positive judgment on the object of the pleasure (pp. 231–32). Hume says: "If they are found to please, they cannot be faults" (p. 232). But as he makes clear, this means what is *generally* found to please. If something is found to please on just one occasion, the pleasure may indeed be at fault. The right answer is independent of what someone feels on any particular occasion; but it is not independent of the disposition of the species to feel pleasure under suitable conditions. That the right answer is independent of what any particular individual happens to think is indeed built into our thought. But that it is independent of what of what we would all think under suitable conditions, where "we" is the whole species, is not obviously built into our thought. Hume can avoid a crude and nasty relativism. But a more subtle form of relativism may be acceptable.

3.5 Other Vices and Virtues?

Given the details of Hume's account, there is a danger that it will turn out that there are vastly more cases of the Ovid/Tacitus kind than we had previously imagined. How realistic is Hume's hope that in all cases of conflicting judgment, where we think that there is a right answer, some defect can be found in the sensibility of at least one of the parties? Whence this optimism about the convergence of uncorrupted and well-functioning sensibilities?

The danger of nonconverging but healthy sensibilities is very real. For there have been certain persistent disputes in criticism which do not seem to fit Hume's optimistic picture. The critics in question appear to have all the virtues which Hume says ought to be possessed by the good critic. Yet these disputes are not like Ovid/Tacitus disputes, they are like Milton/Ogilby disputes. One side thinks of the other as seriously mistaken in their judgment. It seems plausible that a sensibility with all the Humean virtues might still err. Is it really true that where judgments diverge and where we think that there is a right and a wrong answer, the mistaken sensibility must have one of Hume's intrinsic or extrinsic faults? Surely there might be divergences between sensibilities which are excellent by Hume's lights.

However, we need to see Hume's virtues as not merely the absence of defects. Aesthetic sensibilities are not like mechanisms which either function satisfactorily or else have some shortcoming. Instead, aesthetic sensibilities might be like car engines, which are more or less powerful and well tuned. The engines of racing cars can excel with no upper limit. Prejudice and mood are negative considerations. But Hume's other virtues—of fine discrimination, practice, comparison, and good sense—are all respects in which our sensibilities can excel with no upper limit. Moreover, we can make the excellent sensibility more difficult to attain by adding other respects in which it should achieve excellence. We can add to Hume's list of virtues and vices while the basic shape of his theory remains intact. So perhaps there are possible sources of error even in illustrious critics who disagree.

4 THE UNDERLYING PROBLEM

4.1 Sensibilities and Judgments

The teleological account rests on the underlying idea that correct judgments are those made by an excellent sensibility. If an object is naturally apt to produce pleasure, that means that it will do so in a sensibility which possesses the Humean virtues and lacks the Humean vices. There is a relation of fit between the object, on the one hand, and the excellent sensibility, on the other. A particular object is suited for a response of pleasure for a particular sensibility at a particular time if that is how the excellent sensibility would respond.

So let us turn our sights on the underlying idea, where we find the real difficulty with Hume's account. One way to put the problem with the underlying idea would be this: how can we say which aspects of a sensibility are virtues and which are vices, unless we already have some prior grasp of the normativity of aesthetic judgment? But it is important to see that the underlying problem with the underlying idea is not merely epistemological. It is over what it would *be* for a sensibility to be better or worse. If being better or worse does *not* consist in producing or being disposed to produce better or worse judgments or sentiments as the output of the sensibility, then what does it consist in? Hume's predicament is very like that of a nonrealist about science: mere internal coherence allows for radically divergent but nevertheless internally coherent theories. Virtues like simplicity or comprehensiveness are then brought in to explain why certain internally coherent but far-fetched theories should be ruled out. The nonrealist then needs an account of why simplicity and comprehensiveness are virtues which does not appeal to the fact that theories with these properties tend to hit on the truth. And this proves difficult. It is the same with our aesthetic sensibility. What can the virtues or vices of a sensibility consist in if it is not a disposition to produce correct or incorrect judgments or appropriate and inappropriate pleasures? And why should we strive to acquire the virtues and avoid the vices if it is not as a means to acquire correct judgment and appropriate sensibilities and avoid incorrect judgments and inappropriate sensibilities?

4.2 Not Question-Begging

This objection cannot be met with the retort that it is question-begging. Consider the reply that it is just part of sentimentalism that it puts dispositions to respond before the particular responses themselves, whereas the cognitivist will put particular responses before dispositions to respond; so the above objection assumes a cognitivist point of view. This would not be to the point. If we think back, when we read Hume introducing his vices and virtues, we are swept along with him. But this is only because we already have the idea of correctness in aesthetic judgment, and we can then see how his virtues and vices are conducive or unconducive to arriving at correct judgments. But take away the idea of correctness, and the virtues and vices that Hume specifies become utterly cold and neutral. We are left with no reason to think of such features of a sensibility as having any positive or negative value. If so, the project of constructing the idea of better and worse sensibilities has collapsed. In a sense Hume has tricked us. He genially gets us to agree, in a commonsensical way, that the characteristics he cites are virtues and vices, while theoretically withdrawing our tacit reasons for agreeing. If we had known that these characteristics were supposed to have a value quite apart from their manifestation in admirable responses or judgments, then we would not have agreed so readily. Hence, Hume's virtues and vices cannot be the means to *inject* normativity into aesthetics. Without the notion that sensibilities with certain characteristics tend to produce admirable responses, what grounds can we have for thinking of these characteristics as constituting merits in a sensibility, rather than defects?

4.3 Dodging the Circle

I want to distinguish my criticism from the criticism that Hume's account is *circular*. Many have charged Hume with arguing as follows: "(1) Good works of art are works of art approved by good critics; (2) good critics are critics possessing five requisite qualities; and (3) critics possessing the five requisite qualities are critics who approve of good works of art."[8] Peter Kivy argues, in defense of Hume, that this circle can be broken in the case of certain of the qualities of critics, which "are identifiable by marks other than the critic's approval of good art."[9] But although this defeats the circularity objection, it does not remove the difficulty I have in mind. The problem is not merely one of how we are to pick out the qualities of good critics independently of their relation to aesthetic qualities of things; the problem is to see why such a disposition, even if it is one that can be comfortably identified independently of aesthetic qualities, should be admirable apart from its manifestation in admirable judgments or attitudes. The problem is not that Hume is *defining* the qualities of good critics in terms of correct judgments or admirable sentiments, the problem is of seeing how the qualities would *be* virtues apart from their leading to correct judgments or admirable sentiments.

All Hume's techniques face the same problem, which derives from the underlying idea. Hume needs an account of *why* the virtues he cites are virtues, which is independent of the fact that they lead to admirable judgments. This is the fundamental objection to the way Hume goes about things.

CODA

Without the underlying idea, Hume's project collapses. Without it, the teleological account is empty. And without the teleology, there is no basis for

8. This is Peter Kivy's description of the argument in his "Hume's Standard of Taste: Breaking the Circle," *British Journal of Aesthetics* 8 (1968): 60.
9. Ibid., p. 61.

Hume's suggestions. By employing the device of contrast with the nice and the nasty, we initially saw some reason to doubt whether any of Hume's suggestions could be successful. The teleological account seemed to give the suggestions a new lease on life. But with the collapse of the underlying idea, the suggestions are submerged once again. I do not want to dogmatically assert that no noncognitivist theory can capture normativity. But I suspect that if normativity is to be constructed on a noncognitivist basis, it will have to be by beginning from the possible shortcomings of aesthetic responses or judgments themselves, and not from the sensibility which produces them. Hume made a brave effort in his essay to solve the fundamental problem for a sentimentalist aesthetics. Interpreters of Hume's essay have failed to do Hume justice because they have failed to notice its teleological basis. Teleologically interpreted, Hume's account is powerful and interesting. However, while we should have the greatest respect for Hume's project, I have argued that there is a major stumbling block in the way of building an adequate conception of the normativity of aesthetic judgment from the materials that Hume provides. In the end, Hume fails to solve the problem that he set himself. However, perhaps philosophical progress is better measured by the questions that philosophers ask, rather than by the answers that they provide to their own questions.

CHAPTER 10

Metaphor and Realism in Aesthetics

1 THE PROBLEM

1.1 According to aesthetic realism, aesthetic thought and experience represent a range of distinctively aesthetic facts or states of affairs. True aesthetic judgments are true in virtue of the aesthetic facts or states of affairs which they represent. An aesthetic fact or state of affairs is a structured entity consisting of an object or event which possesses a genuine aesthetic property. So if an aesthetic judgment is true, it is because the object or event really does possess the genuine aesthetic property which it is represented as possessing. There are difficult and controversial questions concerning what it is for a property to be a genuine or real property. But I shall assume that this distinction can be drawn.[1] There is more to be said about aesthetic realism, but this characterization will suffice for the purpose of this chapter.

What I want to discuss here is one argument against aesthetic realism. I shall not discuss the reasons for holding this view. I shall be traveling only in one dialectical direction.[2]

1.2 Roger Scruton presents this argument in his book *Art and Imagination*.[3] Novel metaphysical arguments are rare. This is one of them.

---

1. On the distinction between real and projected properties, see my "Quietism," *Midwest Studies in Philosophy*, vol. 17 (1992).

2. The main reason for believing aesthetic realism is that no other theory seems to be able to do justice to the normative aspirations of aesthetic judgments. Once again, there is much more to be said about this motivation. See chapter 9 and chapter 11, section 1.

3. Roger Scruton, *Art and Imagination* (London: Methuen, 1974), pp. 38–44.

His argument takes off from the observation that when we describe things aesthetically, we often use words metaphorically. For example, we might describe a cloud or an insect as "delicate" or "balanced," and we might describe a piece of music as "gloomy" or as "moving" from one note to another. The normal nonmetaphorical use of these words is in the context of ordinary non-aesthetic descriptions. But here their use is metaphorical.[4] Such descriptions contrast with our application of terms like "beautiful," "elegant," and "dainty," which are not used metaphorically in aesthetic contexts. These have no nonaesthetic use except one which is metaphorical. For example, we might speak of "a beautiful hand" in cards or "an ugly mood." There is no significant parallel in moral philosophy, so the ensuing argument could not be developed there.

Having noticed that metaphorical aesthetic description is rife, Scruton adds a certain general doctrine about metaphor. The general doctrine about metaphor which Scruton invokes is one which Donald Davidson developed more fully a few years later in his classic essay "What Metaphors Mean."[5] Davidson argued that the words used in metaphorical contexts have only the literal meaning that they have when used nonmetaphorically. I do not want to review Davidson's very persuasive arguments here. For the most part, I shall assume that such a view is on the right lines.

Given these two premises, Scruton argues that aesthetic realism cannot be maintained—at least in regard to those aesthetic descriptions which are metaphorical.[6]

Why, exactly, is aesthetic realism threatened when we add Davidson's view of metaphor to the observation that many aesthetic descriptions are meta-phorical? An aesthetic fact or state of affairs consists of the existence of an object or event which possesses a real aesthetic property. A realist must, therefore, be committed to the existence of a distinctive range of aesthetic concepts whose role is to pick out real aesthetic properties. If this is the gen-eral view about aesthetic properties, the realist must also hold such a view

4. I do not see why metaphor should be taken to be more important than simile in aesthetics. The two are easily mixed. For example, I might say that the buildings at Knossos float weightlessly due to their downwardly tapering columns, whereas the Parthenon sits heavily due to its upwardly tapering columns, in the way that a stodgy, tepid moussaka sits in one's stomach! But let us stick with metaphor.

5. Donald Davidson, "What Metaphors Mean," in *Inquiries into Truth and Interpretation* (Oxford: Clarendon, 1984).

6. Scruton directs his argument against the idea that there are aesthetic properties (*Art and Imagination*, p. 44), where this means that sentences which ascribe aesthetic properties have truth-conditions in a strong sense (p. 29); and this means that for some sentence 's', "there is some state of affairs which guarantees the truth of 's' " (p. 6).

about those aesthetic properties which are described metaphorically. So, in such cases, there must be distinctively aesthetic concepts which pick out aesthetic properties. Hence, the realist seems to require a difference of meaning between words used in normal and in metaphorical contexts. But this is disallowed by the Davidsonian doctrine about metaphor. If a word means the same in two cases, how can it be that we use it to describe a genuine aesthetic property in one case but not in the other? It is not literally true that music is sad or delicate.[7] So given that in an aesthetic description of music, 'sadness' and 'delicacy' mean what they normally do, they cannot pick out a real aesthetic property of sadness or delicacy.

Scruton sums up his argument in the form of a dilemma:

> The principal objection to the idea of an aesthetic property was this: either terms denoting aesthetic properties have the same meaning as they have when used in their normal contexts, in which case, how can we distinguish aesthetic properties as a separate class? Or else they have a different meaning, in which case, what is the point of naming aesthetic properties as we do? We found that terms used in aesthetic description must have their normal meanings.[8]

The aesthetic realist wants to be realistic about those properties which we describe metaphorically, as well as about properties which we describe as "beautiful," "elegant," or "dainty." If this road is blocked, the realist is faced with an unforeseen and uncomfortable dichotomy among aesthetic judgments. It turns out that in at least some important cases, the sentences do not describe aesthetic facts or states of affairs.[9]

2 AESTHETIC THOUGHT AND AESTHETIC LANGUAGE

2.1   This looks like a powerful argument. How should the aesthetic realist respond? In this section, I present a short-term solution and I then defend it. In section 3, I provide a deeper diagnosis.

I do not recommend denying the Davidsonian doctrine that the words used in metaphorical contexts have no more than the meaning that they have normally. The realist should *agree* with this. Now, Davidson has a posi-

---

7. What is the music sad about? What would delicate music be like if it were broken?

8. Scruton, *Art and Imagination*, p. 44,

9. Notice, however, that the nonrealist will also have to say something about metaphorical aesthetic descriptions and the way in which they relate to nonmetaphorical aesthetic descriptions. But this will not create the same metaphysical problem that it creates for the realist.

tive account of metaphor as well as a negative account. The positive account stresses pragmatic force, as opposed to sense or meaning; in particular, he focuses on what a metaphor makes us notice. It is therefore open to the aesthetic realist to say that what a metaphor makes us notice in aesthetic contexts, as opposed to what it means, is a real aesthetic property, and that this noticing is an intentional state which represents aesthetic facts or states of affairs.

This amounts to querying the "linguistic turn." We should *admit* the thesis of meaning equivalence on the linguistic level, while *denying* it on the level of thought. Although the *sentence* in which the word "delicate" figures means the same in aesthetic contexts as it usually does, the *thought* it expresses is quite different. The thoughts are different in that they employ different concepts. In the aesthetic use of the word, our thought has a realistic aesthetic content that it lacks in the nonaesthetic use. Let us introduce subscripts to mark the difference. The concepts delicacy$_{NA}$ and delicacy$_A$ might both be expressed using the English word "delicacy." When Scruton argues that music does not really move and that it is not really sad, the realist can reply that although 'move$_{NA}$' and 'sad$_{NA}$' do not apply to music, 'move$_A$' and 'sad$_A$' do apply to it.

2.2   It will be objected that it is too mysterious to make such a cleavage. Surely the two uses cannot be pulled apart in this way; for the point of the aesthetic use of such a word is rooted in its usual nonaesthetic use. Why else use the same word? It looks as if we have escaped from the first horn of Scruton's dilemma only to be impaled on the second.

There is something in this complaint. It would certainly be objectionable if the realist implied that the two concepts were completely unconnected—like the financial and fluvial senses of the word "bank." But there is a way that this unpleasant consequence can be avoided: on a realistic account, the connection would be a *causal* one. Acquiring the aesthetic concept would be causally dependent on possessing the nonaesthetic concept. We need to keep the two concepts separate, but not *too* separate. A causal relation achieves this nicely. That there is *some* significant semantic gap at *some* level is plausible.[10] After all, we verify the two judgments in quite different ways. We would not strike a Ming vase with a hammer in order to find out whether or not it is delicate$_A$! We can hold that there is a semantic gap between thoughts

10. If we are talking about sadness$_A$ and delicacy$_A$, then the questions of footnote 7 do not arise. But if we are talking about sadness$_{NA}$ and delicacy$_{NA}$, then they do arise because the sadness$_{NA}$ and delicacy$_{NA}$ of music have the same conceptual connections as the sadness of a human being or delicacy of a Ming vase.

employing the concept of delicacy$_A$ and thoughts employing the concept of delicacy$_{NA}$, but we can preserve some connection between the two thoughts since we can hold that we could not have come to possess the concept of delicacy$_A$ unless we already possessed the concept of delicacy$_{NA}$. On a causal account, the two uses of the word "delicacy" would be separate, but not wholly unrelated.

There is clearly more to be said about the exact causal role that the non-aesthetic concept of delicacy$_{NA}$ might play in the acquisition of the aesthetic concept of delicacy$_A$. I shall say more about this below. So far, all I have done is to gesture in the causal direction. There are problems to be dealt with. Not any causal relation will do. But there is no reason to think that such a story is doomed to failure from the start. The availability of such a causal account enables the realist to evade the second horn of Scruton's dilemma.

2.3   It might be replied that when Scruton talks about metaphorical transference in his essay "Understanding Music," he is referring to a phenomenon at the level of *thought*, not just at the level of *talk*.[11] He claims that in our very experience of music, the same concepts are employed as in non-aesthetic contexts, only they are not used to ascribe properties. Metaphoricalness is said to infect how we *hear* music, not just what we *say* about it. So surely, his argument cannot be met as I have suggested.

This reply would not be to the point. Scruton's essay "Understanding Music" was written almost ten years after the book *Art and Imagination*; and his employment of the idea of metaphorical transference in the essay goes, in one respect, beyond what he wrote in the book, and in another respect not as far. In the book, we have the observation that there is a great deal of metaphorical description in aesthetics, plus an argument against realism based on that observation. In the essay, Scruton's account of musical understanding in terms of metaphorical transference is, in fact, a development of his brand of nonrealism about aesthetics. There is no longer an *argument* against realism to worry about.

2.4   Malcolm Budd, in his essay "Understanding Music," criticized Scruton's essay of the same name for moving from the "uncontroversial thesis" that "There is more to the perception of melody, rhythm and harmony in a succession of sounds than the perception of the succession of sounds" to the positive and "problematic thesis" of "metaphorical transference." Budd is correct to notice that this is an extra step, over which Scruton sometimes

11. Roger Scruton, "Understanding Music," in *The Aesthetic Understanding* (London: Carcanet, 1983).

slides. Budd then asserts a different nonrealist view of music when he says that "rhythm is a sensational, not a representational, property of the experience of a musical work."[12] Budd's view may be coherent (depending on exactly what is meant by a "sensational" property) and he may also be able to explain Scruton's uncontroversial thesis. But he provides as little positive argument for his "sensational" theory as Scruton does for his problematic thesis of metaphorical transference. Argument is needed by both Scruton and Budd because the uncontroversial thesis can also be explained on a realist account, since the representation of melody, rhythm, and harmony, in an experience, would be a different sort of representation from the representation of a succession of sounds (even though *what* they represented might be one and the same).[13] Both Scrunton's and Budd's essays are full of important insights, but neither gives aesthetic realism a decent run for its money.

2.5   There may be some aspects of Davidson's view of metaphor which are in tension with my suggestion that we should locate a difference of meaning at the level of thought, not talk. Davidson writes: "there is no limit to what a metaphor calls our attention, and *much* of what we are caused to notice is not propositional in character."[14] Davidson's example of someone who "mentions the beauty and deftness of a line in a Picasso etching" suggests that he thinks that what metaphorical *aesthetic* descriptions make us notice is *both* unlimited *and* nonpropositional. I agree with the former but not the latter. For if, as Davidson says, "Joke or dream or metaphor can, like a picture or a bump on the head, make us appreciate some fact,"[15] why not an aesthetic fact? Why should aesthetics not be one of the exceptional cases where what we notice *is* propositional in character? The same-meaning doctrine about words is one thing, the nonpropositional view of what we notice is another. The nonpropositional view may be correct in many cases, without being correct in aesthetics. (We can reject a nonpropositional view of what aesthetic metaphors cause us to notice, even though we might want to agree with Davidson that what they make us notice is *unlimited*. These ideas are separate.)

---

12. Malcolm Budd, "Understanding Music," *Aristotelian Society Supplementary Volume* 59 (1985): 241, 244.

13. Budd says that Scruton's uncontroversial thesis is sufficient to show that "melody, harmony and rhythm are not representational properties of musical experience" (ibid., p. 244).

14. Davidson, "What Metaphors Mean," p. 263, my emphasis.

15. Ibid., p. 262.

3 INEFFABLE AESTHETICS

3.1   No metaphor worth its salt admits of a literal paraphrase. This is no less true of aesthetic metaphors. The realist must claim that the content of the noticing which the metaphor causes cannot be stated without metaphor. For the properties that the metaphor draws our attention to cannot be described nonmetaphorically. It may be that what realizes that aesthetic property can be described in purely physical terms. But so long as we are giving an aesthetic description of the aesthetic properties of a thing, the use of metaphor is ineliminable; the metaphor is essential. This is what, parodying John Perry, we might call "the problem of the essential metaphor." Most metaphors are not essential in this way. Although ordinary metaphors cannot be paraphrased, the content of the noticing which they cause *can* be stated without metaphor. In this respect aesthetic metaphors differ from ordinary metaphors.

3.2   However, what we have said so far is not sufficient. We need a deeper diagnosis. We can see Scruton's argument as challenging us to *explain* the ineliminability of metaphorical description. Is it not mysterious to postulate forms of thought which are incapable of literal expression?

To relieve the difficulty, we need to notice that the issue that troubles us in aesthetics also looms large in the description of the phenomenology of inner experience. We are *driven* to use metaphor when we try to describe "what it's like" to be in certain qualitative mental states. Our use of metaphor in describing a pain as "stabbing" or "grinding" is ineliminable.[16] Beyond a certain point—simply describing the pain as "pain"—we cannot express our thought nonmetaphorically. We could invent further classifications of pain; we could artificially construct pain-types (pain$_1$, pain$_2$, and so on.). But there will always be a residue which is not literally describable. Metaphor is not ineliminable in the sense that the object or event which is a pain cannot be described without metaphor. A particular pain might be identical with a particular brain event, and we can describe *that* nonmetaphorically. But *properties* of the pain are another matter. The felt or phenomenological properties of pain are literally indescribable. They can only be described metaphorically. And the contents of our thoughts about pain cannot be linguistically expressed without metaphor. When we think of a particular pain, we can

16. See Russell Hoban's novel *Kleinzeit* (London: Jonathan Cape, 1974) for some superb, imaginatively metaphorical descriptions of pain. See also Elaine Scarry, *The Body in Pain* (Oxford: Oxford University Press, 1985).

think of its exact qualitative character directly, without the aid of metaphor. But the content of such a thought cannot be expressed in language without metaphor. Similarly, in trying to describe the smell of coffee, we run up against the limits of literal language. Thought, however, is not so bound. We can think of the smell of coffee without difficulty.

3.3   It is no accident that aesthetic descriptions and descriptions of the phenomenology of inner experience both manifest the same phenomenon of essential metaphoricalness. What both have in common is subjective grounds, in Kant's sense: such judgments are based on an inner response or feeling.[17] The aesthetic realist can appeal to the ineliminability of our use of metaphor in describing inner experience as a "companion in guilt." We can respond to Scruton's challenge to explain the ineliminability of aesthetic metaphorical descriptions by saying that it arises from the subjective nature of aesthetic judgment.[18] The reason that aesthetic descriptions of objects and events are essentially metaphorical is that descriptions of aesthetic *experience* are essentially metaphorical. And the reason that descriptions of aesthetic experience are essentially metaphorical is that, quite generally, descriptions of the phenomenology of inner experience are essentially metaphorical (beyond an initial classification as pain or pleasure or whatever). This is one reason why the same problem does not afflict moral philosophy; for moral judgments are not subjective in Kant's sense.[19]

Imagine a philosopher who began with the ineliminability of metaphor in the description of the phenomenology of inner experience and who then tried to mount an argument parallel to Scruton's against realism about the qualitative character of those experiences. We would not be impressed. The essentially metaphorical nature of our description of the phenomenology of inner experience does not supply the slightest encouragement for nonrealism about experience. When we think of the exact phenomenological quality of an experience, our thought can only be expressed metaphorically, but we are nonetheless thinking of a genuine property of experience. It is just that the content of such thought defies any literal expression. Similarly, it

17. Immanuel Kant, *Critique of Judgement*, trans. James Meredith (Oxford: Clarendon, 1928), pp. 41–42.

18. See chapter 2.

19. Another area where metaphor is essential and ineliminable is some parts of religion. The classic work on metaphor and religion is, of course, Moses Maimonides' great work *Guide for the Perplexed*, trans. M. Friedlander (New York: Dover, 1956). However, this is hardly an uncontroversial area to which the aesthetic realist can appeal. In addition, it would not be the existence of some supposed religious experience which would explain the ineliminability of religious metaphors.

may be that our thought about certain aesthetic properties, or our experience of them, can be linguistically expressed only by means of metaphor. But it might be that the properties which such metaphors cause us to notice are real and that the noticing has realistic aesthetic content. Thus, the essentially metaphorical nature of much aesthetic description does not endanger a realistic interpretation of aesthetic judgment and experience.[20]

This is mysticism, I admit. My view is that there are some aspects of the *world* which cannot be described without metaphor, for I think that the world has properties that are literally indescribable. And I think that *thoughts* about those properties cannot be linguistically expressed without metaphor. I am unrepentantly embracing the idea of thought content which outruns the possibility of direct literal expression in language.[21] The impossibility is one which derives from the nature of the properties; it does not spring from some contingent limitation of human beings which might one day be remedied.

3.4   This, then, is why aesthetic description is prone to be metaphorical. Given this diagnosis, Scruton's argument to antirealism can be blocked. There is another bonus. The diagnosis helps us to fill in a little more of the causal story of aesthetic concept acquisition.

Assuming the more general principle of the subjectivity of aesthetic judgment, it is plausible that if one judges that something is delicate$_A$, then it must have looked or sounded delicate$_A$. The concept of delicacy$_A$ must enter into the content of such experiences. And in order to have the experience of seeing or hearing its delicacy$_A$, one must possess the concepts of delicacy$_A$. Experiencing its delicacy$_A$ stands to the ascription of the property of delicacy$_A$, just as, according to Kant, disinterested pleasure stands to the judgment of beauty or taste. Now, according to the causal story, the concept of delicacy$_A$ must have its causal origin in the concept of delicacy$_{NA}$. The intermediate step between possessing the two concepts would be the acquisition of the notion that something *looks* or *sounds* delicate$_{NA}$. One can experience something *as* delicate$_{NA}$ without believing that it is. Something can look or sound delicate$_{NA}$ to us even though we know that it is not. Notice that while the judgment that something really is delicate$_{NA}$ is not a subjective judgment,

20. The fact that science sometimes employs metaphorical descriptions in no way compromises a realistic interpretation of scientific descriptions. I cannot see why George Lakoff and Mark Johnson think it does in their book *Metaphors We Live By* (Chicago: University of Chicago Press, 1981).

21. A certain confused linguistic behaviorism in the philosophy of mind would be one source of resistance to this idea.

the judgment that something looks or sounds delicate$_{NA}$ *is*. So the step from judgments of what looks or sounds delicate$_{NA}$ to the aesthetic judgment of delicacy$_A$ is not such a large one: we are stepping from one subjective judgment to another.

This is intended to be no more than a suggestion. The idea is that one could not come to possess the aesthetic concept unless one already possessed the nonaesthetic concept. Aesthetic concepts which cannot be linguistically expressed without metaphor have their causal origin in ordinary concepts which can be linguistically expressed without metaphor. But this is only to isolate a *necessary* causal condition of possessing certain aesthetic concepts. I have said nothing about sufficient conditions. For that we need to consider broader issues. Filling in more details of the causal story would require a general account of the psychology of aesthetic judgment. However, I have said enough to deal with one problem: possessing one concept may be causally dependent on possessing another where we feel no temptation to use the same word to express the two concepts. But we can see why it is natural to use the same word to pick out aesthetic and nonaesthetic concepts of delicacy: given the ineliminability of aesthetic metaphor, there is no other.

CODA

To sum up: the realist should initially meet Scruton's meaning-equivalence argument by retreating to a meaning-difference at the level of thought. The same word with the same conventional linguistic meaning serves to express quite different concepts. But this move needs to be supplemented by a plausible causal account of the connection between the possession of the two concepts. The realist should deny that what aesthetic metaphors cause us to notice is nonpropositional. For, according to the realist, the noticing has realistic aesthetic content, and what is noticed is a range of genuine aesthetic properties. And—digging a little deeper—the realist can explain why the use of metaphors in aesthetic description is ineliminable in terms of the essentially subjective nature of aesthetic judgment. This essential subjectivity poses no special difficulty for the realist. And it gives us some help with filling in the causal account of aesthetic concept acquisition. The aesthetic realist can cope with metaphorical aesthetic descriptions.

What we cannot say literally, we need not pass over in silence.

CHAPTER 11

Skin–Deep or in the Eye of the Beholder?

I shall consider the prospects for a certain kind of aesthetic realism in the light of a difficulty for realism about sensory properties. So I will be discussing three things: the metaphysics of aesthetic properties, the metaphysics of sensory properties, and their connection.

1 PHYSICALIST AESTHETIC REALISM

1.1 As I shall understand it here, aesthetic realism is a purely metaphysical doctrine concerning the contents of reality. The minimal claim of aesthetic realism is that there are mind-independent aesthetic facts or states of affairs—where a mind-independent aesthetic fact or state of affairs is a structured entity, consisting of an object or event which possesses a mind-independent aesthetic property. The object or event might be a natural one, such as a tree or a breaking wave. It might be a human artifact or act, such as a car, or a gesture. It might be a particular work of art, such as a sculpture. It might be a type work of art, such as Beethoven's Fifth Symphony. Or it might be an instance of a type work of art, such as a performance of Beethoven's Fifth Symphony. The aesthetic property possessed by such an object or event might be one of the following: aesthetic merit or demerit, beauty or ugliness, grace, elegance, daintiness, dumpiness, dynamism, balance or unity. I shall take these examples to be paradigmatic aesthetic properties, and I am going to assume that we have an account of the distinction between aesthetic and nonaesthetic properties.[1] And by mind-independence I shall mean that whether something possesses a property does not depend on whether we think it does. This is a rough formulation of mind-independence—for the time being—and I shall return to the idea later on.

Plainly, more needs to be said beyond the bare minimal statement that there are mind-independent aesthetic facts or states of affairs. Flesh needs to be put on the bare metaphysical bones. Most important, we need to know how aesthetic facts or states of affairs stand with respect to other sorts of facts or states of affairs.

I shall begin by making a case for the thesis that aesthetic realism ought to be physicalist in persuasion. It should take the form of an identity thesis, a realization thesis, or a constitution thesis. The claim would be that every aesthetic fact is identical with some physical fact, or that every instantiation of an aesthetic property is realized in or constituted by instantiations of physical properties. For example, we might say that a particular flower's beauty is *identical* with the physical arrangement of its petals, leaves and stem, or that the physical arrangement of its petals, leaves, and stem is the *realization* of its beauty, or that the arrangement *constitutes* its beauty. Let us call such a thesis "physicalist aesthetic realism."

An identity, realization, or constitution claim is, of course, compatible with claiming that aesthetic judgments differ in *meaning* from judgments about physical facts; so judgments about particular relations of identity, realization, or constitution between aesthetic and physical facts or properties are synthetic. Moreover it is plausible that there are no *reductions* or *type identities* because it seems that aesthetic properties can be *variably realized* in physical properties. And some will also say that there are no nomological relations of any kind between aesthetic and physical properties. Those who opt for realization or constitution rather than identity usually do so because they want to eschew reduction or nomological relations between the two kinds of properties.

Some aestheticians ask "What is . . . ?" questions. Other aestheticians thought it better to ask "When is . . . ?" questions. But perhaps we can also ask "Where is . . . ?" ones. We can ask the question: *Where* is beauty? And the physicalist realist's answer is that beauty is part of the physical world. Beauty is where the physical facts are. Heraclitus may not be so far from this position when he writes:

The fairest universe is but a dust-heap piled up at random.[2]

---

1. See chapter 2.
2. Heraclitus, D.K. 124.

What look like opposites—a fair universe and random dust—are in fact one and the same! Beauty, says Heraclitus, just *is* the random arrangement of matter. But not every physical property of a thing is relevant to its aesthetic properties. Only its surface physical properties are relevant. For example, whether a sculpture is hollow or solid makes no difference to its beauty. Beauty resides in the skin of things. It is skin-deep.

This is one kind of aesthetic realist view. There are other rival forms of aesthetic realism. An aesthetic *dualist* denies that there are identity, realization, or constitution relations between aesthetic and physical properties. On such a view, aesthetic properties are mind-independent but also completely independent of physical properties. Another view, which is currently popular, is that aesthetic properties are *response-dependent*—they are dispositions to produce a certain sort of reaction in human beings of a certain sort under certain circumstances.[3] This view sometimes gets classified as realist and sometimes not. I shall return to dualist and response-dependent accounts in due course. But for the moment I want to retain the focus on physicalist aesthetic realism.

1.2   Before we turn to consider a problem that arises for physicalist aesthetic realism, we should appreciate the motivation for holding this view. I shall first look at the motivation for believing *some* form of aesthetic realism, and then for believing physicalist aesthetic realism in particular.

The motivation for believing some form of aesthetic realism is that it is the theory best placed to make sense of ordinary aesthetic *thought*. Aesthetic realism itself is a purely metaphysical doctrine. However, when we come to think of reasons for believing it, we must turn to consider our aesthetic thought. But then, in the search for a philosophical understanding of aesthetic thought, we are inescapably led to consider the metaphysics which is built into it. We are led from the world to the mind, and from there we are led back to the world. What—in the world—are we committed to in thinking aesthetically?

There are certain features of our aesthetic judgments and experience that look as if they can only be explained if aesthetic judgments and experiences represent a realm of mind-independent aesthetic facts or states of affairs. Let us call this a "realistic view" of aesthetic thought. Such a view contrasts with a nonrealist view. A nonrealist view might assign a more expressive or emotive

---

3. See for example, Alan Goldman, *Aesthetic Value* (Boulder, Colo.: Westview, 1995).
4. For an example of the first kind of nonrealist theory, see Hume's "Of the Standard of Taste," in *Essays, Moral, Political, Literary*, ed. Eugene Miller (Indianapolis: LibertyClassics, 1985). For an example of the second, see Roger Scruton, *Art and Imagination* (London: Methuen, 1974).

function to aesthetic judgments, or it might appeal to our capacity to experience one thing *as* another.[4] There are a variety of possible nonrealist views. We need not dwell on them extensively here, since we are concerned with the prospects for realism. But let us briefly note the features of aesthetic thought that encourage realism.

Most prominently, there is the *notion of truth or correctness* that we wield in ordinary aesthetic judgments. In an aesthetic judgment, we think of an object or event as an instance of an aesthetic kind. For example, we judge that the Alhambra of Granada is beautiful or that it is elegant. And it is part of what is involved in making aesthetic judgments that we think that many of them are true or correct, while others are false or incorrect. In a large range of cases, we think that an aesthetic judgment and its opposite cannot both be true or correct. We think that our judgments can be false or in error. When we judge that the Alhambra palace is beautiful, we are committed to denying the truth or correctness of the judgment that it is ugly or mediocre. In *some* cases, we may think that the truth or correctness of aesthetic judgments is indeterminate; but in a significant range of cases, such as that of the Alhambra, we think that there is a truth of the matter or that there is a correct judgment. Of course, there are often considerable aesthetic disagreements between people, and perhaps between cultures. But that only serves to reiterate the point; for disagreement makes no sense unless we presuppose an idea of truth or correctness in judgment. Otherwise there is nothing that the disputants are disputing. There is nothing to which their judgments are aspiring.[5]

Assuming that an error theory is beyond the pale, and we do not think that our aesthetic thought is irrevocably diseased, the task for the aesthetician is to explain how such normative aspirations are possible. And realism about aesthetic thought obviously does well here. For, on this view, true or correct aesthetic judgments are true or correct *in virtue of* the aesthetic facts that they represent, and they are false or incorrect when they fail to represent the aesthetic facts as they are. Aesthetic realism is necessarily allied with such a realistic view of aesthetic thought. Realism does well with the idea that there is a truth of the matter or correctness in judgment. This is not to say that no

5. See Nick Zangwill, "Moral Mind-Dependence," *Australian Journal of Philosophy*, vol. 72 (1994). Note that if a nonrealist appeals to the need for our judgments to be consistent with one another, this consistency ("coherence") would not supply the notion of correctness we need, because consistency between judgments is compatible with the incorrectness or falsity of those judgments. Incorrect judgments might cohere snugly with other incorrect judgments. Consistency is one sort of normative constraint on our judgments, correctness or truth is another. Only the Kantian moral theorist thinks that they amount to the same thing.

other theory can account for it. It *may* be that some variety of nonrealism can succeed in acquiring the right to the normativity of aesthetic judgment. The issue is controversial.[6] But it is unlikely that a nonrealist account will be able to explain normativity as *easily* as realism. For without the world as that in virtue of which aesthetic judgments can succeed or fall short, what other source of normativity could there be? We should think of aesthetic judgments as we think of judgments of the niceness and nastiness of food and drink, where we do not think that there is a right and a wrong in judgment.

1.3   The foregoing gives us a motive for believing aesthetic realism, but not yet for believing *physicalist* aesthetic realism. The ways of thinking that encourage physicalist aesthetic realism in particular are the ways in which we ordinarily conceive of aesthetic properties as *causally and spatiotemporally endowed*. Consider the following examples of the way we speak and think of aesthetic properties as standing in causal relations. The physical structure of seeds is causally efficacious in bringing about the beauty of the flowers that grow from them. Treading on flowers, on the other hand, destroys their beauty. The beauty and elegance of a work of art is brought about by the artist who creates it.[7] The beauty of flowers and works of art cause people to dwell when gazing at them.[8] These are commonsense, nonphilosophical, "Clapham-omnibus" thoughts about beauty. It is true that it is less easy to think of examples where aesthetic properties are themselves causally potent with respect to something other than human reactions.[9] But still, instantiations of aesthetic properties seem to be effects and they seem to cause aesthetic reactions in human beings, and that is a considerable causal role. These commonsense causal explanations, which invoke aesthetic properties, contrast in an interesting way with the following example. There *appears* to be a direct causal relation between the beauty of parents and the beauty of their children, but in fact there is *no* such direct causal relation since both have a genetic common cause. So in this case there is no direct causal link between the aesthetic properties, contrary to appearances.[10] But not all

6. The most famous and probably still the most impressive nonrealist attempt to capture normativity for an aesthetic nonrealist is Hume's essay "Of the Standard of Taste." For discussion see chapter 9.

7. See Nick Zangwill, "The Creative Theory of Art," *American Philosophical Quarterly* 32 (1995).

8. See Kant, *Critique of Judgement*, trans. James Meredith (Oxford: Oxford University Press, 1928), section 12.

9. Apparently listening to classical music helps people to concentrate on repetitive tasks. But the music may not have this effect in virtue of its aesthetic properties.

10. The example comes from Gabriel Segal and Elliot Sober, "The Causal Efficacy of Content," *Philosophical Studies*, vol. 63 (1991).

putative cases of aesthetic/nonaesthetic causal interaction are illusory in this way.

The existence of aesthetic/nonaesthetic causal relations makes physicalist aesthetic realism attractive. For, according to the physicalist realist, physical-aesthetic causal relations are underpinned by purely physical causal relations. Beauty would *be* physical, on another level of description, or else it would be *realized* in or *constituted* by physical states of affairs. However, the identity, realization, or constitution relations cannot capture the causal role of aesthetic properties for the physicalist aesthetic realist, unless these relations bring *strong supervenience* with them. Strong supervenience is the idea that if something has an aesthetic property then it has some nonaesthetic property that *determines* the aesthetic property.[11] But not all conceptions of realization and constitution involve a commitment to strong supervenience, and the appeal to identity usually does not. The claim of strong supervenience must be added to or presupposed by claims of identity, realization, or constitution in order to make good the causal role of aesthetic properties, if they are physicalistically construed. For example, the structure of a seed causally explains the beauty of the flowers that grow from it, only because (a) the seed contains a mechanism by which a certain physical arrangement of petals, leaves, and stem is causally necessitated, and (b) that physical arrangement of petals, leaves, and stem metaphysically determines the property of beauty. A physical state of affairs can only be the cause of an aesthetic state of affairs if the first physical states of affairs causes a second physical state of affairs, and the second physical state of affairs determines the aesthetic state of affairs.[12] The physicalist aesthetic realist must be committed to strong supervenience in order to be able to explain how the instantiation of the property of beauty can stand in causal relations. Some philosophers have argued that strong supervenience is not *sufficient* to explain the causal efficacy of upper-level properties, but it is uncontroversial that, for a realist about the upper-level properties, strong supervenience is *necessary* for causal efficacy. Without strong supervenience, efficacy is lost.[13]

Moreover strong aesthetic supervenience is intuitively plausible inde-

11. See Jaegwon Kim, "Concepts of Supervenience," in *Supervenience and Mind* (Cambridge: Cambridge University Press, 1993). Jerrold Levinson argues against strong aesthetic supervenience in "Aesthetic Supervenience," in *Music, Art and Metaphysics* (Ithaca, N.Y.: Cornell University Press, 1990). His argument turns on what I shall later call a "nonrigid response-dependent" view of aesthetic properties. See section 4 below, especially note 44.

12. See Jaegwon Kim, "Epiphenomenal and Supervenient Causation," in *Supervenience and Mind*.

13. See Nick Zangwill, "Good Old Supervenience: Mental Causation on the Cheap," *Synthese*, vol. 106 (1996).

pendently of the issue of causal efficacy. We have modal intuitions that support the thesis of strong supervenience. For example, Wittgenstein wrote:

Imagine this butterfly exactly as it is but not beautiful.[14]

Wittgenstein is not asking us to imagine another butterfly, but this one; and he is not asking us to imagine this butterfly at a later time, but this butterfly, exactly as it is now. He is rhetorically asking us to consider what is possible for that very thing as it is now. And the force of the rhetorical question is that we should recognize limits on what is possible. Ordinary aesthetic thought entangles us in such modal commitments.[15]

The causal efficacy of aesthetic properties is not all that common sense endorses. We also endow beauty with spatial location. We might say that Virginia is more beautiful than North Carolina; there is more beauty in the one state than in the other. In addition, we think of beauty as being created and destroyed in time: things come to be beautiful and cease to be beautiful. Shakespeare's second sonnet nicely illustrates these points:

> When forty winters shall beseige thy brow,
> And dig deep trenches in thy beauty's field,
> Thy youth's proud livery, so gazed on now,
> Will be a tatter'd weed, of small worth held:
> Then being ask'd where all thy beauty lies,
> Where all the treasure of thy lusty days,
> To say, within thine own deep-sunken eyes,
> Were an all-eating shame and thriftless praise.
> How much more praise deserved thy beauty's use,
> If thou couldst answer "This fair child of mine
> Shall sum my count and make my old excuse,"
> Proving his beauty by succession thine!
> > This were to be new made when thou art old,
> > And see thy blood warm when thou feel'st it cold.

Here we see a commitment to the causal efficacy and spatiotemporality of beauty. And it is this that physicalist realism is in an excellent position to capture.[16]

14. Ludwig Wittgenstein, *Zettel* (Berkeley: University of California Press, 1970), section 199.
15. See Frank Sibley, "Aesthetic/Nonaesthetic," *Philosophical Review*, vol. 74 (1965).
16. In my view, moral realism should also maintain that a realization or constitution relation holds between moral and mental properties. However, whether that would amount to *physicalist* moral realism would depend on the truth about instantiations of mental properties.

1.4   It is often argued that there can be aesthetic differences between works of art which are physically indistinguishable.[17] The history of production of a work might make a difference to its aesthetic properties. And that history of production involves the artist's intentions. If so, the intrinsic physical properties of a work of art are not sufficient for its aesthetic properties. However, what this means is not that we should abandon aesthetic/physical supervenience, but that we must broaden the supervenience base of aesthetic properties in such cases. (The same goes for the relations of identity, constitution, and realization if the physicalist aesthetic realist works with those notions.) This point is not relevant to the aesthetic properties of *natural* objects and events, but it is relevant to the aesthetic properties of works of art that have a representational or contextual point. For example, a work of art might represent Napoleon or make reference to other works of art. In those cases, at least part of what gives a work of art a representational or contextual meaning is the artist's intention. If we include the artist's intention in the broad supervenience base of aesthetic properties, the metaphysics of aesthetic properties will turn in part on the metaphysics of intentions. The aesthetic properties of *uncontextual* and *abstract* works, if there are any, would be *narrowly* supervenient, like the aesthetic properties of natural objects and events. But the aesthetic properties of representational or contextual works would be *broadly* supervenient. (And again, the nonaesthetic terms of the identity, constitution, or realization relations might be narrow or broad.) This means that if one happened to be a psychophysical dualist, one would also be a *partial* aesthetic dualist, since one would be dualist about the aesthetic properties of representational and contextual works. That would be because one thinks that part of what aesthetic properties supervenes on (is identical with, is constituted by or realized in) is nonphysical. But if psychophysical materialism is true, the metaphysics of the aesthetic properties of representational or contextual works would be entirely physical, and thus in line with the metaphysics of the aesthetic properties of uncontextual abstract works and of natural objects and events. In this chapter, I shall, for simplicity, assume some kind of materialism about mental states.

1.5   The metaphysical advantages of physicalist aesthetic realism are clear: unlike aesthetic dualism, we are not stuck with a queer metaphysics, since aesthetic facts or states of affairs are part of the ordinary physical

17. See Kendall Walton, "Categories of Art," *Philosophical Review*, vol. 79 (1970). I critically discuss this essay in chapter 5.

world. Physicalist aesthetic realism is metaphysically economical. It is not problematic, like dualism, on the ground that it postulates something transcending the physical. On the other hand, we certainly need positive reasons for believing physicalist aesthetic realism. The fact that it is not metaphysically problematic is not enough. Response-dependent views are also unproblematic on metaphysical grounds. Moreover, they might be able to capture the normative dimension of aesthetic thought and also the causal role and spatiotemporality of aesthetic properties. So we need some reason to rate physicalist aesthetic realism above response-dependent views. For the time being, however, I want just to focus on physicalist aesthetic realism, and raise a problem for it. I shall address response-dependent views of aesthetic properties in section 4.

2 AESTHETIC/SENSORY DEPENDENCE

2.1   One would expect moral and aesthetic realism to run in tandem. Indeed, most considerations for or against realism apply equally in both areas. But this may not be universally true. There may be some purely metaphysical problems that only afflict aesthetic value. The present problem is one such.[18]

We need two premises to generate the problem. The first is a certain *weak sensory dependence* premise:

> Aesthetic properties depend in part on sensory properties, such as colors and sounds.

Just as something has moral properties only if it has mental ones, and many think that something has mental properties only if it has physical or functional ones, so something has aesthetic properties only if it has sensory properties.

When we think of certain paradigm cases, the thesis seems plausible. For example, it is obvious that a painting would not be beautiful without a certain spatial arrangement of colors; and a performance of a piece of music would not be delicate without a certain temporal arrangement of sounds.

However, this weak aesthetic/sensory dependence thesis faces difficulties

---

18. I dealt with another problem faced only by aesthetic realism in the previous chapter. There is also a purely metaphysical problem, which has no parallel in moral philosophy, about the apparently unexplainable *quantity* of natural beauty. Kant is the only philosopher I know of who has raised this issue.

posed by certain problematic cases: the spatial properties of architecture and sculpture, the representational and symbolic properties of paintings, and the narrative properties of works of literature. In these cases, there seem to be aesthetic properties which are dependent not on sensory properties but on properties of other kinds. In spite of this initial appearance, I think that these cases can be tamed: their aesthetic properties do after all depend on sensory properties. I argued for this thesis at length earlier in this book.[19] In outline, the strategy is to maintain a dilemma: for some cases, such as architecture, sculpture, and representational paintings, although it is true that other properties besides the sensory properties are aesthetically important, in all such cases some sensory manifestation is crucial. That is, in these cases, although sensory properties do not *suffice* for the instantiation of the aesthetic properties, they are *necessary* for their instantiation. However, in other cases, such as the symbolic properties of paintings and narrative properties of works of literature, the properties we value are not *aesthetic* properties. If the dilemma holds, we can maintain the thesis that aesthetic properties always depend on sensory properties, despite the apparently problematic cases. I shall assume this in what follows.

The thesis is not that a painting is beautiful *only* because of a certain spatial arrangement of colors, or that a performance of a piece of music is delicate *only* because of a certain temporal arrangement of sounds. The thesis is not the *strong* dependence thesis that the aesthetic properties of a thing depend *entirely* on its sensory properties. The thesis is that sensory properties are *necessary* for aesthetic properties, but they may not be *sufficient*. Accepting a weak dependence thesis is compatible with admitting that other factors are also important.

2.2   Given the weak dependence premise, if we are to pursue a realist theory, the beauty of a particular painting must, at least in part, be identical with, realized in, or constituted by the spatial arrangement of colors, and the delicacy of a performance of a piece of music must, at least in part, be identical with, realized in, or constituted by a temporal arrangement of sounds. More may be involved. But sensory properties are necessary. No sensory properties, no aesthetic properties.

Why does the metaphysical dependence of aesthetic on sensory properties create a problem for aesthetic realism? Surely all the realist now needs to do is to change tack slightly and say that the aesthetic facts are identical with or realized in or constituted by sensory property facts. For example, a realist might

19. See chapter 8.

say that the beauty of music *is* sound—even though what we *hear* when we hear sound as beautiful is not the same as what we hear when we hear sound as mere sound. The realist can say that the beauty of music is where the sounds are, or perhaps that its beauty is realized in or constituted by sounds. A nonrealist, by contrast, says that, really, there is only sound—the rest is something projected onto it by us.

The problem is: where is sound? What is the right metaphysics of sound?

In both morality and aesthetics, the moral and aesthetic qualities of things cannot be more real than that to which they attach. This is a question of the structural interrelation between different realist theses. In general, if F realism depends on G realism because F facts or states of affairs are identical with, realized in or constituted by G facts or states of affairs, then G nonrealism entails F nonrealism, and we cannot be an F realist as well as a G nonrealist. For example, moral realism is in jeopardy if nonrealism about mental states is true. Similarly, aesthetic realism is in jeopardy if nonrealism about sensory properties is true. The asymmetry between morality and aesthetics is that what aesthetic properties depend on is less secure than what moral properties depend on. We are far more inclined to nonrealism about sensory properties than about mental states. There is considerable pressure to think that minds are part of the world—especially one's own mind! But there is a familiar tradition, dating back to Democritus, according to which sensory properties are not part of the world in the way that other qualities are.

3   THE METAPHYSICS OF SENSORY PROPERTIES

3.1   A *secondary quality* (the older term for a response-dependent property) is, roughly speaking, a property which depends on the experiences of normal humans beings under normal conditions; a *primary quality*, by contrast, is, roughly speaking, one that does not depend on the experiences of normal humans beings under normal conditions. Everyone should agree that there is a significant difference between primary and secondary qualities. The difference is purely stipulative.[20] What is controversial is the assignment of certain sorts of properties to one class or the other. Many philosophers think that sensory properties, such as colors, sounds, taste, and smells, are paradigm examples of secondary qualities and that physical properties are paradigm example of primary qualities. Colors, sounds, tastes, and smells are all secondary qualities, it is said, because they depend on the specific character

20. See Colin McGinn, *The Subjective View* (Oxford: Clarendon, 1983), p. 5.

of the sensory experiences of normal human beings in normal circumstances. What it is to be red, loud, sweet, or pungent depends on what it is for normal human beings to experience them as red, round, sweet, or pungent in normal conditions. Sensory properties are not intrinsic features of things as they are in themselves. What it is to be red, loud, sweet, or pungent is a relational matter. Sensory qualities are not part of the "objective" world—a world that is left over when we subtract human beings.

Beyond this, secondary quality views of sensory properties vary. Some add an actuality operator, so that sensory properties depend on the *actual* experiences and circumstances of normal human beings. That yields a *rigid* theory, which affects certain counterfactuals.[21] More on this later. But all such views accept that being red and looking red are essentially connected. Primary qualities, on the other hand, are independent of the idiosyncrasies of human beings; they are what is there anyway, independently of us. Being square and looking square are not essentially connected. And primary qualities are not tied to a specific sensory modality. It is this independence from our sensory idiosyncrasies which makes such properties the apt object of scientific investigation.

It may also be true that being square disposes something to look square (to normal people in normal circumstances). But the question is not whether some dispositional statement concerning colors or shapes is *true* but whether the dispositional statement captures the *essence* of the property. There is some plausibility in the idea that we can cash this out as a distinction between whether the dispositional statements are necessarily or contingently true. But perhaps we could even admit that the dispositional statements are necessarily true without capturing the essence of the property. As Kit Fine has pointed out, if Socrates exists then so do necessary existents, such as mathematical objects; but those necessarily existing mathematical objects are not part of Socrates' essence.[22] Similarly, perhaps dispositional statements about a property can be necessarily true without capturing its essence. For example, physical properties might yield certain necessarily true dispositional statements with respect to human experiences even though those necessarily true statements do not capture the essence of the properties. Instead those necessary truths might be *consequential* on the physical properties being the properties they are in certain circumstances. But similar dispositional statements *are* supposed to capture the essence of properties such as colors and

---

21. See Martin Davies and Lloyd Humberstone, "Two Notions of Necessity," *Philosophical Studies*, vol. 38 (1980).
22. Kit Fine, "Essence and Modality," *Philosophical Perspectives*, vol. 8 (1994).

sounds. However, if the dispositions only hold contingently in the physical case, then the distinction between the two kinds of properties would be easier to make out.

The issues surrounding primary and secondary qualities are first and foremost issues about *properties*, and not directly about *concepts* or *beliefs* which might pick out those properties. It is sometimes said that we can know a priori that the dispositions hold for secondary qualities or response-dependent properties and we cannot know a priori that the dispositions hold for primary qualities or non-response-dependent properties.[23] But this is a further claim about our *knowledge* of the dispositions, or about the *semantics* of disposition terms. The distinction itself is primarily a *metaphysical* one. But it might also be the case that our concepts of color or sound have the relevant metaphysical wisdom built into them.

3.2   At first sight, the secondary quality view of sensory properties seems to be opposed to the primary quality view of Jack Smart and David Armstrong.[24] On that view, color properties are identical with or realized in or constituted by physical properties of the surface of objects or properties of light. And there is no essential connection between those properties and experiences. Smart and Armstrong deny that colors and sounds are secondary qualities in the sense stipulated. They could happily admit that *other* properties are secondary properties—such as the comfortableness of chairs.[25]

The Smart/Armstrong view is realistic in a strong sense: color properties are independent of the experiences of human beings. Sometimes these theorists add the epistemic or semantic thesis that sensory experiences serve to "fix the reference" of color terms and concepts. But the epistemic or semantic claim that experiences fix the reference of color terms and concepts can figure in both realist and secondary quality theories.

However, the opposition between realist and response-dependent theories may not be clear-cut. Recall the distinction between rigid and nonrigid response-dependent theories. On a rigid view, sensory properties are said to be dispositions to provoke experiences in organisms of the sort that we *actually* are *now*. This allows that a thing has such dispositions solely in virtue of its actual intrinsic properties plus the laws. The idea would be that something

23. See Jim Edwards, "Secondary Qualities and the A Priori," *Mind*, vol. 99 (1992).

24. Jack Smart, *Philosophy and Scientific Realism* (London: Routledge, 1963); David Armstrong, *A Materialist Theory of Mind* (London: Routledge, 1968). See also their essays reprinted in *Readings on Color*, vol. 1, ed. Alex Byrne and David Hilbert (Cambridge: MIT Press, 1997).

25. This is Brian O'Shaunessey's nice example. See his "Secondary Qualities," *Pacific Philosophical Quarterly* 67 (1986): 156.

has a sensory property if and only if it has some intrinsic physical property which, given the laws, determines that it has a disposition to provoke certain experiences in normal people under normal circumstances.[26] So such rigid theories are *not* committed to the counterfactual "if we had different reactions then things would have different sensory properties." By contrast, on a nonrigid view, sensory properties hold partly in virtue of our actual reactions. So such a view *is* committed to that counterfactual.[27]

There is a general distinction between *intrinsic* and *extrinsic* dispositions. Compare the disposition of an iron key to melt at 500°C with its power to open a particular door. The disposition to melt at 500°C is determined just by the key's intrinsic molecular structure plus the laws, whereas the disposition of the key to open a lock is determined by the intrinsic properties of the key plus the laws *plus* what the lock is like. One disposition is intrinsic and the other is extrinsic. This is connected with a modal difference. It is necessary that the key has a disposition to melt at 500°C, given that it is made of iron and that it has a certain shape, but it is not necessary that the key has a disposition to open the door, given that it is made of iron and that it has that shape. The key with those intrinsic properties could easily have lacked that door-opening disposition, but it could not easily have lacked its disposition to melt at 500°C. Either it would have to be made of something different or else the laws would have to be different. The intrinsic dispositions of a thing do not depend on how it is with any contingent thing distinct from it.[28]

For a rigid response-dependence theorist, the disposition to provoke responses is an intrinsic disposition, whereas for a nonrigid theorist it is an extrinsic disposition. Rigid response-dependence theories allow that the disposition is determined by the intrinsic properties of the thing in question plus the laws, and it does not vary with varying responses. Nonrigid response-dependent theories, by contrast, deny that the disposition is determined solely by the intrinsic properties of a thing plus the laws, and they allow that if our responses were to vary then the colors or sounds would vary.

On the face of it, and in principle, the rigid response-dependent theory is compatible with the Smart/Armstrong theory, at least about purely metaphysical issues—though the two theories may diverge over epistemological

---

26. See Frank Jackson and Robert Pargetter, "An Objectivist's Guide to Subjectivism about Color," in *Readings on Color*, ed. Byrne and Hilbert.

27. See further Peter Vallentyne, "Response-dependence, Rigidification, and Objectivity," *Erkenntnis*, vol. 44 (1996).

28. On all these issues, see Sydney Shoemaker's classic "Causality and Properties," in *Identity, Cause and Mind* (Cambridge: Cambridge University Press, 1984); see also his more recent "Causal and Metaphysical Necessity," *Pacific Philosophical Quarterly*, vol. 79 (1998).

or semantic issues. Perhaps they disagree over whether there is an a priori reference-fixing relation between our experiences and the colors. But the metaphysics seems to be the same.[29]

By a "secondary quality" view in what follows I shall just mean a nonrigid response-dependent view. Secondary qualities are by definition mind-dependent properties.

Two other metaphysical options that we should have on the table before we proceed are *projectivism* about color, according to which judgments of color are noncognitive and there are no color properties, and *illusionism*, according to which we conceive of color properties as mind-independent but in fact there are no such properties. (The latter is an error theory, like John Mackie's view of ethics.)[30] On the illusionist view, our sensory judgments are cognitive, but we are subject to a metaphysical error since there are no properties of the sort that are represented in our experiences and judgments. The projectivist option is not at all plausible and no one really holds it. But the illusionist position has considerable plausibility and has able defenders.[31]

3.3   How, then, can we *argue* for the secondary quality (nonrigid) view of sensory qualities, or at least against the Smart/Armstrong and rigid response-dependent views? This topic has had much attention, and I cannot hope to give the matter the discussion that it requires. But I shall employ one very simple and familiar argument. (Margaret Wilson reconstructs Berkeley as maintaining this argument.[32] And Colin McGinn deploys it.[33])

It is an argument from possible divergence, based of two claims. The first point is that it is possible for there to be Martians (the philosopher's favorite pets!) with completely different perceptual mechanisms from ours, such that when they perceive what we perceive, they have qualitatively different but equally fine-grained color experiences. Perhaps their experiences are inverted relative to ours so that their experience of London buses is qualitatively similar to our experience of grass. Since they have different *experiences*, they would also apply their color *concepts* differently and make different color *judgments* from those that we make. What they ascribe when they look at

29. One way to resist this would be to say, following Fine, that there is a necessary connection between the intrinsic physical properties and the rigid disposition to provoke responses, but there is no essential connection between them.

30. John Mackie, *Ethics* (Harmondsworth, England: Penguin, 1977).

31. See the two essays by Paul Boghosian and David Velleman in *Readings on Color*, ed. Byrne and Hilbert.

32. Margaret Wilson, "Berkeley on the Mind-Dependence of Color," in *Mechanism and Ideas* (Princeton: Princeton University Press, 1999).

33. Colin McGinn, *The Subjective View*, pp. 9–11, 119–21.

grass is what we ascribe when we look at London buses. And what they ascribe when they look at London buses is not the same as what we ascribe when we look at London buses.[34] For those with residual verificationist worries about the intelligibility of such possible *inter*subjective color-experi-ence divergence, we can note, with Bill Lycan, that the intuition in favor of this possibility can be reinforced by reflection on the cases of possible *intra*-subjective color-experience divergence, where one's own color experience diverges over time.[35] Moreover, the possibility of divergence is supported by what we know of the physiology and psychology of vision.[36] The point here is merely that this divergence is possible; and I want to emphasize that the point is not that this is possible while the physical or functional states of per-ceivers do not vary. That is a different matter, and it is relevant to a quite dif-ferent debate.

The second claim, to add to the possibility claim, is a normative point. Let us now ask: Would we think that Martians are in *error* to apply their color concepts as they do, if we were fully aware of their situation? I think not. If the Martians experience London buses as green and grass as red, and so judge that London buses are green and that grass is red, we would surely not con-demn them as *mistaken* about their true color.[37] Their experiences are not nonveridical and their judgments are not incorrect or false. We would be *tol-erant* in our judgments about sensory qualities in a way that we are not in our judgments about physical properties.

There is a question about whether the norm of tolerance is built into our concept of color. In the divergence scenario, the concept dictates either tol-erance, intolerance, or neither. If tolerance is built into our concept, then the concept allows that both of the apparently conflicting judgments can be cor-rect or true. Or perhaps our concept of color dictates *in*tolerance but we are led to reject those dictates for independent reasons; so the normative aspira-tions of our color concepts should be rejected. Or it might be that our con-cept dictates neither tolerance nor intolerance, but that we have acquired beliefs about color which license tolerance.

Whichever of the three options we take concerning the locus of tolerance,

---

34. Wilson puts Berkeley's perceptual variability point like this: "the sensible appearances of things alter according to the condition or circumstances of the perceiver" (*Mechanism and Ideas*, p. 232).

35. See William Lycan, "Form, Function and Feel," *Journal of Philosophy*, vol. 78 (1981).

36. See the readings in *Readings on Color*, vol. 2, ed. Alex Byrne and David Hilbert (Cambridge: MIT Press, 1997).

37. Hume writes: "According to the disposition of the organs, the same object may be both sweet and bitter" ("Of the Standard of Taste," p. 278.)

our tolerance in divergent cases rules out sensory quality realism of the Smart/Armstrong sort. *For a real property cannot both attach to a thing and not attach to it.* If redness is a real mind-independent property, London buses cannot be both red and not red. If redness were a real mind-independent property, we would have to be intolerant and condemn the Martians as mistaken. But we surely would not. Moreover, were we to do so, it would be very odd since there is an exact symmetry between our situation and theirs. They could, with as much justice, take the same attitude to us. Call this the "symmetry" point.

The possibility of divergence, by itself, is compatible with a realist view if such divergence were taken to be between veridical and nonveridical perceptions. We need the normative claim to rule this out. First we accept the actuality or possibility of perceivers in different conditions with systematically different experiences of the same things. And then we see that there is no basis for asserting that we are right and that they are wrong in color ascriptions. That would be baseless arrogance, since our situation with respect to them is exactly parallel to their situation with respect to us. So it is not just that we would be tolerant but that we *should* be, for intolerance could have no basis.

Therefore redness is not a mind-independent property of objects and the Smart/Armstrong view is incorrect.[38]

3.4   The reply might be that we should be *externalist* about the content of sensory experiences. According to such a view, the content of both our experiences and those of the Martians is determined by the objective properties of the world that are causally responsible for the experiences. It would follow that we cannot, after all, suppose that the content of the Martian's sensory experiences—and thus the content of their judgments of sensory properties—are radically different from ours. Accepting such an externalist account of the content of color experiences would involve turning our back on a secondary quality account, which is the idea that some properties are determined not just (externally) by the world but also (internally) by the specific mode of our experience of it. However, the purely externalist view seems unintuitive, since it runs up against our firm intuition that Martians and earthlings might have different color experiences of the same physical world. Furthermore, what we know of the physiology and psychology of vision supports this. On a secondary quality view, we can map the Martians' concepts onto ours, so that their concept of that which has the disposition to provoke experiences qualitatively resembling their experience of London

38. As Hume says, once again: "color [is] a phantasm of the senses" (ibid., p. 281.)

buses is the same concept as our concept of that which has the disposition to provoke experiences qualitatively resembling our experience of grass. A purely externalist account cannot allow this. The secondary quality account allows that the Martians apply and withhold the same concepts in systematically different cases from us. And the secondary quality account allows for our toleration of divergence in color judgment.

The realist would have to reply that Martians don't see *colors* at all. We see colors; *they* may have perceptual experiences, but not of color. They don't see the color properties that our experiences reveal to us. The question that this view raises is: What exactly is the similarity between our experience of grass and their experience of London buses? The externalist/realist must deny that there is any similarity. But that is desperate and implausible. For even the externalist/realist grants some such similarities when they think that *some* perceptions of color can be nonveridical. They agree that color-blind or jaundice-ridden people have misleading perceptions, and that when they have misleading perceptions, their experience is like our experience of other things. But once *that* is granted, there can be no ban on the idea that a quite differently constructed creature might have experiences like our experiences but of different things. If a creature can diverge from us some of the time then it can diverge from us most of the time. There is of course a possible extremist position that is not vulnerable to this objection. The extremist says that colors are *always* exactly as they appear to be. So there is no room at all for error. I take it that this position is independently implausible because it violates the commonsense norms that we deploy in our color judgments. But the moderate externalist position, which allows nonveridical experiences but not radically divergent experiences, is unstable. For if nonveridical experiences are allowed, there can no longer be an objection in principle to the idea that another perceiver might have systematically different experiences from those that I have.

So the appeal to externalism does not derail the argument from our tolerance of divergent judgments.

3.5   It is less clear what positive view can be gleaned from our tolerance of divergence. One conclusion would be that sensory properties are secondary qualities and we conceive of them as such. But we might equally be led to illusionism if intolerance of divergence is included in our concept of color.

It tends to be assumed that once we make the rigid/nonrigid distinction, it is obvious that we must say that colors and sounds are rigidly response-dependent. It is assumed that rigid versions of response-dependent theories are preferable. But this is by no means obvious. It depends on whether we want a theory that fits with a norm of tolerance in judgments of sensory properties.[39] Tolerance in the face of systematically divergent judgments fits best with nonrigid response-dependent theories, assuming that we have to have some response-dependent theory. Intolerance in divergent cases would favor a rigid theory. But in fact, we are tolerant, and that favors the non-rigid theory over the rigid theory—although illusionism can also be happy with tolerance.[40] We can conclude that either sensory properties are mind-independent or there are no such properties at all. Either way, sensory properties are not mind-independent and realism is false.[41]

The argument against sensory property realism from our tolerance of divergence is very brief. However, it can be evaded only by saying that we ought to be as intolerant in our judgments of sensory qualities as we are in our judgments of physical properties. But if we were confronted with a very different range of perceivers, it seems that we would be or should be fairly lax. The only way to salvage realism would be to argue that our attitude of tolerance is somehow misguided. But I cannot imagine what such an argument would be, given the symmetry point.[42]

Ultimately, our attitude to color is the same as our attitude to the comfortableness of chairs. The issue is not whether we would think that our chairs had

39. It is often said that rigid theories allow that in a world where our experiences were different, the colors would not be different, because the reference of color concepts is fixed by our actual and present experiences. But when this point is made, the desirability of delivering such counterfactuals is usually assumed to be obvious.

40. Either the tolerance of divergent judgments is built into our concepts or it isn't. If it is, then we arrive at a secondary quality, nonrigid response-dependent account. If it isn't, and intolerance is, then we arrive at an illusionist theory.

41. I am *not* here proposing that we consider the counterfactual "If our experiences were different then the sensory properties would be different." It might be argued that if common opinion delivers such counterfactuals then that supports the nonrigid theory; and if not, then that supports the rigid theory. But in fact I think that it is less obvious whether we think that the counterfactuals hold than whether we are tolerant of divergent judgments.

42. The argument appeals to our *judgments* about sensory properties, rather than the sensory *properties* themselves. But we can get from tolerance in judgment to the metaphysical idea that sensory properties are not mind-independent because if we were making judgments about mind-independent properties then we could not be tolerant of divergent judgments about them. So if tolerance is legitimate, our judgments do not concern mind-independent properties, and realism is ruled out. The reality we think of can be *less* independent than we suppose it to be, but not *more*. That is, if our judgments represent a property as being mind-independent, the property may turn out not to be; but if our judgments represent a property as being mind-*de*pendent, then the property cannot turn out to be mind-*in*dependent. Similarly, if our judgments of a certain sort are projective, then this rules out the existence of properties of a corresponding sort, whether mind-independent or mind-dependent. For example, I take it that judgments of funniness and niceness are either projective or nonrigidly response-dependent; and if so, there could not possibly be mind-independent properties of funniness and niceness given that ordinary thought represents them as being projected or mind-dependent.

become uncomfortable if our buttocks were to change or disappear. I don't know about that. The point is that Martians with different buttocks, or no buttocks at all, would find our comfortable chairs uncomfortable. The Martians would make systematically different judgments of comfort from those that we make. Perhaps by "comfortableness" we really mean comfortableness *for someone*, although we usually suppress the tacit relativization. This would be *why* we are tolerant of divergence in judgments of comfortableness. Or perhaps we think of comfortableness as a simple objective property, but we can see that this is an illusion if we reflect on our attitude to creatures who make divergent judgments of comfort. In that case, we should reform our thought and language so that plain 'comfort' becomes 'comfortable-to-me'. Color and comfort are similar. Color is sensory-experience-relative just as chair-comfortableness is buttock-relative. We should embrace a nonrigid response-dependent theory of comfortableness or else illusionism, depending on whether the buttock-relativity is built into our concepts. Either comfortableness in chairs is nonrigidly buttock-dependent or else there is no such property.[43]

The argument from the tolerance of divergence encourages either nonrigid response-dependent theories of sensory properties or else illusionism, and it discourages Smart/Armstrong realism and rigid response-dependent theories. And with that, we have the second premise of our argument against physicalist aesthetic realism.

4 DERIVING AESTHETIC NONREALISM

4.1   Let us now put the two premises together. Since sensory properties are not mind-independent, they are not identical with, realized in, or constituted by physical properties (since physical properties are mind-independent). And if so, we cannot rely on the transitivity of identity, realization, or constitution to ensure that aesthetic facts are also identical with, realized in, or constituted by physical facts. If sensory properties were mind-independent, then the same would be true of beauty and other aesthetic properties. But since sensory qualities are not mind-independent, the same is true of aesthetic properties. Aesthetic properties are either mind-dependent or nonexistent. The upshot of the metaphysical dependence of aesthetic properties on sensory qualities (the first premise) plus a nonrealist view of sensory properties (the second premise) is that physicalist aesthetic realism is untenable.

---

43. Presumably judgments about the comfortableness of chairs are a posteriori!

Since physicalist aesthetic realism is the most plausible version of aesthetic realism, it means that value realism is markedly less attractive in aesthetics than it is in morality. Aesthetic reality is at greater risk than moral reality to the extent that we are more inclined to nonrealism about sensory qualities than about mental states. And because nonrealism about sensory properties is plausible, that inclination ought to be considerable. Therefore aesthetic reality is at risk, and it is at greater risk than moral reality.

4.2   Should we then get ready to abandon the cognitivist ship in aesthetics? Is Hume's projectivist lifeboat the best we can expect? Perhaps we are being overhasty. Maybe it is true that aesthetic properties depend on sensory qualities, which are not part of the "objective" world. But why can we not still say that aesthetic properties are identical with (or are realized or constituted by) dispositions to provoke sensory experiences? Assume that sensory properties are nonrigidly response-dependent. Instead of abandoning aesthetic properties altogether with sensory qualities, we might be led to change our views about their mind-independence. This revised view would be that aesthetic properties are identical with (realized in or constituted by) the disposition to produce sensory responses that are identical with (realize or constitute) sensory qualities. On this view, then, beauty is "in the eye of the beholder." Beauty is not wholly banished. It is not a quality of *external* reality as before— it is not skin-deep. But it might be a mind-dependent property because of its dependence on sensory properties, which themselves involve dispositional relations between things and our sensory experiences. No one except a nonrealist about mental states would deny that those responses are real.

Is this a way that we can rescue beauty from oblivion? Is this a diluted form of aesthetic realism? Or is it the opposite of realism, since beauty is partly constituted by the mind rather than just properties of the external world? There is no beauty *out there*, independent of us, as pre-theoretically envisaged; and that looks like a nonrealist claim. But perhaps beauty still exists. Is this a form of realism? Or do we have a halfway house, roughly equidistant from both realism and nonrealism? We could call a commitment to mind-independent aesthetic properties *strong* aesthetic realism, and commitment to mind-dependent aesthetic properties *weak* aesthetic realism. Or we could refuse to call the latter a form of aesthetic realism. The reasonable thing to say about *this*, surely, is that it doesn't much matter what we say![44]

---

44. The view I am envisaging here may be close to Jerrold Levinson's view in his "Aesthetic Supervenience," additional note 1, pp. 155–57. Levinson thinks that we should reject the strong supervenience but not the weak supervenience of aesthetic properties on intrinsic physical prop-

4.3   At any rate—realist or not—the view we are considering is that aesthetic properties are response-dependent. But it is important to contrast the
kind of response-dependent view that I have in mind with the sort of
response-dependent aesthetic theory that has recently been popular among
aestheticians. This is a theory to the effect that aesthetic properties are dispositions to provoke a certain kind of *pleasure* or *displeasure* in normal human
beings under certain conditions. Let us call this the "hedonic response-
dependent view."[45]

We can distinguish two kinds of response-dependent theories here, as we
did earlier for sensory properties—rigid and nonrigid theories. The rigid
response-dependent theory says that aesthetic properties are mind-independent
in the sense of being independent of our actual responses, whereas the nonrigid response-dependent theory says that they are mind-dependent in that
sense. By contrast with the line I took concerning sensory properties, I want
to distance myself from the nonrigid hedonic response-dependent view of
aesthetic properties. A response-dependent theory in aesthetics must be rigid
with respect to our actual hedonic reactions.

If the nonrigid view of aesthetic properties were true, it would reinforce
the case against physicalist aesthetic realism. We would then have *two* reasons
to deny that aesthetic properties are mind-independent. But the nonrigid
hedonic response-dependent view is intrinsically implausible. On that view,
aesthetic properties are said to be dependent in part on our actual hedonic
reactions rather than just on the nonaesthetic properties of the object or
event. But it is common sense that what makes a flower beautiful or elegant
is not our actual reactions of pleasure and displeasure but its sensory and
physical properties—the arrangement of colored petals, leaves, and stem. If
the aesthetic properties of a flower were dependent in part on our actual
pleasures and displeasures, how could it be dependent *solely* on its sensory

---

erties plus context. That is, he thinks that two relevantly similar things must be aesthetically similar
if they are in the same possible world but not if they are in different possible worlds. Whether or
not this is right depends on whether there is a rigidification with respect to *time* in the response-
dependent account. Some theories might say that if our experiences were to change then the colors would also change. If so, there *could* be two similar things at different times with different
sensory properties and thus with different aesthetic properties. Levinson must be envisaging an
account that is nonrigid with respect to worlds but rigid with respect to times. However, if we
embrace an account that is nonrigid with respect to both worlds and times, we would then be
committed to abandoning both the strong and the weak supervenience of aesthetic properties on
physical properties.

45. The view is sometimes thought to have its pedigree in Hume and Kant—but in fact on
both their views, beauty is not a property at all and aesthetic judgments are not cognitive. Note that
on such a view, there is no threat of circularity in the analysis, by contrast with dispositional
accounts of color that analyze color as dispositions to produce experiences—of color.

and physical properties? The idea that, when explaining why a flower is beautiful, we ought to refer to our actual reactions, or those of other human beings, is out of line with ordinary aesthetic thought. The sensory and physical properties of the flower are what we *find* beautiful in it. Our reactions may be *warranted* by its beauty, but our reactions are not partly *constitutive* of its beauty. Even if we consider those works of art whose aesthetic properties depend in part on their *context*, it is intuitive that they do not depend on our actual *reactions*. It may be acceptable, in some cases, to think that if a work of art had a different context it would have had different aesthetic properties; but it is not acceptable, in those cases, to think that if we had different hedonic responses, it would have had different aesthetic properties.

Humean projectivist theories can admit that things are not *made* beautiful by our actual reactions, since on those accounts there is no genuine cognition of aesthetic properties. But unlike projectivist theories, hedonic response-dependent theories are *cognitivist*; and they usually hold that the hedonic response-dependent view of aesthetic properties is built into our concepts. So the nonrigid hedonic response-dependence theory says that the content of an aesthetic judgment is that there is a relation between properties of the object and actual properties of the subject. But common sense (folk aesthetics) does not represent aesthetic properties as depending on our actual hedonic reactions. Intuitively aesthetic properties depend on a thing's physical and sensory properties, and maybe on its context as well, but not on our actual pleasures or displeasures.[46]

Rigid response-dependence theories are untouched by this argument since they do not say that aesthetic properties depend on our actual reactions. In section 3, I argued against realist and rigid response-dependent theories of *sensory* properties from our tolerance of divergent judgments. But a similar argument cannot be run against realist and rigid response-dependent theory of *aesthetic* properties because we lack such tolerance in aesthetics. Our normative standards are higher there. Those who fail to appreciate the Alhambra are not just different but defective. We are more tolerant of divergence in sensory judgments than we are of divergence in aesthetic judgment. So the nonrigid hedonic response-dependent theory of aesthetic properties is less plausible than the rigid theory.[47]

4.4   However, in a sense, the falsity of the nonrigid hedonic response-dependent view of aesthetic properties makes no difference to the meta-

46. There is also a difficulty here for aesthetic dualism; for on that view there would be no dependencies tying aesthetic properties to physical or sensory properties.
47. There may also be a counterfactual difference between the two areas. The counterfactual

physics of aesthetic properties. For even if aesthetic properties were rigidly response-dependent with respect to our hedonic reactions, they would still depend on sensory properties which are either nonrigidly response-dependent or illusory. Whether aesthetic properties are rigidly or nonrigidly related to hedonic responses, aesthetic properties are lost to the mind-independent world in virtue of their dependence on sensory properties which are not mind-independent.

Now it might turn out that nonrigid response-dependent view of sensory properties cannot be defended. If so, we would then be led to illusionism about sensory properties. In that case, the illusionist metaphysics would be inherited by aesthetic properties. So beauty would not be mind-dependent; instead, there would be no such thing as beauty. Beauty would be banished. However, whether beauty is illusory or nonrigidly response-dependent, it is not physical.

4.5   Let us note that even if we refuse strong physicalist aesthetic realism on the basis of a rejection of strong realism about sensory qualities plus aesthetic/sensory dependence, many features characteristic of realistic thinking remain.

The response-dependent view of aesthetic properties can capture the commonsense idea that aesthetic properties have a causal role. For dispositions—rigid or nonrigid—can perfectly well stand in causal relations.[48] Such dispositions are also comfortably located in time. On the other hand, I suspect that our pre-theoretic commitment to the spatial location of instantiations of aesthetic properties cannot fully be captured. For in folk aesthetics, we think of aesthetic properties as being instantiated entirely where the things are (apart from contextual cases). A partial error theory is I suspect unavoidable here. But the causality and temporality of aesthetic properties are comfortably captured on the response-dependent view we are considering.

The normative aspirations of aesthetic judgments can be captured by both the response-dependent view and the illusionist view. We can retain a sense in which, if we make an aesthetic judgment, we claim that anyone who has the same visual or aural experiences should make the same judgments of aesthetic value or apply the same aesthetic concepts. We could

---

"If we had different hedonic reactions, beautiful things would not be beautiful" seems to be less plausible than the counterfactual "if we had different sensory experiences, things would have different colors."

48. Given the kind of dispositions that aesthetic properties are according to the nonrigid theory, it is unsurprising that we are more inclined to credit beauty with a causal role with respect to us than with respect to other phenomena (see section 1.3). There is a contrast here between folk aesthetics and folk morality.

still think of aesthetic judgments as aspiring to correctness. For example, imagine that we get the Martians to look at a painting—say, the *Mona Lisa*. Imagine that their sensory experiences are radically different, so that they see it as garishly colored (a psychedelic *Mona Lisa*!). They would surely be entitled to make quite different aesthetic judgments from those that we make. After all, it is not through any defect in their *aesthetic* faculties that they do not accord it the value that we do. However, *given* that they have certain sensory experiences of the painting, their aesthetic judgments may be more or less appropriate to their experience. They can get it wrong. Despite pulling back from the strong physicalist aesthetic realist position about aesthetic properties, facts, or states of affairs, we are not in danger of losing the idea of correctness in aesthetic judgment, given that correctness is relativized to sensory experiences.

On this view, whether some certain sensory quality experiences call for a judgment of beauty is not something to which we would have privileged access. We could be quite unaware of the beauty residing in our sensory experiences. So whatever this position is—realist or not—it is no facile subjectivism which implies that there is no truth of the matter or that our judgments cannot be wrong. The correctness or truth of aesthetic judgments is quite independent of aesthetic *judgments*, even though it is not wholly independent of the *mind*. Aesthetic correctness or truth is not mind-independent, but it is judgment-independent. In this way we can save most of the phenomena of aesthetic thought.

Coda

Strong aesthetic realism of the physicalist variety is untenable. The only plausible alternative that is not antithetical to common sense is the view that aesthetic properties are nonrigidly response-dependent. But the responses that aesthetic properties depend on are not pleasures or displeasures but sensory responses. On this view, aesthetic properties depend on the character of our actual experience of colors, sounds, and perhaps smells and tastes. However, if illusionism is true of sensory properties, then it is also true of aesthetic properties. In that case, beauty and the other aesthetic properties would not exist in the way that we pretheoretically conceive of them. So long as we hold that aesthetic properties depend on sensory properties, we must hold that aesthetic properties inherit the metaphysical status of sensory properties, whatever it may be.

CHAPTER 12

Differences

In this last chapter, I compare my views with those of others, or at least with some others we have not so far encountered. After first commenting on five writers on beauty, I take a skeptical look at skeptical sociological approaches to beauty.

I FIVE LANDMARKS

Among writings on the nature of beauty, three recent landmarks and two classic landmarks have not so far been explicitly addressed in this book. I do not intend this to be a full discussion of these important works and authors: I merely want to locate my views with respect to theirs and to give minimal reasons why I prefer my views.

1.1 Mary Mothersill

There is much that I agree with in Mary Mothersill's book *Beauty Restored*.[1] Like her, I want to restore beauty to its rightful place as a central object of enquiry in aesthetics. Her "First Thesis" is that there are no laws of taste. I probably agree with Mothersill in spirit, although I think supervenience lands us with some harmless necessary universal generalizations. Her "Second Thesis" is that aesthetic judgments are "genuine judgments" and that some of them are true. Again, I probably agree with this on most elu-

---

1. Mary Mothersill, *Beauty Restored* (Oxford: Oxford University Press, 1984).

cidations of 'genuine judgment'. What I don't think is helpful is her analysis of aesthetic properties as those which are shared between perceptually indistinguishable things. The notion of perceptual indistinguishability is insufficiently spelled out (see chapter 5, section 1.1 above), and her definition of it (which involves only unaided ordinary perception) seems to imply that aesthetic properties cannot be possessed by distant galaxies and minute cells that we have only recently been able to perceive by means of telescopes and microscopes. Moreover, Mothersill assumes that aesthetic properties are all narrowly determined by "perceivable" properties, which makes her an extreme formalist of an objectionable sort. Lastly, she says that "beauty is a disposition to produce pleasure in virtue of aesthetic properties."[2] Without the phrase "in virtue of aesthetic properties," this would be a dispositional account, like Alan Goldman's—which I shall turn to in a moment. But with that phrase it is not informative about the metaphysics of beauty. It just delineates a connection between pleasure, beauty, and other aesthetic properties—one that has some plausibility. But it is one which is compatible with most accounts of the metaphysics of aesthetic properties, in virtue of which things have these dispositions. After having read Mothersill's impressive book, I still find myself metaphysically hungry.

1.2 Alan Goldman

Alan Goldman argues for a nonrealist view of aesthetic properties in his book *Aesthetic Value*.[3] He begins with a description of the relation between aesthetic properties and aesthetic values. He thinks that aesthetic properties have an evaluative polarity.[4] I am sympathetic with such a view and with much else that Goldman has to say on this topic. But Goldman thinks he can build an argument for aesthetic nonrealism on this basis. Without offering much in the way of argument, he embraces the view that an aesthetic property is a disposition to elicit responses in ideal critics (in virtue of more basic properties).[5] He calls this view the "Humean Structure." Given the Humean Structure, Goldman argues that ideal critics can nevertheless diverge in their responses,[6] and he draws the conclusion that aesthetic properties are mind-dependent and aesthetic realism is false.[7] However, the Humean Structure is

2. Ibid., p. 349.
3. Alan Goldman, *Aesthetic Value* (Boulder, Colo.: Westview, 1995).
4. Ibid., p. 20.
5. Ibid., p. 21.
6. Ibid., pp. 30–31.
7. Ibid., pp. 36–39.

very far from being uncontroversial. Hume himself, who was a noncognitivist, would have had nothing to do with it. Moreover, those of a realist
inclination can and should also back away from it. An aesthetic realist should
deny that aesthetic properties *consist in* some dispositional relation to critics,
even ideal critics. Perhaps it is true that we are disposed to respond in certain
ways to aesthetic features. But we take our responses to be *warranted*—and we
take them to be warranted in virtue of the aesthetic features that we experience. Even if it is true that ideal critics *necessarily* come to know a thing's aesthetic properties (or else they are not ideal), that would not be part of what
being an aesthetic property *consists in*.[8] To impose the Humean Structure is
to beg the question against aesthetic realism. If an ideal critic is just someone
who makes correct judgments, then the fact that there is divergence in *non-*
ideal aesthetic judgments is unproblematic. And if ideal critics are those with
certain virtues in judgment, then there is no reason why such ideal critics
should not be fallible, since, for a realist, a virtue in judgment is just a *tendency*
to produce correct judgments in appropriate conditions. Again, divergence
in actual judgment is unproblematic. Goldman uses a parallel argument from
ideal critics against the idea of aesthetic/nonaesthetic supervenience.[9] Again
the cure is to reject the ideal critic account.

1.3 Eddy Zemach

Eddy Zemach is one of the few recent authors to resist the lure of dispositional or ideal observer theories. I think this is a virtue of his brand of aesthetic
realism.[10] Zemach is an aesthetic realist because science, he thinks, necessarily
takes aesthetic considerations into account. Aesthetic properties such as elegance are crucial in evaluating scientific theories where adequacy to the data
fails to give us reason to choose between competing theories. Zemach argues
that if we must appeal to aesthetic criteria in evaluating theories, then unless
that appeal is fraudulent, it must be because the theories really have aesthetic
properties. I find this argument problematic on several counts. The first problem follows from my general rejection, in chapter 8, of the idea that abstract
objects can possess aesthetic properties. Scientific theories are presumably
abstract objects.[11] If so, they cannot possess aesthetic properties and talk of
their elegance is merely metaphorical. Second, even if we admit that scientific

8. Kit Fine, "Essence and Modality," *Philosophical Perspectives*, vol. 8 (1994).
9. Goldman, *Aesthetic Value*, pp. 39–44.
10. Eddy Zemach, *Real Beauty* (University Park: Pennsylvania State University Press, 1997).
11. Their beauty presumably does not consist in the beauty of the inscriptions or sounds in
which they are realized.

theories *can* in principle have aesthetic properties,[12] the argument only shows that *scientific theories* have aesthetic properties; it does not show that the *world* in general does. An aesthetic realist thinks that roses and paintings have aesthetic properties, not just scientific theories. Third, even if we concede that scientific theories have aesthetic properties only if the world they describe also has them, that too would fail to include roses and paintings. For it would only show that the laws the theories describe have aesthetic properties, along with the entities postulated in the theories, but not that the commonsensical items bound by the laws, such as roses and paintings, have these properties.[13] Finally, even if the argument shows that the commonsensical items bound by the laws, such as roses and paintings, have aesthetic properties, it only shows that they have aesthetic properties of the sort that figure in the evaluation of scientific theories. But there are many other aesthetic properties that do not. Roses and paintings are sometimes elegant, as (let us concede) are some scientific theories. But are theories delicate, poignant, vibrant, exuberant, vivacious, and so on? The class of aesthetic properties that Zemach's argument covers is too restricted.

1.4 Kant

As I mentioned in the introduction, I think that Kant has a great deal to teach us about the deep psychology of the judgment of taste.[14] However, Kant also has a positive account of aesthetic properties and judgments. It is a nonrealist account, like Hume's. And like Hume's account, it involves a projective element. (Kant writes:"We speak of beauty as if it were a property of things.")[15] Kant's view, however, is not happily classed as noncognitive, since for Kant pleasure in the beautiful is, or is intimately bound up with, the free play of our *cognitive* faculties.[16] But in the judgment of taste the cognitive faculties are not engaged in acquiring *knowledge*. They are on holiday, not engaged in their regular business. Presumably our cognitive faculties include many things besides knowledge or belief. For example, entertaining a thought is cognitive, but not a matter of knowledge or belief. And imagination is similar. Roger Scruton's account is also of this sort.[17]

12. Let us grant Zemach that noncognitive analyses of aesthetic judgments fail; so there is no plausible noncognitivist account of judgments of the elegance of scientific theories.
13. I think there is especially something odd about the idea that *laws* of nature possess aesthetic properties. However, this may be because I am inclined to hold the aesthetic/sensory dependence thesis of chapter 8, so laws of nature themselves have no sensory properties.
14. Kant, *Critique of Judgement*, trans. James Meredith (Oxford: Oxford University Press, 1928).
15. Ibid., p. 52.
16. Ibid., sections 35–39.
17. Roger Scruton, *Art and Imagination* (London: Methuen, 1972).

However, I am skeptical about whether this account has the resources to provide for the 'universal validity' of judgments of taste. For why should this free play of the cognitive faculties be constrained to play freely in one way rather than another? In my view, there is nothing in the *Critique of Judgement* to meet this fundamental question. And if so, Kant's view is in the same boat as Hume's, namely, it is a view which eschews realism, but which fails to be able to capture the normative aspirations of aesthetic judgments. Only full-blooded cognitivism, it seems, can do justice to them.

This dismissal is, I admit, rather too brief, and I hope to have more to say about Kant in future. But I thought I ought to say something about where I stand with respect to Kant's solution to the fundamental problem of how a judgment of taste is possible.

1.5 Plato

This book depends on the idea that things are beautiful because of the way they are in other respects. This seems obvious and fundamental to me, and absolutely everyone seems to accept it—except Plato. In the *Phaedo* (and perhaps elsewhere), Plato says that the form of the beautiful itself is beautiful.[18] This means that beauty itself is beautiful, but not in virtue of other characteristics. This worries me. If the great Plato denies what I take to be obvious, surely it is at least true that my principle of dependence is not uncontroversial after all. Is Plato just confused? (Surely he is too clever for that.) Or is my principle of dependence not mandatory as I assume?

At first sight there seems to be an even worse problem. At one point in the *Phaedo*, Plato seems to go further and *deny* that things are beautiful in virtue of their bright colors and particular shapes, along with other dependencies, such as that something is hot because of fire, or that something is ill because of fever, or that something is odd because it is three. That would run directly contrary to my fundamental dependence thesis. However, Plato does not in fact reject such claims. Instead, rather like Simon Blackburn, Plato says that he finds such dependence claims "confusing" or "unsafe."[19] Plato goes on to say how he thinks we *can* after all say that something is hot because of fire, or that something is ill because of fever, or that something is odd because it is three.[20] As I read him, Plato thinks that one can after all assert the existence

18. Plato, *Phaedo* 100b.
19. Ibid., 100c–d; Simon Blackburn, "Supervenience Revisited," in *Essays on Quasi-realism* (Oxford: Oxford University Press, 1993).
20. Plato, *Phaedo* 105b–c.

of dependence relations among ordinary things and their properties so long as a thing "brings along" a form. (So explanation still appeals to the forms.) Thus threeness brings along the form of oddness (which necessarily excludes its opposite, evenness), and fever brings along the form of illness (which necessarily excludes its opposite, health) and fire brings along the form of heat (which necessarily excludes its opposite, cold). The point is supposed to be that three is not the opposite of evenness even though it excludes it. Plato seems to be reaching for something like the idea of an essential property. He is allowing himself to embrace the idea that there can be a dependency between threeness and oddness, and perhaps between beauty and certain colors and shapes, which is not like the dependency of the oddness of a thing on the form of oddness, or the beauty of a thing on the form of the beautiful.

But this leaves the self-predication problem unanswered. What exactly is it about the beautiful itself which is beautiful? It seems bizarre to answer "nothing except itself." Is the beautiful somehow self-beautifying? I submit that Plato's view is indeed bizarre and implausible, but that he is driven to this view by his fundamental metaphysical commitments. For Plato, the world depends on the forms just as, for a traditional theist, the world depends on God. The forms are the primary being, on which the rest of the world depends. The forms lie at the base of the cosmos, and the forms of goodness and beauty are the most fundamental forms. So, of course, given that metaphysical vision, the good and the beautiful do not depend on anything else. They must be self-sustaining, like God is supposed to be. God is thought of as the only self-sustaining thing and everything else is sustained by God, and for Plato that is true of the forms of the good and the beautiful. So the beauty of the beautiful does not depend on other features which make the beautiful beautiful.

However, I think that Plato would admit that his metaphysical vision is a revision of common sense. Plato has turned the commonsense world upside down, and he might admit that I am right about the concept of beauty. I maintain that we conceive of beauty as a dependent property. Plato holds an error theory about that conception. Since I do not in fact accept Plato's theory of forms, I do not think that the beauty of beauty itself is an exception to the principle that beauty is a dependent property.

2 AGAINST THE SOCIOLOGY OF TASTE

2.1 The Metaphysics of Aesthetics, Error Theories, and Historicism

I have considered a number of views about the nature of aesthetic properties and judgments. On the *realist* and *cognitivist* view, aesthetic properties are as real and mind-independent as biological or chemical properties, and our aesthetic judgments are beliefs about these properties. In many ways this is the natural view in the light of our ordinary aesthetic thought. But aesthetic realism has its problems. On the *noncognitivist* view—Humean projectivism, for example—aesthetic judgments are sentimental responses to beliefs and perceptions. There are views according to which aesthetic properties are real but mind-dependent in one way or another. And there are also those who hold that aesthetic judgments are cognitive but not beliefs, such as Kant or Roger Scruton.

There is quite a choice on the menu. But none of these theories threatens our everyday practice of making aesthetic judgments, so long as central features of aesthetic judgments are respected. Preeminent among these is an aspiration to correctness in judgment and to consistency between our judgments. Consistency here does not just mean that we ought not to assert that something is elegant and that it is not elegant. For that is implied by the aspiration to correctness in judgment. Consistency is something more than this. We aspire to consistency in the sense that we think that we ought not to assert an aesthetic difference between two cases unless it is grounded in a nonaesthetic difference. These two aspirations are essential to aesthetic thought; judgments that lacked them would not be aesthetic judgments. Aesthetic realists explain the aspiration to correctness as stemming from the existence of aesthetic properties, and they explain the aspiration to consistency as stemming from the metaphysical dependence of aesthetic on nonaesthetic properties. Nonrealists, on the other hand, have to struggle to explain the fact that our ordinary aesthetic thought has these aspirations without appealing to aesthetic properties. If they cannot do that, then they are committed to an error theory about aesthetic thought.[21]

This is how I think the debate should be conducted. But there is another kind critique of the aesthetic which is at large in the contemporary intellectual landscape, and it may be worth saying something about it—although I find the intellectual terrain and temper uncongenial. This is the *sociological*

---

21. John Mackie advanced an error theory about moral thought in his *Ethics* (Harmondsworth, England: Penguin, 1977).

perspective on aesthetic judgments. Such a perspective is common (but by no means universal) among postmodernist, Marxist, and feminist aestheticians. These theorists critique the notion of the aesthetic from a sociological point of view. They say that they have recently discovered that the entire tradition in aesthetics, in which I am happy to locate my work, is misguided or at least has a false self-conception. This tradition stretches back to the enlightenment thinkers of the eighteenth century, and I think also way back before them, through medieval thinkers, to the Greeks. The mistake that the sociological critics say that these traditional writers have made is to "dehistoricize" their subject matter. These traditional writers falsely imagine that they are dealing with something timeless and universal when in fact it is the product of a particular era and culture.

Now I agree that traditional aesthetics does make certain substantive ahistorical assumptions. But in my view these assumptions are very plausible indeed, and apart from the dubious pleasures of debunking something held dear by many, or being privy to an esoteric truth to which others are blind, there is little to be said for the sociological critique of the aesthetic. Traditional aesthetics has firm foundations, whereas sociological approaches are flawed.

2.2   Aesthetic Skepticism and Aesthetic Historicism

There are roughly two sociological views that we can distinguish, although both strains can often be found in one author, even in one paragraph. The first, more radical view is that beauty is a myth.[22] It's a charade—an ideological construct thrown up by a certain social system. Not only do these theorists think there is no such thing as beauty, but also that there are no correct (or universal) judgments of beauty and there is no requirement to be consistent in aesthetic judgments. The commitment to deploying a concept of aesthetic value, and its constitutive norms of correctness and consistency, is the product of bourgeois or patriarchal society, together with generous helpings of false consciousness.[23] Such sociological theorists thus end up with an error theory. The idea that things *have* aesthetic value, or that we ought to judge in some ways rather than others, is an illusion. Call this outlook "aesthetic skepticism." Here is an example of this view. Griselda Pollock writes:

---

22. The phrase "the beauty myth" has come to refer to a specific position about *feminine* beauty. However, one could be *locally* skeptical about some such specific kind of beauty while being unskeptical about beauty in *general*.

23. So far as I can tell, this was not Marx's own view; but it is a view that many Marxist art theorists advance.

I am arguing that feminist art history has to reject all this evaluative criticism and stop merely juggling the aesthetic criteria for appreciating art.[24]

For aesthetic skeptics, the only value that art is allowed is nonaesthetic value—art causes or reflects certain social facts which are thought to have an independent value. Perhaps good art is progressive or egalitarian, and bad art is counterrevolutionary or sexist. There are two ways of casting this thesis. The skeptic says either that aesthetic value is a myth which should be rejected (as Pollock says above) or that aesthetic value is really some other value. That is, aesthetic values are either *eliminated* or *reduced* to nonaesthetic values. To give an illustration of the reductionist option, John Berger writes:

> we can only make sense of art if we judge it by the criterion of whether or not it helps men to claim their social rights.[25]

Traditionalist defenders of the aesthetic should not deny that art can have such nonaesthetic values. What I think they should vigorously dispute is the *rejection* or *subordination* of aesthetic values to those other values. For example, much propaganda poster art of the 1930s and during the Second World War had repugnant political messages at the same time as possessing considerable aesthetic values. But that one politically disapproves of something does not mean that we must deny it any further value. We can regret that beauty was not used to promote a more desirable political end. The aesthetic value of works of art may sometimes be outweighed by their nonaesthetic values. But in that case we have a dilemma—a conflict of different values: the aesthetic versus the political, for example. But aesthetic skeptics do not find a dilemma; instead the aesthetic is either eliminated in favor of the political or reduced to it.[26]

The other position is *officially* neutral about whether the concept of the aesthetic embodies an error and whether we should dispense with it. What is foregrounded, however, is the explanatory view which sees the deployment of the concept as culturally and historically *local*, and thus in this sense contingent. These theorists say that there is no innate and culturally universal concept of beauty or the aesthetic. The concept has its source in a specific period of history or specific social arrangements—perhaps bourgeois or patri-

24. Griselda Pollock, *Vision and Difference* (London: Routledge, 1988), p. 27.
25. John Berger, *Permanent Red* (London: Methuen, 1960), p. 18.
26. Theologically minded aestheticians tend to be more tolerant of the aesthetic than politically minded aestheticians.

archal society. Again, a sprinkling of false consciousness will be required, since many people (like me) take the concept to be universal and necessary. Call this explanatory outlook "aesthetic historicism." Here are some examples of this view, Bourdieu writes:

> Kant's analysis of the judgment of taste finds its real basis in a set of aesthetic principles which are the universalization of the dispositions associated with a particular social and economic condition."[27]

In a similar sprit, Eagleton writes:

> The category of the aesthetic assumes the importance it does in modern Europe because in speaking of art it speaks of these other matters too [freedom and legality, spontaneity and necessity, self-determination, autonomy, particularity and universality], which are at the heart of the middle class's struggle for political hegemony.[28]

Although this position is officially neutral about whether the concept of the aesthetic embodies an illusion, the *tone* of the discussion often evinces lofty disdain for the aesthetic. The official theory is merely that we should *explain* its existence or preeminence at one period in history and no negative judgment is intended. All they claim is that the deployment of the concept of beauty or the aesthetic is contingent on certain social circumstances. What is a myth, they say, is the idea that possession of the concept is universal among human beings.

2.3 Straw Men

Both skeptical and historicist theorists make things very easy for themselves by setting up an aesthetic straw man. They increase the prima facie plausibility of their intrinsically implausible thesis by assuming that the target for criticism or historicist explanation is peculiarly narrow. Bourdieu and Eagleton, for example, constantly conflate *the aesthetic* with a *pure aes-*

---

27. Pierre Bourdieu, *Distinction* (London: Routledge & Kegan Paul, 1984), p. 493. See also his "On the Historical Genesis of the Pure Aesthetic," in *The Rules of Art* (Oxford: Polity, 1996). I am unsure how to classify Theodor Adorno's *Aesthetic Theory* (London: Routledge & Kegan Paul, 1984).

28. Terry Eagleton, *The Ideology of the Aesthetic* (Oxford: Blackwell, 1984), p. 3. However, he also writes "The aesthetic . . . is in this sense the very paradigm of the ideological" (p. 93–94), and that *looks* skeptical. Unfortunately he is very muddled about what ideology is in the passages following this quotation. The closest he gets is to say that an ideological statement has an emotive role. But then he also says that ideological statements can be true.

thetic approach to art. Or else they continually vacillate between them. The idea of the "pure aesthetic" embraces a stew of several ideas. Here are three salient ideas that I have managed to extract: (a) We should understand works of art in total detachment from their historical context. (b) Works of art only have aesthetic properties or purposes. (c) Works of art are, or ought to be, fine art or "high" art.

But *of course*, there is absolutely no reason the traditionalist defender of the aesthetic is committed to any of this.

(a) Kant's notion of dependent beauty[29] means that the traditionalist can allow that works of art sometimes need to be understood in terms of their historical and social contexts. For example, where we are dealing with dependent representational beauty, we need to understand the meaning of what we are appreciating, and information about history and society may be crucial here. Kant would certainly have rejected the pure aesthetic approach. But Bourdieu takes Kant himself for a target, not some nebulous Kantian view.[30]

(b) The discussion of these matters is almost always muddied and muddled by a confusion between the *aesthetic* and *art*: just as the aesthetic is a wider category than art (since nature has aesthetic properties), so art has many important nonaesthetic properties as well as aesthetic ones.[31] There is no reason to suppose that a traditionalist about the aesthetic should think that works of art should only have an aesthetic point.

(c) It may be that a classification of art as "high" or "low" involves implicit value judgments that we may or may not wish to defend. Oil painting and women's quilt making may have been ranked differently, and perhaps the unsung glories of women's quilt making has been unfairly done down by classing it as mere *craft* rather than fine art. But I would say that both should be included under an umbrella concept of art and we can judge both in aesthetic terms. I do think that a healthy philosophy of art requires that we operate with a broad concept of art that includes oil paintings as well as quilts, together with advertisements, tattoos, fireworks, and much else. We should respect the diversity of artistic activity. It distorts aesthetics only to have "high" art forms in view, and sociological skepticism is one such distortion. (I think that it also distorts more analytic approaches—for example, in the philosophy of music, where a tendency to take classical music as the paradigm sometimes leads to an overemphasis on notation and an underemphasis on improvisation.) That said, the high/low distinction among art forms supplies absolutely no encourage-

29. See chapter 4.
30. For confirmation, see Bourdieu, "Historical Genesis," p. 295.
31. See note 3 in the introduction to this book.

ment for a quite general skepticism or historicism about aesthetic value. The traditionalist can allow that we make plenty of genuine aesthetic judgments about lowly non–fine art.

So the *pure aesthetic* is one thing and the *aesthetic* is another. That the sociological theorists are right to attack the notion of the pure aesthetic does not cast and doubt on the general notion. Moreover, Kant, who is usually cast as the villain, would have agreed. The sociological theorists set up a conception of the aesthetic which probably no one has ever held (bar perhaps Bell and Fry) and which is not plausible as a general conception.[32]

So let us henceforth assume that we are not dealing with a straw man conception of the aesthetic. We should perhaps concede that the skeptics and historicists are right about such conceptions. But that leaves the entire mainstream tradition in aesthetics completely untouched, and it leaves untouched anything in this book.

2.4 Against Aesthetic Historicism

What considerations have been put forward in favor of aesthetic historicism? The fact is that usually no arguments are thought to be necessary. And when any are offered, they are nugatory. The usual move is simply to *assert* that the deployment of concept of the aesthetic is somehow a particularly bourgeois phenomenon. It is clearly untrue, however, that peasants, proles, plebs (or indeed aristocrats) have no aesthetic sense. The appreciation of natural beauty, in particular, has no social boundaries, whether of class, creed, race, gender, nation, culture, or era. And some kind of music is appreciated across these same boundaries. Moreover, when statistical empirical research is done, anthropologists and psychologists are often surprised at the cross-cultural convergence in taste. For instance, in one study, an anthropologist and a psychologist found that the rankings of tribal masks by Central African BaKwele elders correlated very well with those of Yale University students.[33] The sociologist's article of faith that the concept of the aesthetic must be "historicized" and "relativized" seems to depend on a lack of inter-

---

32. One of the few times that Bourdieu stoops to describe his target, he writes that what is historically specific is the idea that works of art call for "aesthetic perception," which has "the properties of gratuitousness, the absence of function, the primacy of form over function, disinterest, and so on" ("Historical Genesis," p. 285). This is quite a list! We should here critique someone who held such a bad theory of the aesthetic. (Apart from some aspects of Kant's own doctrine of disinterestedness, I would reject the other three features as essentially characterizing the aesthetic.)

33. Irvin Child and Leon Siroto, "BaKwele and American Aesthetic Evaluations Compared," *Ethnology* 4 (1965): 349–60.

est in such historical and sociological facts. In practice, rather than in creed, much writing on the sociology of art is no more empirical than theology.

However, I do not want to pin too much on actual convergence in taste. It is true that our aesthetic judgments are subject to psychological and social forces. And these forces can be empirically investigated. If our aesthetic judgments could be *entirely* explained by sociological factors, then perhaps aesthetic skepticism would be vindicated.[34] But all that we have been presented with so far by sociologists is evidence (if such it is)[35] that our judgments are *affected* by social circumstances. But that is compatible with the fact that these circumstances do not exhaust *all* the causal factors that are at work. If so, our aesthetic judgments cannot be *completely* explained in social terms.

Of course, our aesthetic experience is affected and perhaps partly constructed, in a sense, by social circumstances. We do not come to aesthetic experience with a tabula rasa. Our aesthetic responses and judgments need not be thought of in atomistic terms, as independent of each other. It is plausible that they hang together in systematic ways. And the kinds of experiences we have and which we are offered obviously depend on our social circumstances. All this the traditionalist can happily concede.

One sociological historicist who does adduce some empirical research is Bourdieu. He appeals to data about the way different social classes have different aesthetic taste. And he thinks that this supports his historicism.[36] But it is difficult to reconstruct steps of reasoning between this empirically supported premise and the general historicist conclusion. Incidentally, it is no accident that Bourdieu shows little interest in the fact that aesthetic judgments about *nature* do not vary in the same way with social groupings. But let us put that to one side. It is true that we distinguish high art from more lowly forms, or cultivated taste from crude and shallow taste. There is a kind of classification of art into "fine arts" art (or into Art with a capital *A*) rather than craft. And some of Bourdieu's data reflect this. But the fact that judg-

34. See John Mackie's parallel relativity argument in *Ethics: Inventing Right and Wrong* (Harmondsworth, England: Penguin, 1977), pp. 36–38.

35. I express caution in the light of the fact that the fabled Whorf-Sapir hypothesis, which "proved" that reality is a social construction, was based on fraudulent evidence. (See Benjamin Whorf, *Language, Thought and Reality* [Cambridge: MIT Press, 1976].) Whorf claimed that the Hopi have a radically different conception of time from that of Europeans. But Whorf's writings are found amusing by the Hopi themselves and also somewhat insulting. My Hopi students (I worked at Northern Arizona University for one year) read Whorf's account with as much dismay and distance as any European. Many Hopi have written essays debunking Whorf. But sociologists have showed little interest in what the Hopi have to say. The myth is too valuable. It has a function in the life of certain academics.

36. See Bourdieu, *Distinction*.

ments vary with social grouping could not possibly show that the aspiration to correctness in aesthetic matters is an illusion or even culturally local. It may be true that opera and country-and-western music have a different appeal and that their popularity varies with social groupings. But so what? Of course, aesthetic tastes vary. It would be surprising if they did not. These are precisely variations in aesthetic taste—that is, a sort of attitude and judgment that aspires to correctness and consistency. The facts speak in favor of the universal deployment of the *concept* of the aesthetic; but there is no reason why that should mean universal agreement in *judgment*. None of Bourdieu's data supports the historicist conclusion that the *conception* of the aesthetic is historically and culturally local.[37]

We might note that the role that Bourdieu and others give to Kant's *Critique of Judgement* is very odd. It somehow gets introduced into the argument as if Kant personally defined the ordinary concept of the aesthetic that is deployed by Outer Mongolian shepherds. However, that some *theorist* is mistaken about the aesthetic is hardly the exciting conclusion the sociologists seek. All it would show is that we need a better theory of the aesthetic, not that the category of the aesthetic is a bourgeois illusion. Is it the *theorists* who are supposed to be operating with the defective second-order theory about the ordinary concept of the aesthetic, or is it the concept of the aesthetic deployed by ordinary folk that is supposed to be defective? The skeptics slide between the two.[38]

Bourdieu says that we should look at the historical conditions under which aesthetic judgments and experiences come into being.[39] Well if this means that the *pure* aesthetic sensibility is in question, then I simply deny that this has anything essential to our *general* capacity to have aesthetic experiences and make aesthetic judgments. That general capacity, I see as a human universal, which may require biological or evolutionary explanation, but not a sociological explanation. There is nothing "bourgeois" about the aesthetic, although specific aesthetic tastes may vary with social groupings. Of course aesthetic responses will be socially conditioned, in the sense that the *sort* of

37. So when Bourdieu writes, "The oppositions structuring aesthetic perception . . . are historically produced and reproduced" ("Historical Genesis," p. 299), the traditionalist should agree. On other occasions, however, we should be suspicious of the philosophical gloss he puts on his data. For example, Bourdieu thinks that working-class people prefer pleasure in the agreeable to pleasure in the beautiful. I cannot see that his data in any way support this.

38. Kant's distinction between pleasure in the beautiful and pleasure in the agreeable has absolutely nothing to do with the contrast between High and Low art forms, as Bourdieu says. Bourdieu seems to have an almost willful or pathological blindness to the content of Kant's *Critique of Judgement*.

39. Bourdieu, "Historical Genesis," p. 286.

aesthetic response we have is subject to societal pressures and influences. But our general capacity to have some aesthetic response or other is innate and universal.[40]

Even if it were true that the category of the aesthetic is historically and culturally local, that would not in any way undermine the notion of the aesthetic. Presumably science is historically and culturally local. It only exists in certain social circumstances. Nevertheless, science tells us about a mind-independent world. Similarly, perhaps the sociological theorists are right that the aesthetic is a bourgeois or patriarchal notion. Still, it might be a feather in the cap of bourgeois or patriarchal society that only in such a society do people deploy the concept of the aesthetic in judgments and experiences! Perhaps only in bourgeois or patriarchal society are the glories of the aesthetic revealed. I don't believe this for a moment, but the possibility is wide-open, even granted the dubious historicist thesis.

2.5 Against Aesthetic Skepticism

Let us now put the historicist sociological approach to one side and return to aesthetic skepticism.

40. Nancy Etcoff has recently argued that there are evolutionarily programmed culturally universal responses to the opposite sex (Etcoff, *The Survival of the Prettiest: The Science of Beauty* [New York: Doubleday, 1999]). Contrary to the academic consensus that such responses are socially conditioned and constructed, she argues that they are biologically implanted, which is why they are culturally universal. So in a sense, some people just *are* more beautiful than others. (Let us assume that what is in question here is a kind of beauty rather than something like sex appeal, which might contrast with beauty.) Many feminists want to reject this claim since they claim that conceptions of female beauty are entirely socially constructed (Naomi Wolf, *The Beauty Myth* [New York: Doubleday, 1991]). Of course, such conceptions are *partly* socially constructed (long earlobes being in one year or out the next); the question is whether conceptions of female beauty are *entirely* a social construction. Science is sometimes biased, but I think that feminists should be wary of always crying bias when the science doesn't come out how they like, for then they will look like creationists. The question is: Should Etcoff's views be found disturbing from a broadly feminist point of view? Is it reactionary science? I would urge that nothing of political consequence immediately follows from her claims. Compare John Rawls: he takes for granted that some people are more talented than others, but he insists that how one factors that into ones political theory is another matter (Rawls, *A Theory of Justice* [Cambridge: Harvard University Press, 1971]). He famously argued that people have no inherent right to benefit from their natural talents. (He thought that they should be allowed to do so only if it benefits the worst off.) Analogously, some people might indeed be more beautiful than others, but how one factors that into one's political theory is another matter. It could be argued that the more beautiful among us have no inherent right to benefit from their looks, or they have a right to do so in certain cases but not in others. It could still be true that we all have a right to equal respect however beautiful we are. We could still believe in decent values despite admitting that some really are more beautiful than others and their beauty is not a social construction. Etcoff's science does not threaten core liberal values of fairness and respect. And if it threatens social-constructionist dogmas, then the dogmas should go, not the science.

Although I do not offer the following considerations as knockdown arguments, I do think that they put pressure on aesthetic skepticism.

First, aesthetic skeptics should pause to reflect on the scale of what they
are asserting. The aesthetic is not just a mode of *talk* but a mode of *thought
and experience*. Aesthetic judgment and experience are part of the lives of
billions of denizens of this planet. Sociological skeptics condemn their
experiences as an error because those experiences involve impossible and
indefensible aspirations to correctness and consistency. It follows that they
should all stop making aesthetic judgments and having aesthetic experiences,
or at least recognize their error. This is surely a tall order! It is not as if we
could remove the *judgments* with their normative aspirations, leaving the
experiences in place. For aesthetic judgments are based on aesthetic experiences, and aesthetic experiences are such as to warrant aesthetic judgments.
The normativity is implicit within the experience. That's why we say that it
is the experience of beauty. Moreover, it would not just be people's experience of *art* that is denigrated but also their experience of the beauty of
nature.[41]

Second, the aesthetic skeptic has the same pragmatic problem that a skeptic
has in morality: he cannot *live* his skepticism. He cannot apply it to his own
judgments and experiences. The average skeptic makes countless aesthetic
choices every day—choices forbidden by his own theory. The possessions he
chooses betray him. He could condemn himself, like the moralizer who con-
demns lust even in his own person when he cannot suppress the awful tendency. But can the skeptical sociologist really believe his own theory—about
how the aesthetic is an ideological delusion and a product of false consciousness—at the very moment that he chooses a cushion cover for himself in a
shop?[42]

Given that the experience of billions is denigrated by the skeptic, and given
the dangers of pragmatic inconsistency, we need to see strong arguments for

41. At one point, Iris Murdoch nicely draws attention to the fact that although nothing could
be more common and apparently mundane than those who love potted plants, in fact theirs is a
spiritual pastime (Murdoch, *The Sovereignty of the Good* [London: Routledge & Kegan Paul, 1970],
p. 85). There is also the insightful passage about the morose person who suddenly glimpses a hov-
ering kestrel outside his window (p. 84). What wonderful examples!

42. Many theorists use the word "transcendental" to describe the idea, roughly, that art has an
aesthetic value, or that different sorts of people ought to make certain aesthetic judgments rather
than others. Thus the word "transcendental" is used to describe any nonrelativist view of beauty.
But this is rhetoric in the pejorative sense. It gives a misleading and unflattering label to the view
they oppose. The so-called new art historians trade on this maneuver. See, for example, Tom Gret-
ton, "New Lamps for Old," in *The New Art History*, ed. A. L. Rees and Frances Borzello (London:
Camden, 1986), p. 69. Most of the other essays in this collection are similarly crude.

the skeptical view. But we do not even get weak arguments. We usually get an appeal to a tendentious sociological account about the role of the aesthetic in society, for which little or no empirical evidence is offered, and then a leap into theoretical hyperspace to arrive at the skeptical conclusion.

It might be replied that there is nothing wrong with denigrating the thoughts and experiences of billions of people. The atheist does exactly that. It might be an intellectually respectable thing to do. But the aesthetic case is different from the case of atheism. First, there are powerful arguments for atheism (the problem of evil and the problem of the lack of evidence). Second, atheists do not convict themselves of pragmatic inconsistency—except for the odd expletive. Third, beauty is not something transcending the world around us, as God is supposed to be. Beauty is instantiated by ordinary objects and events.

Aesthetic pleasure, and aesthetic experience more broadly, is a fundamental part of the human psyche—like the concerns of friendship or family. We might go as far as to say that aesthetic concerns, like these other concerns, are important if not central to our "identity," although I am not sure that I understand that use of the word. It is often said that our identity, in this sense, is constituted by the loyalties we feel and which bind us. It is said that our fundamental commitments to some extent make us who we are. But we can also feel loyalty to things and their properties as well as to people, institutions, and cultures. And some of our reactions to things are also integral to who we are. Our aesthetic sensibilities are important to the particular human being that we are. A person with a completely nonfunctioning aesthetic sensibility would, I believe, lack something fundamental in human life. Let us hope that the sociological skeptics do not describe many actual people. And if they are presenting a norm for humans to pursue, let us hope that they are thoroughly ignored.

Let us stop being defensive. Instead, we should celebrate beauty and our experience of it. Our experience of beauty is, after all, one of the things that makes life worth living.

Author Index

Subject Index